WINNING AND KEEPING POWER IN CANADIAN POLITICS

Do negative campaigns win elections? Do voters abandon candidates accused of scandalous behaviour? Do government apologies affect prospects for re-election? While many people assume the answer to each of these questions is yes, there is limited empirical evidence to support these assumptions. In this book, Jason Roy and Christopher Alcantara use a series of experiments to test these and other commonly held beliefs.

Each chapter draws upon contemporary events and literature to frame the issues and strategies. The findings suggest that not all of the assumptions that people have about the best strategies for winning and keeping political power hold up to empirical scrutiny. In fact, some work in ways that many readers may find surprising.

Original and innovative in its use of experimental methods, *Winning and Keeping Power in Canadian Politics* is a persuasive analysis of some of our most prominent and long-standing political myths. It will be a "go to" resource for journalists, strategists, scholars, and general readers alike.

JASON ROY is an associate professor in the Department of Political Science at Wilfrid Laurier University.

CHRISTOPHER ALCANTARA is a professor in the Department of Political Science at Western University.

Winning and Keeping Power in Canadian Politics

JASON ROY AND CHRISTOPHER ALCANTARA

UNIVERSITY OF TORONTO PRESS
Toronto Buffalo London

© University of Toronto Press 2020
Toronto Buffalo London
utorontopress.com
Printed in the U.S.A.

ISBN 978-1-4875-0731-2 (cloth)   ISBN 978-1-4875-3600-8 (EPUB)
ISBN 978-1-4875-2501-9 (paper)   ISBN 978-1-4875-3599-5 (PDF)

Library and Archives Canada Cataloguing in Publication

Title: Winning and keeping power in Canadian politics / Jason Roy and
    Christopher Alcantara.
Names: Roy, Jason J., 1974– author. | Alcantara, Christopher, 1978– author.
Description: Includes bibliographical references and index.
Identifiers: Canadiana (print) 20200209426 | Canadiana (ebook) 20200209450 |
    ISBN 9781487525019 (softcover) | ISBN 9781487507312 (hardcover) |
    ISBN 9781487536008 (EPUB) | ISBN 9781487535995 (PDF)
Subjects: LCSH: Political campaigns – Canada. | LCSH: Elections – Canada. |
    LCSH: Canada – Politics and government. | LCSH: Politics, Practical –
    Canada.
Classification: LCC JL193 .R69 2020 | DDC 324.70971–dc23

This book has been published with the help of a grant from the Federation for the Humanities and Social Sciences, through the Awards to Scholarly Publications Program, using funds provided by the Social Sciences and Humanities Research Council of Canada.

University of Toronto Press acknowledges the financial assistance to its publishing program of the Canada Council for the Arts and the Ontario Arts Council, an agency of the Government of Ontario.

  Canada Council   Conseil des Arts
for the Arts   du Canada

In memory of Barry Kay

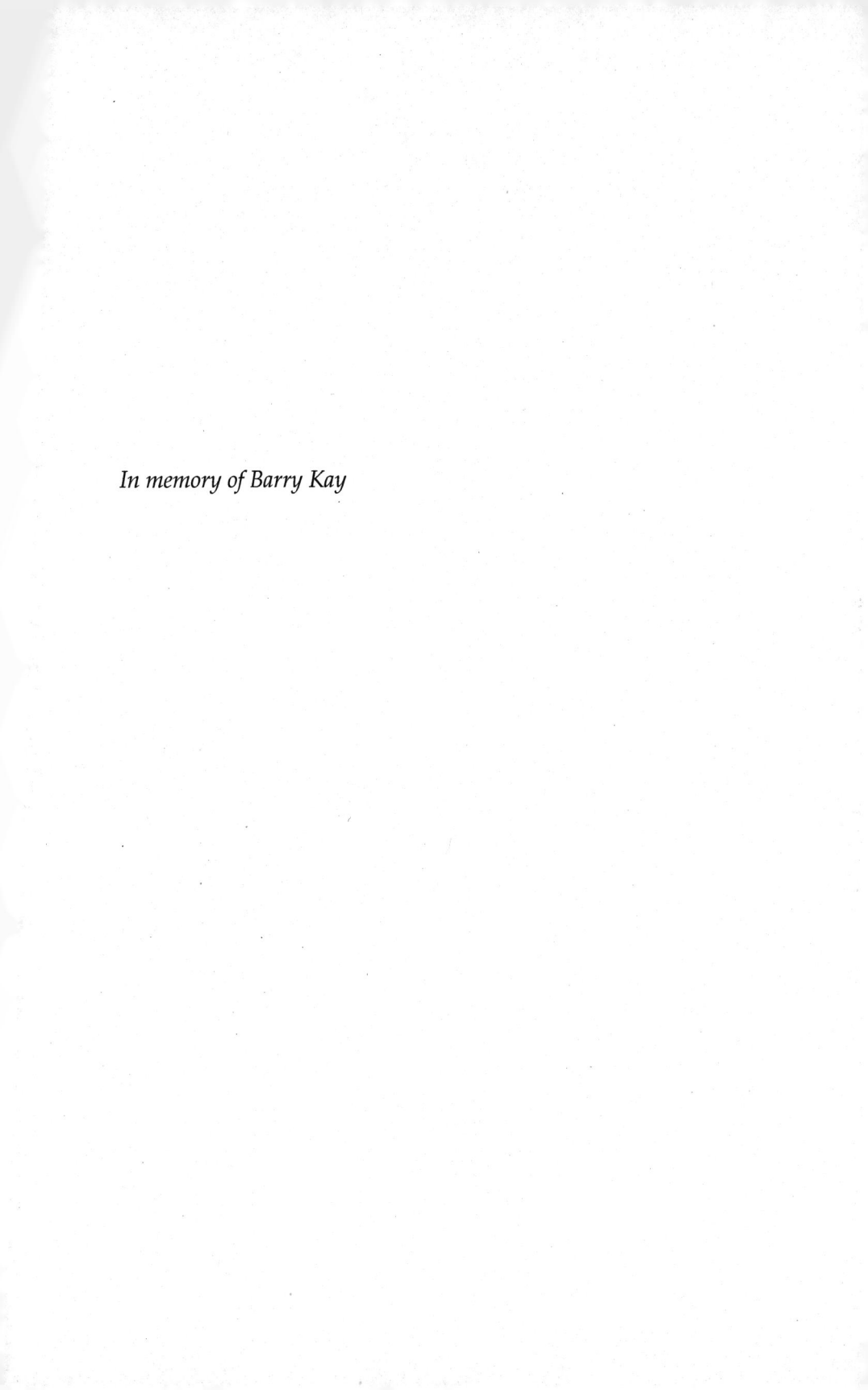

Contents

List of Figures   ix

List of Tables   xi

List of Appendices   xiii

Preface   xv

Acknowledgments   xvii

1 An Overview of *Winning and Keeping Power in Canadian Politics*   3

Part One: Winning Power – Election Campaigns

2 Going Negative in Canadian Federal Elections   19
3 Political Scandals   45
4 Candidate Endorsements   73
5 The Quality of Local Candidates   103

Part Two: Keeping Power – Public Opinion and Incumbency

6 Parliamentary Configurations and Assigning Political Responsibility   129
7 Election Timing   149
8 The Supreme Court of Canada, Parliament, and the Role of Experts   168
9 Framing Public Budgeting   188
10 Political Apologies   207
11 Reflections, Recommendations, and Future Research   223

Index   235

List of Figures

1.1 The effect of negative campaign tone on vote choice   11
3.1 Election campaign information screen   53
3.2 Treatment effects on the information search by party   55
3.3 Treatment effects on the information search by party and type of scandal   56
3.4 Treatment effects on the information search by party and by type and sphere of scandal   57
3.5 Treatment effects on vote choice by party   58
3.6 Treatment effects on vote choice by party and type of scandal   59
3.7 Treatment effects on vote choice by party and by type and sphere of scandal   59
4.1 Election campaign information screen   80
4.2 Treatment effects on the information search by party   83
4.3 Treatment effects on the information search by party and level of endorsement   83
4.4 Treatment effects on the information search by party and level of political sophistication (PS)   84
4.5 Treatment effects on the information search by party, level of political sophistication, and level of endorsement   85
4.6 Treatment effects on vote choice by party   86
4.7 Treatment effects on vote choice by party and level of endorsement   87
4.8 Treatment effects on vote choice by party and level of political sophistication   88
4.9 Treatment effects on vote choice by party, level of political sophistication, and level of endorsement   89
5.1 Election campaign information screen   109
5.2 Treatment effects on vote choice by partisanship   111

x   List of Figures

5.3   Candidate effect by voter type and election context   115
6.1   Impact of legislation passing on incumbent vote   139
7.1   Election campaign information screen   155
7.2   Electoral timing and incumbent vote share   160
8.1   Support for the SCC determining Canadian laws relative to the PoC   176
8.2   Support for the SCC determining Canadian laws relative to the PoC when one institution overrules a decision by the other   176
8.3   Change in PoC support when it overrules the SCC   177
8.4   Change in SCC support when it overrules the PoC   177
8.5   Change in SCC support after an expert says that the SCC overruling the PoC is a bad decision   177
8.6   Change in SCC support after an expert says that the SCC overruling the PoC is a good decision   178
8.7   Change in PoC support after an expert says that the PoC overruling the SCC is a bad decision   178
8.8   Change in PoC support after an expert says that the PoC overruling the SCC is a good decision   178
8.9   Impact of expert cues by political sophistication (PS)   179
9.1   Impact of cueing a funding mechanism   194
9.2   Support for infrastructure investment when individuals are given actual versus anticipated costs   195
9.3   Treatment effects on infrastructure investment   196
10.1   Change in public satisfaction with government response compared with "No comment"   214
10.2   Change in public satisfaction with government response, compared with "No comment," by number of elements   215
10.3   Change in public satisfaction with government response, compared with "No comment," by type of element   216

List of Tables

1.1 Vote probability according to campaign tone 9
2.1 Campaign tone treatments 27
2.2 Number of information links accessed after first tone-cueing link 31
2.3 Vote probability according to campaign tone 32
2.4 Number of information links accessed after first tone-cueing link by number of negative campaigns 33
2.5 Vote probability by number of negative campaigns 35
3.1 Political scandal treatments 52
4.1 Political endorsement treatments 79
5.1 Support for a strong local candidate according to information search undertaken and strength of partisan attachment 112
5.2 Average vote probability by type of candidate and strength of partisan attachment 116
6.1 Government configuration treatments 137
6.2 Estimated vote share by party and treatment 140
7.1 Election-timing treatments 158
8.1 Public support for the PoC and SCC treatments 174
9.1 Support for infrastructure spending treatments 193
10.1 Government apology treatments 211

List of Appendices

2.1 Election campaign information screen 40
2.2 Examples of positive and negative newspaper stories, quotes from campaign, and statements from Campaign Watch Canada 41
2.3 Summary statistics 43
2.4 Multinomial logistic regression results for test of random assignment to treatments 44
3.1 Summary statistics 65
3.2 Multinomial logistic regression results for test of random assignment to treatments 67
3.3 Election instructions 69
3.4 Sample cueing links 69
3.5 Full results for figures 3.2 to 3.7 70
4.1 Political-endorsement cueing links 94
4.2 Summary statistics 97
4.3 Multinomial logistic regression results for test of random assignment to treatments 98
4.4 Full results for figures 4.2 to 4.9 99
5.1 Candidate profiles available to participants 121
5.2 Newspaper story available to participants 123
5.3 Summary statistics 124
5.4 Multinomial logistic regression results for test of random assignment to treatments 125
5.5 Full results for figure 5.2 126
6.1 Election campaign information screen 145
6.2 Sample newspaper story and voting record cues 145
6.3 Summary statistics 146
6.4 Multinomial logistic regression results for test of random assignment to treatments 147

xiv List of Appendices

6.5 Full results for figure 6.1   148
6.6 Full multinomial logistic regression results for table 6.2   148
7.1 Summary statistics   166
7.2 Multinomial logistic regression results for test of random assignment to treatments   166
7.3 Full results for figure 7.2   167
8.1 Summary statistics   184
8.2 Multinomial logistic regression results for test of random assignment to treatments   185
8.3 Full results for figures 8.1 to 8.4   186
8.4 Full results for figures 8.5 to 8.8   186
8.5 Full results for figure 8.9   187
9.1 Wording of questions about infrastructure-spending-experiment control and treatments   199
9.2 Summary statistics   202
9.3 Multinomial logistic regression results for test of random assignment to treatments   204
9.4 Full results for figures 9.1 to 9.3   206
10.1 Summary statistics   220
10.2 Multinomial logistic regression results for test of random assignment to treatments   221
10.3 Full results for figures 10.1 and 10.2   222
10.4 Full results for figure 10.3   222

Preface

We never planned to write a book. In fact, we never planned to write anything together. The catalyst for this project was Alcantara's – ultimately misguided – frustration with the praise that most Canadian commentators and scholars seemed to heap on fixed election dates despite there not being any strong, empirical evidence to suggest that they were necessary. This frustration led to our first experiment and co-authored publication in *Electoral Studies*. That study, published in 2012, and the reactions it received from reviewers and readers, were very encouraging, and we saw an opportunity to use experiments to test a wide range of political "myths" and assumptions in Canada. The result is the monograph you see before you.

This book is not your typical scholarly monograph. While most university-press books engage in a deep exploration of a single theme or argument using some sort of cohesive theoretical framework, this book was written to serve as a collection of experimental tests of various assumptions and ideas that we had encountered in our research, in the academic literature, and in the media. The assumptions we test are not unique to any single election or government, although the idea for many of the studies was prompted by political events that took place in Canada since 2004. While there is a broad, unifying theme to our book, which is an investigation into some of the tactics thought to be effective at winning and keeping power in Canadian politics, we do not advance a sustained or novel theoretical claim about the nature of Canadian elections or the political competition for power. This was never our goal. Instead, we wanted to write a sort of handbook – first and foremost, for social science researchers interested in the various topics and debates that are at the heart of each chapter, and, second, for political strategists and journalists in the hope that they might use our findings to make better decisions or provide better analysis of current events, election campaign tactics and outcomes, and government actions. We also hoped that course instructors might use our book in its entirety or by assigning individual chapters in their graduate and undergraduate courses on Canadian politics, elections, political behaviour, and the like.

Given the diverse audiences that might take an interest in this book, we wrote it in standalone chapters, realizing that not everyone will have an interest in every study. We also included a simplified presentation of the findings in each chapter, along with an explanation of the results in the text and, in the introductory chapter, a guide to reading the tables and graphs. For those interested, the more complex statistical analyses are included as appendices. In short, while this book may not fit the classic mould of what some think a scholarly monograph should look like, we hope that readers will forgive us and see this book for what it is: an empirically informed handbook written primarily for academics, but also for course instructors and students in the classroom, politicians in the corridors of Parliament Hill, and political strategists on the ground in election campaigns.

Acknowledgments

Writing a book requires a significant amount of support from a variety of sources, and we are grateful to the many individuals, organizations, and programs that helped us complete this book. Thank you to Daniel Quinlan and the rest of the staff at University of Toronto Press for shepherding our manuscript through the peer review and publication process. Thank you as well to our anonymous reviewers for their excellent feedback and suggestions during the review process and to Stephanie Stone for her superb copy editing. As far as funding is concerned, the authors would like to thank the Laurier Institute for the Study of Public Opinion and Policy at Wilfrid Laurier University in Waterloo, Ontario, and the Petro-Canada Young Innovator Awards program, housed at the University of Western Ontario in London, Ontario. Both provided much needed research support to run the experiments and hire research assistants.

Many of our friends, colleagues, and students were instrumental in agreeing to serve as (sometimes reluctant) sounding boards as we worked on this book, listening to our many ideas, reading drafts, answering questions, adjudicating our many intellectual disagreements, and the like. In particular, we thank Cameron Anderson, Loleen Berdahl, Christopher Cochrane, Patrick Fournier, Elizabeth Goodyear-Grant, Loren King, Andrea Perrella, Shane Singh, Laura Stephenson, and Melanee Thomas for their feedback. We also wish to thank our colleagues in the political science departments at Wilfrid Laurier University and the University of Western Ontario for providing a rich and stimulating research environment in which to complete this book. Some of the chapters also benefited from the feedback we received from audience members and discussants (especially Peter Loewen and Jonathan Rose) at the annual conferences of the Canadian Political Science Association, the Midwest Political Science Association, and the Southern Political Science Association. Finally, we wish to acknowledge the excellent work of our student research assistants – Shereen Arcis, Abigail Gorrell, Kourtney Koebel, and Rachel Weiss – for their help with this project.

Some portions of our book draw upon our previously published material, and we thank the publishers for their permission to reuse some of those works, along with the anonymous reviewers who provided useful feedback for each article. These papers are: Jason Roy and Christopher Alcantara, "Fighting Fire with Fire: The Implications of (Not) Going Negative in a Multiparty Election Campaign," *Canadian Journal of Political Science* 49, no. 3 (2016): 473–97, reprinted with permission from Cambridge University Press; Jason Roy and Christopher Alcantara, "The Candidate Effect: Does the Local Candidate Matter?," *Journal of Elections, Public Opinion and Parties* 25, no. 2 (2015): 195–214, reprinted with permission from Taylor & Francis Ltd (http://www.tandfonline.com); and Jason Roy and Christopher Alcantara, "The Election Timing Advantage: Empirical Fact or Fiction?," *Electoral Studies* 31, no. 4 (2012): 774–81, reprinted with permission from Elsevier.

Most importantly, we wish to express our deepest gratitude to our families, who have had to put up with our Skype meetings, text exchanges, phone calls, disappointments, and celebrations over the course of writing this book. This work could not have been completed without your support. Thank you!

WINNING AND KEEPING POWER IN CANADIAN POLITICS

Chapter One

An Overview of *Winning and Keeping Power in Canadian Politics*

To be frank, politics is about wanting power, getting it, exercising it, and keeping it. (Jean Chrétien 2008, 2)

For Mr. Harper, politics is first and foremost about tactics. Tactics, tactics, tactics. He immerses his mind not so much in grand designs or great policies for the country but in grand designs for outfoxing his opponents. (Lawrence Martin 2008, A15)

For many people, Canadian politics is fundamentally about the pursuit of state power and the quest to hold on to it for as long as possible. Elections are crucial mechanisms for accomplishing these goals, and they play a significant role in influencing the kinds of public policies pursued and enacted by the state. In short, who wins office, what kinds of promises are made, and what party elites decide to do once they form the government and wield the levers of the state matter greatly for those who desire and exercise power and for those who must live with the outcomes.

Which electoral strategies are effective for winning power in Canada? What tactics are likely to succeed at fostering public support and allowing governments to keep power? In this book, we address these timeless questions using experimentation and statistical analysis to examine a series of claims commonly made about how politicians can win office and maximize their chances of re-election. Our underlying assumption is that the primary goal of politicians and political parties is to win and maintain power for as long as possible. We also assume that who wins and is able to keep power has significant consequences for Canadians.

Taking these assumptions as given, our primary task in this book is to empirically assess the validity of a number of widely held beliefs among pundits, practitioners, and academics about the kind of strategies that are effective at influencing vote choice and behaviour during general elections. For example, do negative campaigns and political scandals affect vote share? Do candidate endorsements and the quality of a local candidate matter? We also assess a number of strategies commonly thought to be effective at maintaining a government's public approval rating and thus increasing its chances of keeping power. Each of these strategies is based on contemporary issues in Canadian politics that have come to the forefront in recent years, such as parliamentary configurations, election timing, and political apologies, for example.[1] We draw upon existing literature and theories as the basis for our assumptions, which we then test using a series of experiments. The evidence we marshal allows us to empirically analyse the utility of each strategy as a means to win and keep power, and it enables us to assess the extent to which the empirical evidence supports anecdotal claims. However, before outlining our studies and the results that follow from our work, we wish to directly address the advantages and disadvantages associated with experimental techniques like the ones employed in this book.[2]

Advantages and Disadvantages of Using Experiments to Study Political Behaviour

The use of experiments to study political behaviour is by no means new (Druckman et al. 2011). But what has changed in recent years is the prevalence of experimental designs and the types of experiments that researchers are employing to advance our understanding of political behaviour and politics more generally.[3] We fully embrace this growth and the variety of innovative experimental research designs that have been developed to address research questions. The primary advantage of an experiment is its ability to isolate causal relationships. This is possible due to the control that researchers have over the environment during the experiment, allowing them to rule out other potential factors that may influence what they are studying. For example, we

---

[1] We note that the topics examined here are by no means exhaustive. Our choices fall broadly within the two main themes of the book: how parties or candidates come to power and, once they have won, the efforts they make to stay in power.
[2] See also Druckman et al. (2011) for a more detailed discussion about the application of experimental research to studying political behaviour, including the advantages and disadvantages of experimental designs.
[3] One need only look to the *Journal of Experimental Political Science*, launched in 2014, for a sampling of the array of experiments being used to address a range of research questions.

can (and do) develop an experiment where half the participants read a candidate's statement that criticizes an opponent, while the other half read a similar statement, except that, in it, the candidate outlines his or her personal strengths. Given that everything else is the same in each group, which we know to be true because we control the environment and the information that is available, any difference in the level of support for the candidate across scenarios can be due only to the difference in the tone of the message. Thus, we can determine the extent to which campaign tone *causes* changes in voting behaviour.

Put differently, experiments give researchers increased confidence in the "cause" of a change given the control they have over the environment, which allows them to rule out other factors.[4] Of course, it is fair to ask, how can we be sure that the individuals in the two groups are, in fact, similar? This is achieved by randomly assigning the participants to each of the groups. Assuming a large enough sample, the two groups should, on average, be very similar to one another.[5]

A common critique of experimental designs is that the findings do not necessarily allow inferences to be drawn about the "real world," given the artificial nature of the experimental environment.[6] In a majority of the studies that follow, we created a fictitious electoral environment, devoid of political history or context. We used fictitious candidates and, in some studies, excluded partisan cues, such as party affiliations and labels. Quite simply, it is true that our experiments do not necessarily match a number of the electoral conditions likely to be observed in the real world. Nonetheless, we believe that there are considerable advantages to this strategy, and we designed our studies being fully aware of these choices and their merits and consequences. We contend that what we may have lost in *external validity* is offset by the ability of our design to isolate the cognitive effects of processes that are not otherwise measurable (Druckman et al. 2011).

Do incumbent parties benefit by controlling election timing? Does the tone of a campaign matter? Do high-quality local candidates win elections? To answer these questions, we believe it is necessary to first

---

4   This is referred to as *internal validity*, one of the main strengths of experimental designs.
5   In the studies that follow, we use statistics to test our assumption that the groups are indeed similar. Another option is to use a statistical procedure called *matching*. As the name suggests, the participants across the groups are matched on any number of characteristics. The values of the outcome variable (e.g., the level of support for the candidate, based on our example) are then compared to isolate the impact of exposure to the treatment stimulus.
6   This is referred to as *low external validity*.

isolate the effect of each factor, net of other individual and contextual factors that are likely to influence how individuals process election campaigns and how this ultimately influences the vote that they cast. Our research design allows us to do just that. What we are left with, in our controlled environment, are observable measures of changes in behaviour, given various stimuli. While we acknowledge that we are unable to confirm the extent to which these findings will hold in the larger population or under real-world conditions, the evidence we marshal here offers, at the very least, a first step in recognizing whether such effects are likely to exist, and it allows us to identify factors that may influence the magnitude of these effects. Insomuch as one adheres to the belief that the potential influence of the factors we consider in this work matter, our experimental designs offer a means by which we can directly test these effects and their implications for Canadian democracy.

The Two Types of Experiments Used in the Book

In the work that follows, we employ two types of experiments. The first presents the respondents with a stimulus (treatment) that is delivered using a static online information board, what we refer to as the Election campaign information screen (chapters 2, 3, 4, 5, 6, and 7). We then observe how both the information search and the vote preference change according to the treatment to which an individual is exposed. For example, in chapter 2, the participants are randomly assigned to treatments, with one to three candidates engaging in a negative election campaign. By monitoring how their information search and the probability of voting for a candidate differ according to the tone of the campaign (negative or positive), as well as the number of other candidates engaged in a similar campaign tone, we can isolate the direct effect of negativity in a multiparty election setting.

The second type of experiment we employ is wording experiments (chapters 8, 9, and 10). In these studies, the participants are randomly assigned different text or statements to identify how the framing of the question or the information presented might alter behaviour. For example, in chapter 10, we test how political apologies influence approval ratings according to the extent to which the government accepts responsibility, offers an apology, and/or offers to compensate citizens for the mistake. By controlling the stimulus that the participants receive, we can directly identify the impact of each criterion, independently or combined, and the impact it has on public opinion. In each chapter, we provide a detailed outline of the experimental design developed, along with the reasoning for the various stimuli.

One caveat about the experiments that follow is that all the fictional candidates are presented as middle-aged, white, heterosexual men with Anglo-Saxon names. This choice was intentional: we wanted to eliminate any potential candidate effects – those based on candidates' characteristics – as opposed to treatment effects – those based on how candidates are treated.[7] For example, a growing body of literature has investigated the gendered and racial implications of political campaigns in Canada and other similar contexts, finding that public opinion and voting behaviour vary significantly when candidates differ from the typical profile (Bird et al. 2016; Carroll and Sanbonmatsu 2013; Goodyear-Grant and Tolley 2017; McMahon and Alcantara 2019; Spicer, McGregor, and Alcantara 2017). Investigating those dynamics is beyond the scope of this book but could make for a fascinating sequel. How might our results differ if half or all the candidates were women? Does a candidate's name suggest racial differences? If so, do these differences influence the results we report from our studies? We hope that this book encourages further study into these differences and their effects on voting behaviour.

The Participants

For all but two of our studies (chapters 5 and 7, discussed below), the respondents were recruited from proprietary panels set up by Survey Sampling International (SSI)[8] from 23 November to 8 December 2016. The participants were incentivized to complete the study as part of SSI's reward program: it offered points for completed surveys, which could then be exchanged for prizes through its online marketplace as well as entered into a quarterly monetary draw. Sampling was performed within strata for gender, age, region, and household income to ensure that, based on these characteristics, the sample was reflective of the Canadian population, outside Quebec.[9] The participants were randomly assigned to one treatment group or the control group in one

---

7 This candidate profile was chosen because it reflects the typical demographic profile for political candidates at the Canadian federal and provincial levels for much of Canada's history (see Thomas and Bodet 2013).
8 Since we conducted our research, SSI has become Dynata. See http://www.dynata.com for information about the panel and rewards program.
9 Given that our study was available only in English, and given the difference in the number of competitive parties in Quebec, only respondents in Canadian provinces outside Quebec were included. While designed to be representative, the sample is not random.

of the four information-board experiments (chapters 2, 3, 4, and 6). The same respondents were also assigned to one treatment group or the control group in each of the wording experiments (chapters 8, 9, and 10).

For chapters 5 and 7, we draw upon a student sample. For these studies, we sent an email invitation to the entire student population at Wilfrid Laurier University in Waterloo, Ontario.[10] The study was open from 17 October until 5 November 2012. As an incentive to participate, we offered individuals a chance to win an iPad. As in the 2016 study described above, each participant was randomly assigned to one treatment group or the control group from only one of the information-board experiments. There were no wording experiments with this sample. We report the number of usable cases for all studies in the methodology section of each chapter.

Interpreting the Tables and Graphs

In each chapter, we present our findings in tables and/or as graphs. Below each one, we include a note that explains what is being reported. In the text, we also provide a full explanation of the results. While we recognize that some readers may not have the experience to fully understand the coefficients reported or the type of statistical models we employed, we hope that our explanations will suffice and provide readers with the key points that can be drawn from our results. For readers familiar with the statistical procedures we use to test our assumptions, we provide the full set of results either in the chapter or as an appendix.

In general, the tables show that any value above zero (*positive coefficient*) represents a positive relationship – that is, when the independent variable (the *cause*) increases in value, the dependent variable (the *effect*) also increases in value. Any value below zero (*negative coefficient*) indicates a negative relationship – when the independent variable increases

---

10 We note that the characteristics of an opt-in sample drawn from a university population differ from what we might expect in the larger population (see, e.g., chap. 7). This difference creates another potential challenge to the external validity of our study. Should we expect the effects observed from a student-only sample to be similar to those in the larger population? While we cannot know for sure (at least, not with the data available), previous research suggests that we should not be too concerned about external validity when using a student sample in the way that we have in this book (Druckman and Kam 2011). Thus, we maintain that our results are still useful for identifying potential relationships and encourage future efforts to test the robustness of our findings beyond a student population.

Table 1.1. Vote probability according to campaign tone

	Model 1
Negative campaign	−0.82 (0.20)***
	[−0.12]
Constant	−0.47 (0.14)***
Pseudo R^2	0.26
N	769

Note: The cells report logistic regression coefficients, with standard errors in parentheses. Marginal effects/discrete changes are reported in square brackets. Party identification is included in the models as a control but is not reported.
***$p < 0.001$; **$p < 0.01$; *$p < 0.05$; ª$p < 0.10$.

in value, the dependent variable decreases in value. In models where the independent or dependent variable, or both, are dichotomous (coded as "1" if true and "0" if not), a positive coefficient means that, when true, the value of the dependent variable will increase (or its likelihood of being true will increase). For example, if we were assessing the results from a logistic regression model (used when the dependent variable is dichotomous) that looked at whether there was a relationship between negative campaigns (the independent variable, coded "0" for *positive campaign* and "1" for *negative campaign*) and voting for a candidate (the dependent variable, coded "0" for *did not vote for the candidate* and "1" for *voted for the candidate*), a positive coefficient for *negative campaign* would suggest that when a candidate engaged in a negative campaign, the respondents were more likely to vote for him or her. A negative coefficient would suggest the opposite (see table 1.1, drawn, in part, from chapter 2).

In this example, we can see that the coefficient, −0.82, indicates that the respondents were *less likely* to vote for a candidate when he or she ran a negative campaign relative to taking a positive tone. This coefficient represents the change in the *log odds* of voting for the candidate, a value that is difficult to interpret even for those well versed in statistical methods. However, we can convert this value to one that is more meaningful – namely, the marginal effect (for continuous variables) or, in the case of a dichotomous (binary) variable, the discrete change (reported in the square brackets below the log odds coefficient) in the probability of a dependent variable being "true." Thus, instead of reporting that the log odds of voting for a candidate engaged in a negative campaign decreased by 0.82 points, it is more meaningful to report that going negative decreased the likelihood of a respondent voting for the candidate by 12 percentage points.

The value reported in parentheses next to the coefficient is the standard error. This value can be used to assess statistical significance using both *probability values* (*p*-values) and confidence intervals. The superscript text after the standard error provides an indication of how confident we can be that the results from the sample reflect the actual value in the larger population from which the sample was drawn (e.g., statistical significance). In the example (table 1.1), *** means that there is only a 0.1% chance that if the true relationship between two variables were zero (did not exist) in the population from which we sampled, the analyses of the data in our sample would return the relationship that we found or a stronger relationship. We report this as a probability of less than 0.1% ($p < 0.001$) that we have committed a Type 1 error (i.e., we assume that a relationship exists in the population when, in fact, it does not). In other words, we would state that there is a statistically significant relationship between the campaign tone and the likelihood of voting for a candidate.

The other information that is reported in the table is the constant, the pseudo R^2 value, and N. The N reports the number of cases (respondents) that were included in the model. The pseudo R^2 value can be interpreted, loosely, as an indication of how much of the variance in the dependent variable we have explained with our independent variable(s). The constant can be interpreted as the mean value of the dependent variable when all other variables in the model are at zero.

We could report the same result in graphical form (see figure 1.1). In the graph, the solid circle is the point estimate (the 12-percentage-point change reported in table 1.1), representing the difference in the likelihood of voting for a candidate when he or she engages in a negative campaign relative to if the campaign tone were positive. The horizontal line on each side of the point estimate represents the 90% confidence interval for this coefficient: we can be 90% sure that the true population value will fall between the end points of these two lines. If the point estimate is to the left of the broken vertical line that crosses the horizontal axis at "0," the relationship is negative. If the point estimate is to the right of the vertical line, the relationship is positive. If the two end points of the confidence interval are to the left or to the right of the vertical line, the relationship is statistically significant (see the discussion of table 1.1 above). If either crosses over the line, we cannot be sure that a similar relationship would be observed in the larger population from which we sampled.

As noted, we offer an interpretation of the results in the text but believe that this basic overview of how to read the results will be helpful. There are a number of online resources, books, and courses

Figure 1.1. The effect of negative campaign tone on vote choice

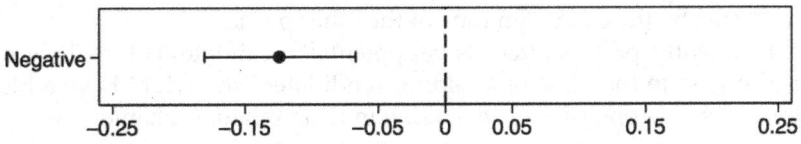

available for those wishing to develop a more advanced understanding of statistics.

Chapter Outline

The chapters that follow are divided into the two broad categories of winning and keeping power in Canadian politics.[11] The first considers strategies for winning power. Each of the chapters within this section follows from events that took place in the lead-up to, or during, contemporary Canadian federal election campaigns. We begin by considering the impact of campaign tone in a multiparty context. After he won the leadership of the Liberal Party of Canada (LIB) in 2013, Justin Trudeau made a public statement, claiming that the party would maintain a positive message throughout the 2015 election campaign.[12] This statement led us to question whether such a strategy would be effective, especially if only one party ran a positive campaign while other parties chose to attack. The bulk of the literature on the effects of negative campaigns is based on the two-party US system, where any losses or gains at the ballot box resulting from campaign tone are directed toward the other party. However, the impact of such behaviour in a multiparty system is much more complicated: the potential effects may be spread across all the other parties, directed toward only one of the other parties, or cancelled out under the more complex electoral environment. In chapter 2, we test these possibilities directly by examining

---

11 We introduce chapter-specific abbreviations as needed in each chapter. However, readers should take note of the following political party abbreviations that are used throughout this book: Bloc Québécois (BQ), Conservative Party of Canada (CPC), Green Party of Canada (GRN), Liberal Party of Canada (LIB), and New Democratic Party (NDP). We also make numerous references to partisanship or party identification, which we shorten to PID.
12 We leave it to the reader to decide whether Trudeau and his party were successful at maintaining a positive campaign.

how the attention and vote share that a party receives vary according to the campaign tone employed and the extent to which these effects are mediated by the campaign tone of the other parties.

Frequently, party strategists vet potential candidates before the writ is dropped in the hope of avoiding candidates who might have a history of, or a propensity for, engaging in unacceptable behaviour, which might prevent them from winning a riding or might harm the party's general popularity. In chapter 3, we examine how the public reacts at the ballot box in the wake of political scandals and focus on two types of scandal: financial and sexual. We further explore the impact of each type of scandal according to whether the scandalous behaviour takes place in private or public life. In doing so, we provide empirical evidence of the costs of political scandals as well as how the type and context of a scandal mediates such effects.

Chapter 4 considers how endorsements affect electoral outcomes. Do political parties gain support through endorsements? Does the level of support vary according to the endorser? While the general assumption is that political endorsements benefit political parties and candidates, little research has been done that assesses this claim directly. It seems plausible that the impact of an endorsement may vary, in part, according to who is doing the endorsing. Our study allows us to examine the impact of receiving an endorsement and whether its effects differ according to who is offering an endorsement. On this latter point, we compare local- with national-level endorsements to assess how much, if anything, parties gain from each level of public statements of support.

When the LIB announced that Chrystia Freeland would run in the 2015 election for the riding of Toronto Centre, critics of the party and political pundits were quick to note the hypocrisy of Justin Trudeau's involvement in supporting Freeland and how such efforts usurped the authority of the local riding association to choose its own candidate. Are such efforts to find star candidates effective for winning power? Chapter 5 considers how candidate quality affects vote share. Our experimental design offers evidence of the potential electoral costs and benefits of high-quality, star candidates.

It is one thing to win power, but once obtained, how is it maintained? The second section of this book addresses this question by presenting empirical evidence on how a governing party's efforts while in office can shape public support. The studies in this section also provide an indication of the fluidity of Canadian public opinion when it comes to support for public policy. As a point of departure, chapter 6 examines how voters reward or punish parties at the ballot box based on the parties' behaviour under majority, minority, or coalition governments. Although Canada has limited experience with coalition governments at the federal level, efforts to defeat and replace the Conservative (CPC) minority government in 2008–9 led to considerable debate about not only the constitutional legality of such an alliance but also the political consequences that each party might face if it were involved in a coalition. In this chapter, we test how voters react to the action that political parties take under different parliamentary configurations and the extent to which citizens assign blame or credit to parties for their actions under majority, minority, or coalition government configurations.

Chapter 7 considers how much incumbent governments actually gain by controlling the timing of an election. The issue of election timing has been prominent in Canada for some time, with critics claiming that an incumbent party gains an unfair electoral advantage by having the power to call a general election when it suits it. In 2007, the CPC government passed legislation that established a four-year election cycle, although many question the extent to which this legislation constrains governments to set election dates, as exemplified by the early calls of the 2008, 2011, and 2015 federal elections. We witnessed similar behaviour at the provincial and territorial levels, with most of these subnational governments passing partially fixed election-date legislation beginning in 2001 (Alcantara and Roy 2014). That chapter provides empirical evidence of how much incumbents stand to gain by controlling the timing of the election and how this advantage is influenced by the political context in which an election is called.

Chapter 8 examines public support for Parliament versus the Supreme Court in deciding public policy. A shift in the concentration of power following the entrenchment of the Canadian Charter of Rights and Freedoms in 1982 has increased the power of the courts to curtail government action when such action is viewed as violating the rights defined in the Charter (Morton and Knopff 2000; Hogg and Bushell 1997). Does the Canadian public support this shift in power? Can governments maintain public support by avoiding controversial policy decisions and handing them off to the Supreme Court? To answer these questions, we use a wording experiment to measure the public appetite for parliamentary versus judiciary authority in defining and changing legislation. The findings offer empirical evidence for the claim that the judicial branch of government has become more powerful, at least in the minds of citizens, as well as the potential for governments to maintain popular support by deferring to the courts on controversial issues. We also include a secondary experiment in this chapter, testing whether expert opinion affects how citizens interpret judicial and parliamentary authority over legislative and constitutional interpretation. In this study, we find that experts have little effect on public opinion.

In chapter 9, we consider public support for various government spending mechanisms, focusing on infrastructure spending. During the 2015 federal election, the LIB campaign presented Canadians with a promise to address depleting infrastructure through increased infrastructure spending. However, it was not immediately clear from where the funding for these projects would come. In this chapter, we consider the level of public support for infrastructure spending in Canada and test how such support varies according to different public budgeting mechanisms. More generally, this chapter allows us to explore how support for government policy can be influenced by the way in which the options are presented to the public. The results suggest that governments have considerable power to appease the public (and thus keep power) according to how spending mechanisms are framed.

At the time of writing this manuscript, Canadian federal, provincial, and municipal governments have made thirty-seven official apologies since 1988 (see chapter 10). Do Canadian citizens accept these kinds of apology as sufficient for addressing government wrongdoing? In our final study, we test public support for various types of apology to assess the extent to which simply acknowledging an act, as opposed to accepting responsibility and providing compensation to victims, resonates within the Canadian population. Our results suggest that, as a means of maintaining public support (and keeping power), recognizing past shortcomings can be effective, although the effectiveness of such recognition can vary by the willingness of the government to accept responsibility and address the needs of those affected.

Drawing upon the evidence collected from our experiments, our concluding chapter assesses how well assumptions about what it takes to win and keep power in Canadian politics holds up to empirical scrutiny. Our findings offer academics, students, pundits, practitioners, and the public insight into Canadian politics and the nuances that define our Canadian political identity. We now turn to our first study, which examines the effect of a negative election campaign tone on *winning and keeping power in Canadian politics*.

REFERENCES

Alcantara, Christopher, and Jason Roy. 2014. "Reforming Election Dates in Canada: Towards an Explanatory Framework." *Canadian Public Administration* 57 (2): 256–74. https://doi.org/10.1111/capa.12067.

Bird, Karen, Samantha D. Jackson, R. Michael McGregor, and Aaron A. Moore. 2016. "Sex (and Ethnicity) in the City: Affinity Voting in the 2014 Toronto Mayoral Election." *Canadian Journal of Political Science* 49 (2): 359–83. https://doi.org/10.1017/S0008423916000536.

Carroll, Susan J., and Kira Sanbonmatsu. 2013. *More Women Can Run: Gender and Pathways to the State Legislatures*. New York: Oxford University Press.

Chrétien, Jean. 2008. *My Years as Prime Minister*. Toronto: Vintage Canada.

Druckman, James N., Donald P. Green, James H. Kuklinski, and Arthur Lupia, eds. 2011. *Cambridge Handbook of Experimental Political Science*. New York: Cambridge University Press.

Druckman, James N., and Cindy D. Kam. 2011. "Students as Experimental Participants: A Defence of the 'Narrow Data Base.'" In *Cambridge Handbook of Experimental Political Science*, edited by James N. Druckman, Donald P. Green, James H. Kuklinski, and Arthur Lupia, 41–57. New York: Cambridge University Press.

Goodyear-Grant, Elizabeth, and Erin Tolley. 2017. "Voting for One's Own: Racial Group Identification and Candidate Preferences." *Politics, Groups, and Identities* 7 (1): 131–47. https://doi.org/10.1080/21565503.2017.1338970.

Hogg, Peter W., and Allison A. Bushell. 1997. "The Charter Dialogue between Courts and Legislatures (or Perhaps the Charter of Rights Isn't Such a Bad Thing after All)." *Osgoode Hall Law Journal* 35 (1): 75–124. https://digitalcommons.osgoode.yorku.ca/ohlj/vol35/iss1/2.

Martin, Lawrence. 2008. "There's Nothing Like an RCMP Raid to Get the Irony Flowing." *Globe and Mail*, 17 April 2008, A15.

McMahon, Nicole, and Christopher Alcantara. 2019. "Running for Elected Office: Indigenous Candidates, Ambition and Self-Government." *Politics, Groups, and Identities*. https://doi.org/10.1080/21565503.2019.1584750.

Morton, F.L., and Rainer Knopff. 2000. *The Charter Revolution and the Court Party*. Peterborough: Broadview Press.

Spicer, Zachary, Michael McGregor, and Christopher Alcantara. 2017. "Political Opportunity Structures and the Representation of Women and Visible Minorities in Municipal Elections." *Electoral Studies* (48): 10–18. https://doi.org/10.1016/j.electstud.2017.01.002.

Thomas, Melanee, and Marc André Bodet. 2013. "Sacrificial Lambs, Women Candidates, and District Competitiveness in Canada." *Electoral Studies* 32 (1): 153–66. https://doi.org/10.1016/j.electstud.2012.12.001.

PART ONE

Winning Power – Election Campaigns

Chapter Two

Going Negative in Canadian Federal Elections[1]

By any means possible, see that your competitors are smeared with an evil reputation – which fits their characters – for crime, vice, or bribery. (Cicero 1970, para. 52)

"I personally would be very embarrassed if he were to become prime minister of Canada," said a Progressive Conservative Party television ad depicting Jean Chrétien's face in 1993. (Flanagan 2014, 145)

Many politicians and strategists believe that the path to power is easier if you attack your opponents. By smearing or discrediting the opposition, the hope is that voters will shift their support to the attackers or not vote at all, thereby increasing the attackers' chances of winning. According to Jeffrey Simpson (2011), "Attack ads work. And as long as they work, parties will use them." In British Columbia (BC), the New Democratic Party (NDP) suffered a major defeat in the 2013 provincial election, prompting then NDP campaign director Brian Topp to argue that the party needed to run "a more aggressive, bloody-minded campaign" in the next election (Culbert 2013). The rise of the federal Conservative Party of Canada (CPC) under the leadership of Stephen Harper was also partly attributed to its increased use of attack ads. According to Tom Flanagan (2007, 285), who was CPC national campaign manager in 2004 and senior communications adviser from 2005 to 2006, "The Conservatives were ambivalent about playing hardball in 2004. Because we feared that negative ads might feed into the 'scary' image that the Liberals had pinned on Harper, we

---

1 This study modifies the original design and draws upon a new sample to re-examine the findings that we reported in an article that was first published in the *Canadian Journal of Political Science* (Roy and Alcantara 2016).

made whimsical ads such as 'Carousel' and 'Cookie Jar'" (Rose 2004, 95). In 2006, however, CPC advertising went for the jugular with an unflattering picture of Paul Martin, and it paid off. Since then, the CPC's strategy has continued to rely heavily on running "hard-hitting, fact-based negative ads; and [to] do whatever is legally possible to jam our opponents' communications and disrupt their operations" (Flanagan 2007, 285).

Attack ads target not just political parties and party leaders but also individual candidates and politicians during and outside election campaigns. In March 2018, one report uncovered 240 federal CPC social media ads attacking "16 different Liberal MPs [in Ontario and New Brunswick] by name for supporting what the Conservatives call 'Trudeau's values test' – the rule put in place by the Trudeau government that organizations applying for federal summer job grants had to affirm that they supported a women's right to choose." One ad contained the following message: "Did you know that Liberal MP Ruby Sahota voted to impose a values test on Canadians? ... We think this is wrong – sign if you agree" (Akin 2018). Similarly, in the city of Burlington, Ontario, mayoral candidate Marianne Meed Ward was the target of a flyer by "Ward 3 city councilor [sic] candidate Peter Rusin" in October 2018 that called her "Self-Centred," "Disruptive," "Negative and Pessimistic," and "Calculating" and claimed that she had a "Poor understanding of numbers" (Craggs 2018).

Negative campaigning has become a major feature in Canadian politics. Surprisingly, however, little empirical research has been published on its effects in the context of the Canadian political system (Daignault, Soroka, and Giasson 2013, 168; Haddock and Zanna 1997; Jerit 2004). Instead, the basis for much of our assumptions about the effectiveness of negative messages stems from anecdotal evidence (Flanagan 2014; Rose 2004) or from American studies, which focus on two-party contests (Lau, Sigelman, and Brown Rovner 2007; Fridkin and Kenney 2011; Krupnikov 2014; Krupnikov and Piston 2015; Krupnikov and Bauer 2014; Marks, Manning, and Ajzen 2012; Wu and Dahmen 2010). As a result, politicians and commentators have very limited empirical evidence to support their claims that attack ads work in Canada.

In two-party races, the outcomes are relatively easy to predict. Negative ads will either decrease or increase support for the attacker or the target. But what happens in a multiparty system if one or more parties run a negative campaign, while others maintain a more positive message? How do voters respond to differing campaign tones in a multiparty context? Adding additional parties or candidates increases the complexity of the potential effects, making it difficult to translate the findings of the American literature to multiparty systems such as those in Canada (Flanagan 2014, 158–9).

In this chapter, we analyse original data collected from an online voting experiment to answer two sets of questions relating to negative campaigning in a multiparty context. First, to what extent do the attention and vote share that a candidate receives vary according to the tone (positive or negative) of his or her election campaign? Second, do a candidate's vote share and the attention that he or she receives change depending on the tone of the other candidates' campaigns? Although we have provided a preliminary answer to these questions in previous work (Roy and Alcantara 2016), this chapter takes that research further by collecting a new and independent sample and by using actual party labels (e.g., CPC, Liberal, and NDP) to assess the effects of negative messages on Canadian voter behaviour at the federal level.

Background, Theory, and Expectations

Generally speaking, studies of negative election campaigns have tended to focus less on the nature of an attack (e.g., issue-based attacks versus character-based ones) and more on the overall tone of the campaigns being waged by the candidates and/or parties (Lau, Sigelman, and Brown Rovner 2007). In John Geer's (2006, 23) influential book, he defines negativity as "any criticism leveled by one candidate against another during a campaign." Following his work, the literature has tended to define a negative campaign in two ways. One body of scholarship has favoured a *directional* definition, conceptualizing negativity in broad terms: as any election campaign in which a candidate or a party *criticizes an opponent* rather than *emphasizing their own positive aspects* (Curini and Martelli 2010, 636; Hansen and Pedersen 2008, 409; Nai 2013, 44). These criticisms usually focus on a candidate's personal traits and characteristics, or a candidate's or political party's policies, ideas, and voting record (Lau and Brown Rovner 2009, 286). In this sense, negative campaigning is directional because the candidates or parties use negativity in the hope of attracting support for themselves and diminishing support for their opponents (Walter, van der Brug, and van Praag 2013).

Other researchers have conceptualized negative campaigns more narrowly, in an *evaluative* manner. For these scholars, negativity is defined as including only "those critiques that are unfair, illegitimate, dishonest and deal with trivial issues" (Walter, van der Brug, and van Praag 2013, 369). To be classified as negative, campaign messages must violate certain democratic norms, such as fair play, civility, and mutual respect (Dermody and Hanmer-Lloyd 2011, 739; Fridkin and Kenney 2011, 308; Pattie et al. 2010, 334). These messages can range from more "innocuous efforts," which are purely cognitive, to more direct, purposive, and cognitive-emotional *ad hominem* attacks (Dermody and Scullion 2003, 82; Jackson, Mondak, and Huckfeldt 2009, 56; Fridkin and Kenney 2008, 699).

Positive campaigns, on the other hand, have received less conceptual scrutiny in the literature, and, as a result, they have tended to be defined as being opposite to the evaluative and directional negative definitions outlined above. Positive campaigns, for instance, are usually defined as situations or strategies in which a candidate or party focuses mainly on promoting their own policies, agendas, voting records, characteristics, and experiences (Carraro, Castelli, and Gawronski 2013; Sullivan and Sapir 2012, 294). This definition would be a directional conception of a positive campaign. Positive campaigns have also been defined as situations or strategies in which a candidate or party has offered "a legitimate critique of an opponent's policy stands, qualifications, or other substantive information" (Stevens et al. 2008, 528). This definition would be an evaluative conception of a positive campaign.

In terms of the extent to which negative campaigns affect vote choice, the evidence is mixed. Although some studies have found that negative messages can be effective, depending on their content and tone and the timing with which they are deployed (Wu and Dahmen 2010; Fridkin and Kenney 2011; Marks, Manning, and Ajzen 2012; Krupnikov 2014), on the whole, researchers have yet to demonstrate definitively that "going negative" in the American context is an effective strategy for winning votes (Lau, Sigelman, and Brown Rovner 2007, 1183; Lau and Brown Rovner 2009). Indeed, in some cases, negative campaigns can actually harm their users (this is called the backlash effect) far more than their intended targets (Lau, Sigelman, and Brown Rovner 2007, 1182–3).

These findings are somewhat surprising because they are seemingly at odds with a large body of research on the prevalence of a "negativity bias" among human beings. According to this research, humans, on the whole, tend to emphasize negative entities and phenomena over positive ones (Krupnikov 2012, 391; Rozin and Royzman 2001; Soroka 2014). Some experiments, for instance, have found that "an angry face 'pops out' of a crowd of happy faces, but a single happy face does not stand out in an angry crowd. The brains of humans and other animals contain a mechanism that is designed to give priority to bad news" (Kahneman 2011, 301). Moreover, and crucial to our study, is the finding that negativity induces the human brain to classify phenomena as immediately threatening, even if there is no real threat or if the threat is merely symbolic. Negativity repels the human brain and pushes individuals to engage in loss aversion to avoid potential dangers and threats (300–1).

As a result, we should expect to find that negative campaign messages not only reduce support for their intended targets but are also more memorable to voters. The literature, on the other hand, suggests that negative messages do not reduce such support (see Lau, Sigelman, and Brown Rovner 2007), partly because the effects of the negativity bias may be tempered by the nature of the actor delivering the message and his or her intentions for doing so. Although citizens may pay more attention to and be more apt to recall negative campaign messages, the effects of these messages are likely to be mitigated by the fact that they are being delivered by an opponent whose main goal is to defeat the other candidates and win office (as opposed to running for the greater good). Thus, negative tones may produce a backlash against the deliverer rather than reducing citizen support for the party or individual being attacked (Lau, Sigelman, and Brown Rovner, 1182–3).

These assumptions and findings are consistent with the research on negativity bias, negativity dominance, and loss aversion. Voters who punish the deliverers of negativity in a political campaign may be doing so because they recognize that these deliverers are likely more dangerous than the target(s) of the attack. Absent other information, individuals will be suspicious of an attacker's motives, especially in a political campaign, in which the main goal of the participants is to win power and influence policy. Put another way, voters with no information other than the negative messages will respond negatively to the producer of the attacks because of the nature of the contest (i.e., to win power) and our inherent predispositions to negativity and loss aversion. Of course, political campaigns involve all sorts of other informational (e.g., partisanship) and contextual (e.g., the economy) dynamics that interact with the negative messages, so much of the research on this topic has produced a rich yet mixed set of results. If we strip away these contextual factors and consider only the effects of negative tones on vote choice, it is reasonable, from a theoretical standpoint, to expect voters to punish the producers of negativity and to reward targets who remain positive.

An additional consideration is how parties and candidates respond to the tone of their opponent's campaign. Studies have found "that people explicitly dislike and condemn the use of negative campaigning during political races, also when the negative messages represent a reaction to a previous attack. Indeed, as expected, the participants evaluated more positively (i.e., more competent and warmer) the candidate who ignored the attacks as compared with the candidate who counter-punched" (Carraro et al. 2012, 795). Craig, Rippere, and Silber

Grayson's (2014) findings are more nuanced; they discovered that different types of responses (e.g., counter-attacks, denials, counter-imaging, justifications, and charges of mudslinging) could mitigate the effects of negative advertising to different degrees. All this research, while useful and informative, has focused on two-party and two-candidate races rather than multiparty and multi-candidate ones.

In sum, although the literature on negative campaigning in two-party and two-candidate races is large, well-developed, and diverse (e.g., Lau, Sigelman, and Brown Rovner 2007), the scholarship on multiparty systems is not (Walter and Vliegenthart 2010; Walter 2014; Nai 2013; Walter, van der Brug, and van Praag 2013; Hansen and Pedersen 2008; Daignault, Soroka, and Giasson 2013; Soroka and McAdams 2015; Haddock and Zanna 1997; Rose 2004). Accordingly, very little is known about the effects of negative campaigning in multiparty systems such as those found in Canada, Europe, and New Zealand, for example. We build upon existing work by considering how voters react to the way candidates respond to negative campaigning in multiparty systems. In particular, our study allows us to assess the impact of mixed candidate messages and responses (e.g., one candidate ignores an opponent's negative campaign, while another responds with a counterattack) relative to the impact when all candidates employ a similar tone.

Answering these questions is important for teasing out the effects of different choice sets and levels of informational complexity on voting behaviour. In two-candidate races, the choice set available to voters is much smaller compared with the choice set in multi-candidate races. In two-candidate races, different campaign tones (e.g., positive and negative) will either increase or decrease support for the candidate or increase or decrease support for the opponent. They may also increase or decrease voter turnout. As well, voters in these situations face relatively limited levels of informational complexity, making their decision about whom to vote for relatively simple (Lau, Sigelman, and Brown Rovner 2007). In multiparty races, however, the choice set and informational demands are much more complex. It is unclear, given the greater number of options and informational complexity in these contests, how voters will react to additional candidates adopting different campaign tones. Multiparty settings, therefore, are valuable sites for assessing how voters deal with more choices and more information from multiple candidates (e.g., $N > 2$).

Rather than drafting a speculative set of expectations based solely on the limited literature on negativity in multiparty systems, we draw upon the American literature as our starting point and apply its findings to the Canadian setting. While there is some evidence that negative campaigning potentially increases campaign knowledge and interest (Lau, Sigelman, and Brown Rovner 2007), the majority of the research findings show that it tends to produce no advantage and, in some cases, may result in significant backlash against the attacker, with voters voting against him or her. Similarly, research in the Canadian context suggests that while negative information might heighten interest (Daignault, Soroka, and Giasson 2013; Soroka and McAdams 2015), it may also move voters away from the candidate engaged in the negative campaign (Haddock and Zanna 1997). Given our experimental design, in which it is the candidate who delivers the negative message, we expect voter backlash to decrease the vote share for the attacking candidate. Combined with earlier evidence of negative messages increasing interest and attention, we put forth our first two hypotheses:

> H1: The amount of attention that a candidate receives will be greater when he or she engages in a negative campaign relative to the attention received when offering a more positive message.
> H2: The vote share that a candidate receives will be lower when he or she engages in a negative campaign relative to the vote share received when offering a more positive message.

How might the relationship between campaign tone and the attention and vote share that a candidate receives change when moving from a two-party to a multiparty context? For example, in a three-way race, there are numerous possible combinations of the number of parties adopting positive or negative messages.[2] One combination might involve all three parties going negative; another might see all the parties deciding to go positive. We might also expect a situation where one party goes negative and the other two go positive and another instance where one party goes positive and the others go negative. In the first two scenarios (all parties go negative or all go positive), all else being equal, we should see no difference in vote support among the parties because the effects of the messages should cancel each other out. In the third and fourth scenarios, however (one party goes negative, the others positive, or vice versa), we should see some important differences in each party's vote support. Specifically, we expect that the party that goes negative against two positive campaigns will lose more vote support compared with the

---

2 While we use a three-party competition to develop our argument and test our assumptions, we believe that our findings can be extended to other multiparty contexts with more than three competitive parties.

scenario in which two or more parties adopt negative campaign messages (see Carraro et al. 2012). We believe that the contrast in campaign tone across parties will become more apparent to voters in a multiparty context, especially when one of the parties stands out as the only one to engage in a negative (or positive) campaign. Thus, in a multiparty setting, we expect the relationship between campaign tone effect and the number of parties to be linear, with the effects most evident when only a single candidate engages in negative (or positive) campaigning and weakest when all three candidates engage in similar campaign styles. This forms the basis of our third and fourth hypotheses:

H3: The amount of attention that a candidate receives when engaged in a negative campaign will decrease as the number of candidates engaged in similar campaign tone increases.

H4: The loss of vote share that a candidate receives when engaged in a negative campaign will decrease as the number of candidates engaged in similar campaign tone increases.

Before turning to our research design and analysis, we should note that our focus in this chapter is on the impact of campaign tone generally, not examining the effects of particular attack ads or changes in tone over the course of a campaign. In other words, we are interested in the effects of consistent campaign tones (positive or negative) on voting behaviour. Certainly, there are instances where candidates may adopt a positive campaign tone (e.g., in their door-to-door canvassing, commentary to the media, and political speeches), while at the same time running one-off or more sustained negative ads on radio, television, and the Internet. Candidates may also choose to start a campaign with a generally positive tone and then eventually go negative. In this chapter, however, we focus solely on consistently positive versus negative campaigns to isolate the baseline effects of campaign tone in multiparty systems. We hope that others will build upon the findings reported here to assess the robustness of our results under alternative conditions.

Methodology

To test our hypotheses, we employed a web-based experiment using Canadian respondents (see chapter 1 for additional sample information and study dates).[3] After consenting to participate in our study,

---

3 Although our sample consists only of Canadians, given the design of our study, we have no reason to believe that the findings would differ in most other multiparty contexts.

Table 2.1. Campaign tone treatments

Treatment	CPC	LIB	NDP	N
1	Positive	Positive	Positive	104
2	Positive	Positive	Negative	94
3	Positive	Negative	Negative	98
4	Negative	Positive	Negative	86
5	Negative	Negative	Positive	103
6	Negative	Positive	Positive	100
7	Positive	Negative	Positive	98
8	Negative	Negative	Negative	86
Total				769

Note: The cells indicate the tone of the campaign for each candidate. The number of participants in each group is listed in the last column.

they completed a brief survey, which allowed us to capture a host of individual-level characteristics, including socio-demographic information, political interest, ideology, and so forth. Following the pre-survey, the participants were randomly assigned to one of eight experimental conditions, allowing every combination of positive–negative campaign tone across the candidates. Table 2.1 summarizes the campaign tone of each candidate in each treatment as well as the number of respondents in each group. (Note that each respondent participated in only one treatment; see the discussion below for further explanation.)

All eight treatments began with a pre-campaign instruction screen that introduced the participants to three fictional candidates, representing the CPC, LIB, or NDP, contesting an upcoming federal election.[4] Departing from our earlier study on this topic (Roy and Alcantara 2016), we included actual party labels in an effort to test the robustness of our earlier work, which had employed fictional party labels, as well as to increase external validity. We accounted for potential candidate bias by presenting candidates who were all male, approximately fifty years of age, and with similar profiles in regard to marital status, children, education, and experience (see chapter 1 for a discussion of the homogeneity of the candidates). All candidates had Anglo-Saxon names and surnames.

Once the participants had reviewed the instructions, they advanced to the Election campaign information screen, which provided five

---

[4] Given the increased number of treatments that would have been required to include additional parties, we limited our study to the three largest Canadian political parties, outside Quebec, at the time of this study.

information links, with identical titles, for each candidate (see appendix 2.1). The presentation order of the parties and candidates as well as the list of information links were randomized for each individual to guard against ordering effects. The participants could choose to access candidate information by clicking on the links. Unbeknown to them, we recorded the information links that they investigated.

The first manipulation was to vary the tone (negative or positive) of the campaign for each candidate. To do so, we altered three pieces of information: a newspaper story covering the candidate during the campaign, a direct quote from the candidate drawn from a TV debate, and a statement from a fictitious advocacy group named Campaign Watch Canada (see appendix 2.2). The manipulation reflected the tone of the information. For positive campaigns, the newspaper story and the quote contained content in which the candidate spoke only about his own qualifications. Under the negative treatments, the stories and the debate quote presented the candidate as attacking his opponents, commenting on their lack of qualifications for political office. The statement from Campaign Watch Canada simply summarized the tone of the campaign (negative or positive) that the candidate had adopted.

Our initial sample consisted of 1,275 individuals, but 392 of these respondents did not view any of the information links before voting. Of the remaining 883 participants who accessed information on the candidates, 783 (approximately 89%) viewed at least one of the cueing campaign-tone links. Given the focus of our research questions, we included in the analyses that follow only those who viewed at least one of the cueing links. The reason for doing this was simple: we could not assess changes in the number of information links accessed and the probability of voting for each of the candidates according to the tone (positive or negative) of the campaign if a respondent was not exposed to information conveying tone. Because all other factors were held constant, and the tone was assigned randomly, we could assess the impact of campaign tone by comparing differences in the information search and vote choice according to treatment.[5] Given the use of actual party

---

[5] We do not consider individual-level differences in the sequence in which the respondents accessed the links, either in this or in any of the subsequent chapters that include an assessment of the information search that voters undertook before casting their ballot. We focus primarily on "depth of search" – the number of factors each participant considered – as opposed to the type and/or style of information search that he or she chose (see Lau 1995, 2003; Lau and Redlawsk 2006; Redlawsk 2004). See chap. 1 for further discussion about the strength of experimental designs to isolate causal relationships.

labels, we also included controls for partisanship (PID). Our assumption was that partisan behaviour could vary regardless of treatment.[6] After adding these controls, we removed another 14 respondents who had not answered any of the partisan questions in the pre-survey; this reduced our sample to 769 individuals.

The second manipulation in this experiment reflected the number of candidates engaged in similar campaign tone. To fully test hypotheses 3 and 4, we designed a treatment for every combination of candidates engaging in negative or positive campaigns. Our treatments included all candidates running positive or negative campaigns (elections 1 and 8, respectively), a single candidate running a negative campaign (NDP in election 2, CPC in election 6, and LIB in election 7), and two candidates engaging in a negative campaign (LIB and NDP in election 3, CPC and NDP in election 4, and CPC and LIB in election 5). This design enabled us to test how the number of candidates employing similar campaign tone affected the vote decision process and choice.

Results

Appendix 2.3 summarizes the distribution of respondent characteristics for each treatment. To test whether random assignment to our treatments produced similar samples, we use a multinomial logistic regression model to predict the participants' assignment to treatment group as a function of socio-demographic characteristics, ideology, political knowledge (a scale based on their responses to five factual, political-knowledge questions), satisfaction with the way democracy works in Canada, PID (strong or very strong partisans), and political interest as well as whether they correctly answered a careless-response question administered during the survey. Our likelihood ratio statistic (χ^2 statistic, 83.93) indicates that assignment to treatment condition is independent of the respondents' characteristics, suggesting that there is balance on observables between conditions ($p = 0.99$; see appendix 2.4). In simpler terms, our test indicates that our random assignment process worked: the treatment groups are similar to each other.

Following on from earlier work (e.g., Daignault, Soroka, and Giasson 2013; Lau, Sigelman, and Brown Rovner 2007; Soroka and McAdams

---

6 Estimating different treatment effects according to party and strength of partisanship may also reveal how campaign tone affects both the information search and vote choice. However, due to sample size, with fewer than ten NDP partisans in half the treatments, we were unable to accurately assess such effects.

2015; Roy and Alcantara 2016), our first hypothesis contends that the amount of attention a candidate receives will be greater when he or she engages in a negative campaign relative to the attention received when offering a more positive message. To test this hypothesis, we set as our dependent variable the number of information links that a respondent accessed after clicking on the first link, which conveyed campaign tone.[7] Modelling the number of links accessed after exposure to the stimulus, as opposed to the overall number of links viewed, serves to further validate our causal mechanism; as noted above, our assumption that the treatment affected behaviour can be true only if the change in behaviour occurs following exposure to the stimulus (e.g., after a respondent read the positive or negative message). We run separate Poisson regression models for each candidate as a test of the robustness of our results as well as a means of identifying differences across the parties.[8]

To test the impact of negative versus positive campaigns, we add a dichotomous measure that takes the value of "1" if a respondent viewed at least one of the information links that conveyed the negative tone of the campaign (newspaper story, debate quote, or statement from Campaign Watch Canada) for the candidate and "0" otherwise. The results from this first set of analyses are presented in table 2.2.[9]

The results offer evidence that the tone of the campaign did influence the attention that the candidates received in our experiment: all three candidates experienced *increased* attention from voters when they criticized their opponents relative to the attention they received when they spoke of their own strengths. For the CPC, going negative increased the number of links that the individuals viewed, after being exposed to the tone of the CPC campaign, by nearly one full link (0.88). For the LIB

---

7 Note that nine of the fifteen links available cued the campaign tone. It is possible that the number of links that an individual accessed before the first cueing link might affect the outcome variable. We tested this possibility by adding a count of the number of links that he or she viewed before accessing the first cueing link to the model. The results were nearly identical to those without the additional control variable. Thus, we report only the results from the more parsimonious model.
8 We employ a Poisson regression specification since our dependent variable is a count of the number of information links viewed. We do not offer any a priori hypotheses about differences across parties but do consider the possible implications of any such observations in our discussion.
9 See chap. 1 for an overview of how to read the results reported in the tables and graphs. While the type of model used here (Poisson) differs from the example in chap. 1, the general interpretation of the values is the same. The interpretation of the results is also presented in the text that follows.

Table 2.2. Number of information links accessed after first tone-cueing link

	CPC	LIB	NDP
Negative campaign	0.31 (0.04)***	0.16 (0.04)***	0.20 (0.04)***
	[0.88]	[0.45]	[0.52]
Constant	0.96 (0.04)***	1.03 (0.04)***	0.96 (0.04)***
Pseudo R^2	0.02	0.01	0.01
N	769	769	769

Note: The cells report Poisson regression coefficients, with standard errors in parentheses and marginal effects/discrete changes reported in square brackets. PID is included in the models as a control but not reported.
***$p < 0.001$; **$p < 0.01$; *$p < 0.05$; a$p < 0.10$.

and the NDP candidates, going negative resulted in a 0.45 and 0.52 link increase, respectively.[10]

The results from this first assessment support our hypothesis: voters are more likely to access information about a candidate who goes on the attack relative to the attention the same candidate receives when offering a positive message. These findings also confirm earlier work that found that negative campaigns heightened interest (Daignault, Soroka, and Giasson 2013; Lau, Sigelman, and Brown Rovner 2007; Soroka and McAdams 2015), offering external validation of these results. It would seem that our participants were drawn to negative messages, thereby increasing the attention they paid to a candidate attacking his opponents. It is also noteworthy that these findings are similar to those reported in our earlier work (Roy and Alcantara 2016), which employed fictional party labels as opposed to the actual party labels used in the current study.

To further examine the implications of campaign tone, we turn to hypothesis 2, which states that the vote share a candidate receives will be lower when he or she engages in a negative campaign relative to the vote share received when offering a more positive message. Once again, we run separate models for each candidate, this time employing

---

10 To confirm the magnitude and significance of the treatment effects, we also tested our models using Stata's nearest-neighbour matching technique, matching on partisanship and the number of links accessed before the first cueing link. The results are very similar to those reported, with an increase of 0.91, 0.47, and 0.55 ($p < 0.001$) links for the CPC, LIB, and NDP candidates, respectively. We used the same technique for our vote choice models presented below and found similar consistency.

Table 2.3. Vote probability according to campaign tone

	CPC	LIB	NDP
Negative campaign	−0.82 (0.20)***	−1.07 (0.17)***	−1.34 (0.21)***
	[−0.12]	[−0.20]	[−0.20]
Constant	−0.47 (0.14)***	0.02 (0.14)	−0.31 (0.14)*
Pseudo R^2	0.26	0.18	0.20
N	769	769	769

Note: The cells report logistic regression coefficients, with standard errors in parentheses. Marginal effects/discrete changes are reported in square brackets. PID is included in the models as a control but is not reported.
*** $p < 0.001$; ** $p < 0.01$; * $p < 0.05$; a $p < 0.10$.

a logistic regression specification, with a vote for the candidate equal to "1." As with our first set of models, our sole explanatory variable is a dichotomous measure of whether a participant viewed at least one of the information links that conveyed the negative tone of the campaign, with controls for partisanship included in all models. The results from these models are presented in table 2.3.

Clearly, the voters in our study were put off by negative campaigns. In all three of our models, we find support for our second hypothesis, with the vote probability decreasing by a statistically significant ($p < 0.001$) 12 points for the CPC candidate and a drop of 20 points for both the LIB and NDP candidates when they engaged in a negative campaign compared with the vote share these candidates received when offering a positive message. Combined with the results above, we take this as clear evidence that the tone of a campaign affects the vote-decision process and vote choice. While voters may be more likely to pay attention to a candidate attacking his or her opponents, it appears that this added interest has negative consequences for the vote. These results mirror the conclusion drawn by Lau, Sigelman, and Brown Rovner (2007) in their assessment of published studies in the United States. They are also consistent with the findings of our previous study, except that the magnitude of the effect is weaker when real party labels are included. In our previous study, the likelihood of voting for the fictional candidates representing fictional parties decreased by 27 to 29 points (Roy and Alcantara 2016, 485).

While our first set of findings supports the results of earlier work (along with offering external validation of our experiment-based results), the primary objective of this study was to assess the impact of campaign tone in a multiparty context. To do so, we rerun both sets of models, this time taking into account the number of parties engaged

Table 2.4. Number of information links accessed after first tone-cueing link by number of negative campaigns

	CPC	LIB	NDP
One negative	0.46 (0.06)***	0.16 (0.07)*	0.18 (0.07)*
	[1.31]	[0.47]	[0.46]
Two negative	0.24 (0.05)***	0.14 (0.05)**	0.17 (0.06)**
	[0.68]	[0.40]	[0.46]
All negative	0.30 (0.07)***	0.19 (0.07)**	0.26 (0.07)***
	[0.85]	[0.56]	[0.68]
Constant	0.97 (0.04)***	1.04 (0.04)***	0.96 (0.04)***
Pseudo R^2	0.03	0.01	0.02
N	769	769	769

Note: The cells report Poisson regression coefficients, with standard errors in parentheses and marginal effects/discrete changes reported in square brackets. PID is included in the models as a control but is not reported.
***$p < 0.001$; **$p < 0.01$; *$p < 0.05$; ª$p < 0.10$.

in negative campaigns by adding three dichotomous variables to each model: one in which a candidate is the only one engaged in a negative campaign, a second that controls for conditions in which two candidates are engaged in negative campaigns, and a third for the condition in which all three parties are engaged in negative campaigns. As above, each of these dichotomous variables takes the value of "1" only if a respondent has viewed at least one of the information links conveying the negative campaign tone for the candidate under examination. In all cases, the elections in which a candidate employs a positive message are set as the reference. Once again, by running these models separately for each candidate, we are able to offer additional evidence of the robustness of our results as well as control for cross-candidate differences in the number of information links considered. Our assumption is that the impact of the campaign tone will vary according to the tone of the other candidates. Quite simply, we are testing to see whether candidates in multiparty systems are better off "fighting fire with fire" by countering negative messages with a similar tone or whether candidates are rewarded for maintaining a positive message even when being attacked by their opponents. According to our third hypothesis, the amount of attention a candidate receives when engaged in a negative campaign will decrease as the number of candidates engaged in a similar campaign tone increases. These results are presented in table 2.4.

The results offer partial support for our third hypothesis: the level of attention that the CPC candidate receives is reduced by nearly half when a second candidate opts to take on a negative tone. However, the relationship is not linear. When all three candidates engage in negative campaigns, the level of attention that the CPC candidate receives increases by 0.85 links. While this result is less than the 1.31 link increase we find when the CPC is the only party opting to go negative, it seems that the CPC candidate, as well as the LIB and NDP candidates, benefit when all parties opt for a negative tone relative to what we observe when only two candidates do so. For the LIB and the NDP candidates, the difference in the amount of attention received is similar when they are the only ones taking on a negative tone compared with the treatments when the CPC candidate takes on a similar tone. For these parties, having all three campaigns go negative appears to yield the strongest effects, at least in regard to the level of attention they receive relative to when they opt to maintain a positive tone. However, while increased attention has the potential to benefit a party and candidate, is this the case when it comes to the vote?

Our final hypothesis states that the loss of vote share that a candidate experiences when engaged in a negative campaign will decrease as the number of candidates engaged in a similar campaign tone increases. Here we rerun the models we used to test hypothesis 2, with the addition of controls for the number of candidates engaged in negative campaigns. Once again, each of these dichotomous variables takes the value of "1" only if a respondent has viewed at least one of the information links conveying the negative tone of the campaign for the candidate under consideration. We control for PID in all models. *Table 2.5* reports these findings.

The vote models offer intriguing results: the candidates in our study suffered at the ballot box for going negative, but the cost varied according to the number of other candidates engaged in similar behaviour. In all three models, we find a statistically significant drop in the probability of voting for the lone candidate who goes on the attack. The magnitude of this drop is substantial, ranging from a 23-percentage-point decrease in vote probability for the LIB candidate to a full 31-percentage-point decrease in the case of the NDP candidate. With the exception of the two-candidate condition for the LIB candidate, the results conform to expectations: the reduction of the vote share that a candidate receives when opting to go negative decreases as more parties take on a similar tone. In fact, for the CPC candidate, the coefficient when all parties engage in a negative campaign is positive, suggesting an increased vote probability of 3 percentage points under this condition, although this result is not statistically significant. The

Table 2.5. Vote probability by number of negative campaigns

	CPC	LIB	NDP
One negative	−1.90 (0.43)***	−1.24 (0.30)***	−2.08 (0.43)***
	[−0.28]	[−0.23]	[−0.31]
Two negative	−1.08 (0.26)***	−1.41 (0.23)***	−1.19 (0.27)***
	[−0.16]	[−0.26]	[−0.18]
All negative	0.22 (0.29)	−0.28 (0.27)	−1.05 (0.35)**
	[0.03]	[−0.05]	[−0.16]
Constant	−0.49 (0.14)***	0.02 (0.14)	−0.32 (0.14)*
Pseudo R^2	0.29	0.19	0.21
N	769	769	769

Note: The cells report logistic regression coefficients, with standard errors in parentheses. Marginal effects/discrete changes are reported in square brackets. PID is included in the models as a control but is not reported.
***$p < 0.001$; **$p < 0.01$; *$p < 0.05$; a$p < 0.10$.

one exception to the pattern, which is when the LIB candidate faces two parties that go negative, shows an additional 3-percentage-point reduction in vote probability relative to the treatment when the LIB candidate wages the sole negative campaign. However, we find that this 3-percentage-point difference is not statistically significant ($p = 0.60$).

Based on these results, it appears that the best strategy is for candidates to maintain a positive message, especially when the other candidates opt for a negative one. However, if one must go negative, it is advantageous if the others do likewise. While voters in our study paid more attention to candidates on the attack, with some variation according to the number of candidates engaged in similar campaigns, this increased attention was met with lower support at the ballot box.

Discussion and Conclusion

This research set out to test the impact of campaign tone in a multiparty setting. Our results show that campaign style can influence the attention that voters allot to candidates and the vote share that these candidates receive. In the case of the former, campaign tone influenced the amount of candidate information that the individuals sought: engaging in a negative campaign increased the attention that a candidate received. However, while candidates received more attention when they opted for a negative tone, this effect did not translate into increased vote share. For example, in the treatment in which the NDP candidate was the sole individual to engage in mudslinging, his vote probability decreased by 31 percentage points (see table 2.5). We find similar results for all our candidates, results that offer additional evidence of the robustness of our conclusions. Similar to what occurs in the United States, our results suggest that voters in multiparty settings are put off by negativity when it comes to vote choice. Importantly, the impact that campaign tone has on the information search and vote share is conditioned by the number of parties engaged in similar campaign behaviour.

What are the implications of these results for party strategists and leaders interested in winning power in Canada? At a broad level, our evidence suggests that the effects of negative campaign messages are much more nuanced than party strategists and journalists would have us believe. Generally speaking, it is advantageous to maintain a positive message throughout an election campaign. If one must go negative, then one should do so only when all the other parties have adopted a negative tone as well. Strategically, it may be optimal to use a negative tone early in the campaign to encourage voters to seek out information about one's candidate and party; but as election day looms, one should switch to a positive tone to maximize voter support at the ballot box. Testing the impact of the timing and the shifting of tone across the campaign are promising areas for future research.

These important nuances may help explain the vigorous debate in Canada regarding whether going negative is an effective campaign strategy. CPC strategists argue that negativity was the key tool that helped Harper finally slay Paul Martin and the LIB dragon (Flanagan 2007). LIB strategies, on the other hand, suggest that Justin Trudeau's "sunny ways my friends. Sunny ways" campaign tone during the 2015 federal election is undeniable proof that going positive is the more effective strategy (*CBC News* 2015). Our study suggests that perhaps both arguments are correct, depending on the tone adopted by rival parties during the election campaigns.

REFERENCES

Akin, David. 2018. "Notebook: In 240 Facebook Ads, the Conservatives Take Aim at 16 Liberal MPs." *Global News*, 25 March 2018. https://globalnews.ca/news/4098917/david-akin-facebook-political-ads-canada/.

Carraro, Luciana, Luigi Castelli, Ioana Breazu, Giulia Campomizzi, Antonella Cerruto, Massimiliano Mariani, and Ivano Toto. 2012. "Just Ignore or

Counterattack? On the Effects of Different Strategies for Dealing with Political Attacks." *European Journal of Social Psychology* 42 (6): 789–97. https://doi.org/10.1002/ejsp.1884.

Carraro, Luciana, Luigi Castelli, and Bertram Gawronski. 2013. "Explicit and Implicit Effects of Attacking the Electorate of the Opposite Party." *Psicologia Sociale* 8 (2): 279–96. 10.1482/74264.

CBC News. 2015. "Justin Trudeau's 'Sunny Ways' a Nod to Sir Wilfrid Laurier." *CBC News*, 20 October 2015. http://www.cbc.ca/news/canada/nova-scotia/ns-prof-trudeau-sunny-ways-1.3280693.

Cicero, Quintus Tullius. 1970. *A Short Guide to Electioneering*. Lactor Series. London Association of Classical Teachers.

Craggs, Samantha. 2018. "Burlington Attack Ad Says Female Mayoral Candidate Is 'Irrational' and Bad at Math." *CBC News*, 16 October 2018. https://www.cbc.ca/news/canada/hamilton/meed-ward-flyer-1.4863431.

Craig, Stephen C., Paulina S. Rippere, and Marissa Silber Grayson. 2014. "Attack and Response in Political Campaigns: An Experimental Study in Two Parts." *Political Communication* 31 (4): 647–74. https://doi.org/10.1080/10584609.2013.879362.

Culbert, Lori. 2013. "NDP Report Calls for More 'Bloody-Minded Campaign' Next Time Around." *Vancouver Sun*, 20 September 2013. http://www.vancouversun.com/news/report+calls+more+bloody+minded+campaign+next+time+around/8935933/story.html#ixzz2gEnuf8KO.

Curini, Luigi, and Paolo Martelli. 2010. "Ideological Proximity and Valence Competition: Negative Campaigning through Allegation of Corruption in the Italian Legislative Arena from 1946 to 1994." *Electoral Studies* 29 (4): 636–47. 10.1016/j.electstud.2010.06.004.

Daignault, Pénélope, Stuart Soroka, and Thierry Giasson. 2013. "The Perception of Political Advertising during an Election Campaign: A Measure of Cognitive and Emotional Effects." *Canadian Journal of Communication* 38 (2): 167–86. https://doi.org/10.22230/cjc.2013v38n2a2566.

Dermody, Janine, and Stuart Hanmer-Lloyd. 2011. "An Introspective, Retrospective, Futurespective Analysis of the Attack Advertising in the 2010 British General Election." *Journal of Marketing Management* 27 (7–8): 736–61. https://doi.org/10.1080/0267257X.2011.587826.

Dermody, Janine, and Richard Scullion. 2003. "Exploring the Consequences of Negative Political Advertising for Liberal Democracy." *Journal of Political Marketing* 2 (1): 77–100. https://doi.org/10.1300/J199v02n01_04.

Flanagan, Thomas. 2007. *Harper's Team: Behind the Scenes in the Conservative Rise to Power*. Montreal and Kingston: McGill-Queen's University Press.

– 2014. *Winning Power: Canadian Campaigning in the 21st Century*. Montreal and Kingston: McGill-Queen's University Press.

Fridkin, Kim L., and Patrick J. Kenney. 2008. "The Dimensions of Negative Messages." *American Politics Research* 36 (5): 694–723. https://doi.org/10.1177/1532673X08316448.

– 2011. "Variability in Citizens' Reactions to Different Types of Negative Campaigns." *American Journal of Political Science* 55 (2): 307–25. https://doi.org/10.1111/j.1540-5907.2010.00494.x.

Geer, John G. 2006. *In Defence of Negativity: Attack Ads in Presidential Campaigns*. Chicago: University of Chicago Press.

Haddock, Geoffrey, and Mark P. Zanna. 1997. "Impact of Negative Advertising on Evaluations of Political Candidates: The 1993 Canadian Federal Election." *Basic and Applied Social Psychology* 19 (2): 205–23. https://doi.org/10.1207/s15324834basp1902_4.

Hansen, Kasper M., and Rasmus Tue Pedersen. 2008. "Negative Campaigning in a Multiparty System." *Scandinavian Political Studies* 31 (4): 408–27. https://doi.org/10.1111/j.1467-9477.2008.00213.x.

Jackson, Robert A., Jeffrey J. Mondak, and Robert Huckfeldt. 2009. "Examining the Possible Corrosive Impact of Negative Advertising on Citizens' Attitudes toward Politics." *Political Research Quarterly* 62 (1): 55–69. https://doi.org/10.1177/1065912908317031.

Jerit, Jennifer. 2004. "Survival of the Fittest: Rhetoric during the Course of an Election Campaign." *Political Psychology* 25 (4): 563–75. https://doi.org/10.1111/j.1467-9221.2004.00387.x.

Kahneman, Daniel. 2011. *Thinking, Fast and Slow*. Toronto: Penguin Canada.

Krupnikov, Yanna. 2012. "Negative Advertising and Voter Choice: The Role of Ads in Candidate Selection." *Political Communication* 29 (4): 387–413. https://doi.org/10.1080/10584609.2012.721868.

– 2014. "How Negativity Can Increase and Decrease Voter Turnout: The Effect of Timing." *Political Communication* 31 (3): 446–66. https://doi.org/10.1080/10584609.2013.828141.

Krupnikov, Yanna, and Nichole M. Bauer. 2014. "The Relationship between Campaign Negativity, Gender and Campaign Context." *Political Behavior* 36 (1): 167–88. https://doi.org/10.1007/s11109-013-9221-9.

Krupnikov, Yanna, and Spencer Piston. 2015. "Accentuating the Negative: Candidate Race and Campaign Strategy." *Political Communication* 32 (1): 152–73. https://doi.org/10.1080/10584609.2014.914612.

Lau, R.R. 1995. "Information Search during an Election Campaign: Introducing a Process-Tracing Methodology for Political Scientists." In *Political Judgment: Structure and Process*, edited by M. Lodge and K.M. McGraw. Ann Arbor: University of Michigan Press.

– 2003. "Models of Decision Making." In *Handbook of Political Psychology*, edited by D.O. Sears, L. Huddy, and R.L. Jervis. London: Oxford University Press.

Lau, Richard R., and Ivy Brown Rovner. 2009. "Negative Campaigning." *Annual Review of Political Science* 12: 285–306. https://doi.org/10.1146/annurev.polisci.10.071905.101448.

Lau, Richard R., and David P. Redlawsk. 2006. *How Voters Decide: Information Processing during Election Campaigns*. Cambridge Studies in Public Opinion and Political Psychology. Cambridge: Cambridge University Press.

Lau, Richard, Lee Sigelman, and Ivy Brown Rovner. 2007. "The Effects of Negative Political Campaigns: A Meta-analytic Reassessment." *Journal of Politics* 69 (4): 1176–209. https://doi.org/10.1111/j.1468-2508.2007.00618.x.

Marks, Eric, Mark Manning, and Icek Ajzen. 2012. "The Impact of Negative Campaign Ads." *Journal of Applied Social Psychology* 42 (5): 1280–92. https://doi.org/10.1111/j.1559-1816.2012.00912.x.

Nai, Alessandro. 2013. "What Really Matters Is Which Camp Goes Dirty: Differential Effects of Negative Campaigning on Turnout during Swiss Federal Ballots." *European Journal of Political Research* 52 (1): 44–70. https://doi.org/10.1111/j.1475-6765.2012.02060.x.

Pattie, Charles, David Denver, Robert Johns, and James Mitchell. 2010. "Raising the Tone? The Impact of 'Positive' and 'Negative' Campaigning on Voting in the 2007 Scottish Parliament Election." *Electoral Studies* 30 (2): 333–43. https://doi.org/10.1016/j.electstud.2010.10.003.

Redlawsk, David P. 2004. "What Voters Do: Information Search during Election Campaigns." *Political Psychology* 25 (4): 595–610. https://doi.org/10.1111/j.1467-9221.2004.00389.x.

Rose, Jonathan. 2004. "Television Attack Ads: Planting the Seeds of Doubt." *IRPP Policy Options*. September. 92–6.

Roy, Jason, and Christopher Alcantara. 2016. "Fighting Fire with Fire: The Implications of (Not) Going Negative in a Multiparty Election Campaign." *Canadian Journal of Political Science* 49 (3): 473–97. https://doi.org/10.1017/S0008423916000548.

Rozin, Paul, and Edward B. Royzman. 2001. "Negativity Bias, Negativity Dominance, and Contagion." *Personality and Social Psychology Review* 5 (4): 296–320. https://doi.org/10.1207/S15327957PSPR0504_2.

Simpson, Jeffrey. 2011. "The Truth about Attack Ads: They Work." *Globe and Mail*, 9 March 2011. http://www.theglobeandmail.com/globe-debate/the-truth-about-attack-ads-they-work/article623025/.

Soroka, Stuart. 2014. *Negativity in Democratic Politics: Causes and Consequences*. New York: Cambridge University Press.

Soroka, Stuart, and Stephen McAdams. 2015. "News, Politics, and Negativity." *Political Communication* 32 (1): 1–22. https://doi.org/10.1080/10584609.2014.881942.

Stevens, Daniel, John Sullivan, Barbara Allen, and Dean Alger. 2008. "What's Good for the Goose Is Bad for the Gander: Negative Political Advertising,

Partisanship, and Turnout." *Journal of Politics* 70 (2): 527–41. https://doi.org/10.1017/S0022381608080481.

Sullivan, Jonathan, and Eliyahu V. Sapir. 2012. "Modelling Negative Campaign Advertising: Evidence from Taiwan." *Asian Journal of Communication* 22 (3): 289–303. https://doi.org/10.1080/01292986.2012.681667.

Walter, Annemarie S. 2014. "Choosing the Enemy: Attack Behaviour in a Multiparty System." *Party Politics* 20 (3): 311–23. https://doi.org/10.1177/1354068811436050.

Walter, Annemarie S., and Wouter van der Brug. 2013. "When the Gloves Come Off: Inter-party Variation in Negative Campaigning in Dutch Elections, 1981–2010." *Acta Politica* 48 (4): 367–88. https://doi.org/10.1057/ap.2013.5.

Walter, Annemarie S., and Rens Vliegenthart. 2010. "Negative Campaigning across Different Communication Channels: Different Ball Games?" *International Journal of Press/Politics* 15 (4): 441–61. https://doi.org/10.1177/1940161210374122.

Wu, H. Denis, and Nicole S. Dahmen. 2010. "Web Sponsorship and Campaign Effects: Assessing the Difference between Positive and Negative Websites." *Journal of Political Marketing* 9 (4): 314–29. https://doi.org/10.1080/15377857.2010.522454.

Appendix 2.1. Election campaign information screen

☐ Election
☒ Research
☐ Group

Canadian Political Opinion

0% ▬▬▬▬▬ 100%

Election Campaign

Click on a link below to view more information.

Robert Johnson - NDP	Paul Smith - Conservative	George Stevens - Liberal
Campaign Information	Campaign Information	Campaign Information
Professional Biography	Professional Biography	Professional Biography
Campaign Watch Canada Comment	Campaign Watch Canada Comment	Campaign Watch Canada Comment
Newspaper Story – Politics	Newspaper Story – Politics	Newspaper Story – Politics
Voting Record	Voting Record	Voting Record
Quote from TV Debate	Quote from TV Debate	Quote from TV Debate

Going Negative in Canadian Federal Elections 41

Appendix 2.2. Examples of positive and negative newspaper stories, quotes from campaign, and statements from Campaign Watch Canada

Positive:

George Stevens
Liberal

NEWSPAPER STORY

Stevens continues whirlwind tour, talks 'Big Ideas'

METCALF – George Stevens of the Liberals spent the weekend meeting with voters in what has come to represent a whirlwind tour through the community. Speaking by phone last night, Stevens suggested that, "The only way to get a sense of the issues that matter to voters is to get out into the community." Stevens apparently spent the evening canvassing the neighbourhood for support, in an effort to drum up additional support for his candidacy.

For Stevens, the past few weeks have been a great learning experience. "I know that I have a great platform. But to be out in the community like this, I really get to talk to the average voter about the big ideas that matter" he noted.

At an earlier public engagement event, Stevens was overheard encouraging voters to consider his long-time record of community engagement. "I roll up my sleeves for this community each and every day," he stated. His campaign tour will soon take him to a number of neighbouring communities.

George Stevens
Liberal

Quote from Candidate's Debate

"I am confident that my platform best represents the interests of voters. I know this because I have spent time in the community, identifying the issues that really matter"

-George Stevens, candidate for the Liberals in this month's elections, speaking on KRJR television.

George Stevens
Liberal

CAMPAIGN WATCH CANADA COMMENT

George Stevens of the Liberals has appeared to invest most of his energies into emphasizing his active presence within the community, as well as his ability to best connect with the average voter. He has largely avoided any references to his opponents while on the campaign trail. Stevens continues to emphasize his long-term ties to the community, pointing out that his ability to represent the average voter is the core strength of his campaign.

Negative:

George Stevens
Liberal

NEWSPAPER STORY

Stevens takes aim at rivals as campaign tour heats up

METCALF – George Stevens of the Liberals has used a recent campaign tour to suggest that his opponents are "unfit for office" and "out of touch with the community". The message was delivered by Stevens himself, who took the opportunity to go door-to-door in an effort to reach local voters.

Speaking to media in Central Metcalf, Stevens remarked, "It is about time that the average voter saw the dangers in electing my opponents. They are not capable of stepping up to the challenge of holding office in this community". For Stevens, the past few weeks have provided ample opportunity to call into question the integrity of his rivals.

Following an earlier public engagement, Stevens asked local voters, "Would you let candidates so unfit make such important decisions?" When pushed to clarify the intention of the question, Stevens accused his opponents of being absent from the community. "They are ghosts," he charged. "I do not recall the last time I actually saw them out here talking to voters."

George Stevens
Liberal

Quote from Candidate's Debate

"*I roll up my sleeves to do work for this community, day in, day out. The last time my opponents were out here was for a photo op. They are not principled and could care less about representing the average person.*"

-George Stevens, candidate for the Liberals in this month's elections, speaking on KRJR television.

George Stevens
Liberal

CAMPAIGN WATCH CANADA COMMENT

George Stevens of the Liberals has tended to criticize his opponents wherever possible. His recent public appearances have been marked by a number of barbs directed at other candidates, ranging from accusations of being "unfit for office", to being "out of touch with the community". Stevens has also been present in a number of neighbourhoods delivering campaign flyers attacking his opponents.

Appendix 2.3. Summary statistics

	Election 1	Election 2	Election 3	Election 4	Election 5	Election 6	Election 7	Election 8
Age	45.92 (17.02)	47.86 (17.55)	46.22 (16.60)	46.08 (17.31)	48.23 (16.49)	47.22 (16.71)	48.45 (17.28)	48.03 (17.04)
Female	0.54 (0.50)	0.54 (0.50)	0.52 (0.50)	0.54 (0.50)	0.49 (0.50)	0.52 (0.50)	0.58 (0.50)	0.47 (0.50)
No high school	0.03 (0.17)	0.02 (0.15)	0.03 (0.18)	0.01 (0.11)	0.05 (0.22)	0.03 (0.17)	0.05 (0.22)	0.02 (0.15)
University graduate	0.36 (0.48)	0.41 (0.49)	0.41 (0.50)	0.44 (0.50)	0.39 (0.49)	0.40 (0.49)	0.32 (0.47)	0.43 (0.50)
Income	3.79 (1.86)	3.71 (1.93)	3.74 (1.83)	4.11 (1.82)	3.82 (1.69)	4.09 (1.95)	3.81 (1.67)	4.05 (1.97)
Prairies	0.27 (0.45)	0.22 (0.41)	0.26 (0.44)	0.33 (0.47)	0.23 (0.42)	0.29 (0.45)	0.28 (0.45)	0.34 (0.48)
Ontario	0.52 (0.50)	0.43 (0.50)	0.48 (0.50)	0.40 (0.49)	0.52 (0.50)	0.50 (0.50)	0.55 (0.50)	0.48 (0.50)
Atlantic	0.10 (0.30)	0.16 (0.37)	0.15 (0.36)	0.10 (0.30)	0.13 (0.34)	0.09 (0.29)	0.09 (0.29)	0.09 (0.29)
Satisfaction	0.78 (0.41)	0.80 (0.40)	0.81 (0.40)	0.77 (0.42)	0.78 (0.42)	0.80 (0.40)	0.79 (0.41)	0.80 (0.40)
Political interest	6.61 (2.28)	6.37 (2.38)	6.33 (2.31)	6.35 (2.41)	6.52 (2.12)	6.41 (2.54)	6.57 (2.48)	6.84 (2.38)
Political knowledge	0.59 (0.31)	0.58 (0.31)	0.55 (0.30)	0.57 (0.30)	0.61 (0.29)	0.60 (0.31)	0.57 (0.32)	0.59 (0.30)
Political ideology	4.70 (2.10)	4.65 (2.41)	5.02 (2.04)	4.91 (2.17)	4.89 (2.28)	4.73 (2.13)	4.96 (2.30)	5.20 (2.04)
CPC PID	0.20 (0.40)	0.18 (0.39)	0.14 (0.35)	0.23 (0.42)	0.22 (0.42)	0.15 (0.36)	0.23 (0.43)	0.20 (0.40)
GRN PID	0.03 (0.17)	0.02 (0.15)	0.04 (0.20)	0.02 (0.15)	0.04 (0.19)	0.01 (0.10)	0.02 (0.14)	0.05 (0.21)
LIB PID	0.24 (0.43)	0.27 (0.44)	0.23 (0.43)	0.26 (0.44)	0.21 (0.41)	0.29 (0.46)	0.23 (0.43)	0.20 (0.40)
NDP PID	0.11 (0.31)	0.13 (0.34)	0.11 (0.32)	0.09 (0.29)	0.06 (0.24)	0.14 (0.35)	0.08 (0.28)	0.08 (0.28)
Response check	0.98 (0.14)	0.95 (0.22)	0.94 (0.24)	0.91 (0.29)	0.93 (0.25)	0.90 (0.30)	0.90 (0.30)	0.94 (0.23)
N	106	95	99	88	103	103	100	89

Note: The cells report averages, with standard deviations in parentheses. Age is the respondents' age in years. Female, no high school, university graduate, regional variables, PID, and response check are dichotomous measures, coded "1" in correspondence with the variable name. Political interest and political ideology are self-reported positions on an eleven-point scale running from "No interest" to "Great deal of interest" and "Left–Right," respectively. Political knowledge is an index (alpha = 0.61) based on five factual questions: the name of the British prime minister, the level of government that has primary responsibility for education and health care in Canada, the name of the federal finance minister, the name of the governor general, and the number of seats in the House of Commons. The respondents received one point for each correct response. The variable was then rescaled to fit between 0 and 1. N = number of usable cases in each treatment.

Appendix 2.4. Multinomial logistic regression results for test of random assignment to treatments

	Election 2	Election 3	Election 4	Election 5	Election 6	Election 7	Election 8
Age	0.01 (0.01)	0.00 (0.01)	0.00 (0.01)	0.01 (0.01)	0.01 (0.01)	0.01 (0.01)	0.01 (0.01)
Female	−0.15 (0.31)	−0.29 (0.32)	−0.06 (0.33)	−0.16 (0.31)	−0.06 (0.31)	0.15 (0.32)	0.00 (0.32)
No high school	−0.47 (0.96)	−0.05 (0.88)	−1.00 (1.21)	0.48 (0.79)	−0.31 (0.96)	−0.09 (0.87)	−0.16 (0.96)
University graduate	0.36 (0.33)	0.42 (0.33)	0.38 (0.34)	0.15 (0.33)	0.07 (0.33)	−0.13 (0.34)	0.15 (0.34)
Income	−0.03 (0.09)	−0.03 (0.09)	0.07 (0.09)	0.01 (0.09)	0.09 (0.09)	0.03 (0.09)	0.06 (0.09)
Prairies	−0.85 (0.52)[a]	−0.39 (0.54)	−0.19 (0.52)	−0.32 (0.52)	−0.19 (0.52)	0.38 (0.56)	0.72 (0.60)
Ontario	−0.71 (0.46)	−0.21 (0.49)	−0.61 (0.49)	−0.17 (0.47)	−0.28 (0.48)	0.31 (0.52)	0.47 (0.56)
Atlantic	−0.06 (0.60)	0.38 (0.62)	−0.25 (0.66)	0.16 (0.61)	−0.30 (0.66)	0.32 (0.68)	0.40 (0.73)
Satisfaction	−0.19 (0.40)	0.15 (0.42)	−0.55 (0.41)	−0.22 (0.39)	−0.24 (0.40)	−0.10 (0.40)	0.05 (0.42)
Political interest	−0.12 (0.07)[a]	−0.05 (0.07)	−0.07 (0.08)	−0.07 (0.07)	−0.09 (0.07)	−0.01 (0.07)	0.04 (0.08)
Political knowledge	0.25 (0.53)	−0.32 (0.54)	−0.30 (0.55)	0.48 (0.53)	0.47 (0.53)	−0.09 (0.53)	−0.09 (0.55)
Political ideology	−0.05 (0.08)	0.10 (0.08)	0.01 (0.08)	0.01 (0.08)	0.00 (0.08)	0.02 (0.08)	0.10 (0.08)
CPC PID	0.14 (0.47)	−0.83 (0.50)[a]	0.32 (0.48)	0.03 (0.44)	−0.31 (0.48)	−0.06 (0.46)	−0.55 (0.48)
GRN PID	−0.56 (0.98)	−0.01 (0.87)	−0.42 (0.98)	−0.02 (0.83)	−1.40 (1.21)	−0.54 (0.97)	0.25 (0.82)
LIB PID	0.24 (0.40)	−0.42 (0.40)	0.19 (0.42)	−0.13 (0.39)	0.21 (0.39)	−0.14 (0.40)	−0.59 (0.42)
NDP PID	0.49 (0.52)	0.18 (0.53)	0.19 (0.56)	−0.83 (0.65)	0.45 (0.51)	−0.26 (0.56)	−0.39 (0.59)
Response check	−1.49 (1.14)	−1.72 (1.11)	−2.24 (1.09)*	−1.91 (1.09)[a]	−2.38 (1.07)*	−2.18 (1.08)*	−1.73 (1.11)
Constant	2.32 (1.49)	1.78 (1.48)	2.80[a] (1.48)	2.01 (1.44)	2.19 (1.45)	1.41 (1.47)	−0.08 (1.53)

N = 701
χ^2 (df = 119) = 83.93
Pseudo R^2 = 0.03

Note: The cells report multinomial logistic regression coefficients, with standard errors in parentheses. Election 1 is set as the base outcome. Age is the respondents' age in years. Female, no high school, university graduate, regional variables, PID, and response check are dichotomous measures, coded "1" in correspondence with the variable name. Political interest and political ideology are self-reported positions on an eleven-point scale running from "No interest" to "Great deal of interest" and "Left–Right," respectively. Political knowledge is an index (alpha = 0.61) based on five factual questions: the name of the British prime minister, the level of government that has primary responsibility for education and health care in Canada, the name of the federal finance minister, the name of the governor general, and the number of seats in the House of Commons. The respondents received one point for each correct response. The variable was then rescaled to fit between 0 and 1. N = number of cases with full response set.
*** $p < 0.001$; ** $p < 0.01$; * $p < 0.05$; [a] $p < 0.10$.

Chapter Three

Political Scandals

"I issue this statement reluctantly. ... The incident referred to in the editorial did occur, as reported." (Rose Knight, former journalist on the allegation that Justin Trudeau in 2000 had touched her inappropriately, quoted in Tasker 2018)

"It's not about what you did," he [Mike Duffy] quoted [Stephen] Harper as saying. "It's about the perception of what you did that's been created in the media. The rules are inexplicable to our base." Harper ordered him, Duffy said, "Pay the money back. End of discussion." (Hall 2013)

In 2012 and again in 2013, the auditor general of Canada, Michael Ferguson, announced that a number of Canadian senators had failed to properly support and document their various expense claims relating to housing, travel, and hospitality. The media immediately pounced on this news and focused mainly on the problems of four senators, Mac Harb, Patrick Brazeau, Pamela Wallin, and especially Mike Duffy, whose situation quickly morphed into a larger scandal due to allegations of political interference from the Prime Minister's Office (PMO). Sensing that this scandal could seriously harm the re-election chances of the prime minister and his Conservative Party (CPC), the PMO tried to diffuse and then distance itself from the scandal but failed to do so. Instead, the scandal dominated the headlines for much longer than expected and likely contributed to a noticeable decline in public support for the prime minister and his party. Some commentators believed that Harper's eventual defeat in the 2015 general election was partly the result of this scandal (*National Post* 2013; Pammett and Dornan 2016).

Political scandals can take many forms. They can be committed by groups, such as some members of the public works department during the federal sponsorship scandal in the early 2000s (Blais et al. 2010), or they can be committed by individual politicians and public servants, such as when former BC premier Bill Bennett, ten years after his time in office had ended, sold his shares of a company based on inside information that he had received during the Doman scandal in the late 1990s. The scandals can be of a financial nature, such as when several members of the Saskatchewan provincial caucus submitted false expense claims from a number of shell companies that they owned (*Canadian Encyclopedia* 2013) or when BC Premier Glen Clark was accused of accepting a new sun deck for his home in exchange for encouraging his government to approve a casino licence (*CBC News* 2000). Or they can be of a sexual nature, such as when federal minister Art Eggleton had to resign in 2002 because he "gave a defence contract to a former girlfriend" worth $36,500 or when it was reported in 2015 that Bloc Québécois [BQ] candidate VirJiny Provost would bring a "cellphone, a penis and chips" with her if a nuclear attack was imminent (*CBC News* 2015).

Given the numerous examples of scandal in Canada and the potentially negative impact it can have on one's electoral fortunes, political parties today are very careful to vet potential candidates before every election and nomination contest. Party strategists frequently interview potential candidates and comb through their social media sites, the Internet, and any other public databases for potentially scandalous information (Flanagan 2007, 241–2; Hazan and Rahat 2010, 30). In short, political parties want to reduce the possibility of fielding and promoting candidates who are prone to scandals or have committed them in the past.

In this chapter, we investigate whether there is an empirical basis for these concerns in Canada by considering two types of scandal emphasized in the literature as having a potentially significant effect on voting behaviour and public opinion: financial and sex scandals (Barnes, Beaulieu, and Saxton 2018; Carlson, Ganiel, and Hyde 2000; Doherty, Dowling, and Miller 2011; Funk 1996).[1] Our study adds to the literature by not only considering the impact of each type of scandal in the Canadian context but also investigating whether voting behaviour (both the information considered before casting a ballot and the vote that is cast) is affected by the location of the scandal – that is, whether it occurs in the public or the private sphere. Commentators frequently claim that Canadian public officials caught in financial and sex scandals in

---

1 Note that these types of scandal are also referred to in the literature as *corruption* and *moral scandals*, respectively. We believe that financial scandals also reflect low moral principles and, as such, use the more direct terms *financial* and *sex* scandals throughout this chapter.

the private sphere are unlikely to be punished politically by the public because of an unwritten rule among journalists that such topics are off limits; they are also supposedly not of any interest to everyday Canadians (Cohen 2014; Mancuso et al. 2006; Williams 2014). To explore these dynamics, we consider how the attention and vote share that a candidate receives varies according to whether he or she is involved in taking money (financial scandal) from his or her constituency office (public sphere) or a family member (private sphere). We also look at the attention and vote share received when a candidate has an extramarital affair (sex scandal) with an MP (public) versus a neighbour (private). All treatments are modelled against a control condition in which there is no reference to any scandal whatsoever.

Background, Theory, and Expectations

According to John Thompson (2000, 13), the term *scandal* has come to denote "actions or events involving certain kinds of transgressions which become known to others and are sufficiently serious to elicit a public response." This definition is similar to the one that Joseph Nye gives for *corruption* in "Corruption and Political Development," which appeared in the June 1967 issue of *American Political Science Review*: "behavior which deviates from the formal duties of a public role because of private-regarding (personal, close family, private clique) pecuniary or status gains; or violates rules against the exercise of certain types of private-regarding influence" (quoted in Anduiza, Gallego, and Muñoz 2013, 1665). In short, political scandals emerge when the general public becomes *aware* of a politician or public servant engaging in self-serving behaviour that breaks the law or violates public values, norms, or moral codes (Pattie and Johnston 2012; Redlawsk and McCann 2005).

Most of the time, such behaviour involves a politician or public servant using his or her position of power for illegal and/or self-serving purposes. In BC, a number of ministerial aides were arrested for "trading in stolen government documents related to B.C. [sic] government plans to sell B.C. Rail and Roberts Bank, a bulk coal-loading facility connected to the railway. The case summary alleged that David Basi and Mr. [Robert] Virk delivered confidential documents to a third party, apparently in the hopes of furthering their aspirations to win chief-of-staff positions with the Liberal government in Ottawa" (Hume 2004). At other times, a political scandal involves politicians and public servants simply making choices in their personal lives that are not illegal but are seen by at least some members of the public as morally offensive, such as engaging in an extramarital affair or frequenting strip clubs. There have been some cases in Canada of politicians having affairs with other politicians (*CBC News* 2016; *Maclean's* 2012) and even fewer stories of affairs with private citizens, but, in general, extramarital affairs are not reported as often as they are in other advanced democratic countries, like Britain and the United States (Cohen 2014; Williams 2014).

Generally speaking, the academic literature suggests that scandals tend to decrease public support for those politicians connected to the scandals, whether directly or indirectly (Hirano and Snyder 2012; Praino, Stockemer, and Moscardelli 2013, 1047), but that scandals by themselves rarely prevent candidates or parties from winning re-election (Choi and Woo 2010; Peters and Welch 1980). Peters and Welch (1980, 697), for instance, found that although "most candidates accused of corruption are reelected," those candidates still lose somewhere between 6% and 11% of their expected support as a result of the accusation. Drawing on data from the 1992 American National Election Study, Dimock and Jacobson (1995, 1157) found that "our best estimate of the cumulative impact of the House bank scandal is that it reduced the reported vote for incumbents by about five percentage points." Praino, Stockemer, and Moscardelli (2013, 1051) uncovered much larger effects: "On average, involvement in a scandal reduces an incumbent's margin of victory by about 14.5 points," and this effect lingers through to subsequent elections, although not to the same degree as when the scandal first emerged. Finally, using an experiment involving a real political scandal in Bavaria, Maier (2011, 293) found that "support significantly declined between the pre- and post-test not only for the politician involved in scandal but for other politicians not involved in the scandal."

Overall, the majority of studies suggest that the effect of scandals on public opinion and vote choice is modest or marginal. This variation may be partially explained by the nature of the scandal itself – whether it involves financial and sexual malfeasance. Doherty, Dowling, and Miller's (2011) review of the literature suggested that experimental studies favoured financial scandals as having a stronger effect, whereas observational studies found the opposite or no significant difference at all. Carlson, Ganiel, and Hyde (2000, 747), for instance, found that "both male and female candidates received lower character scores in the presence of a financial scandal than in the presence of a sex scandal." Similarly, Funk (1996, 11) found that "politicians involved in the tax evasion scandal were evaluated more negatively than those in the marital infidelity scandal." In terms of observational studies, Welch and Hibbing's (1997, 236) analysis suggested that sex scandals produced a decrease of 13 percentage points compared with 6 to 8 points for financial scandals. Brown's (2006, 163) study found no significant difference between financial and sex scandals in terms of vote share loss in US primary or general elections.

To reconcile these different findings generated by experimental and observational studies, Doherty, Dowling, and Miller (2014) examined both types of scandal in the context of whether a scandal involved an abuse of power. For the sex scandals, one scenario involved a politician having an extramarital affair with a fictional woman that resulted in her being employed in his office, whereas the other scenario simply reported a long-standing affair. For the financial scandals, one scenario involved a politician engaging in tax evasion and attempted bribery of the state auditor, while the other scenario simply reported the tax evasion. The results of that study suggested "that people respond more negatively to scandals that involve abuses of power (striped bars) than those that do not (solid bars)" (Doherty, Dowling, and Miller 2011, 751). We are unaware of any studies that examine the impact of the location – public versus private sphere – of a scandal.

Other studies suggest that partisanship can mediate the effects of scandals on vote choice. While it is both intuitive and likely empirically true that "voters unanimously prefer non-corrupt politicians, they disagree about other aspects of politics, such as which party should be in power; in many situations, their ability to deter corruption is undermined by their determination to achieve other political goals" (Eggers 2013, 1). In other words, partisans are more likely to ignore political scandals involving candidates from their own party, relative to non-partisans, when deciding how to vote. They do so because they prioritize other objectives, such as winning power, as opposed to sending a strong signal about the presence of scandal in their party.

Partisanship can also affect the willingness of voters to either accept wholeheartedly or with suspicion scandalous news about their party and candidates. Using data from the 2004 and 2006 Canadian Election Studies in relation to the federal sponsorship scandal, Blais et al. (2010, 7) found that "partisanship is a determining factor in people's opinion about whether Martin knew about the [sponsorship] scandal. Liberal partisans are significantly more likely to think that he was unaware. Opposition partisans, by contrast, are much more prone to believe that he was aware."

In terms of our formal expectations, we have constructed hypotheses using the above literature and the literature on negative campaigns outlined in chapter 2, at least for how we expect voters will likely search for information once they become aware of a scandal. We draw on the negative campaigning literature for two reasons. First, the literature on scandals is much less developed than the literature on negative campaigns, so very few studies have examined the effect of scandals on information searches conducted by voters.[2] Second, scandals, at their core, are a negative campaign message, and so it makes sense to expect findings similar to what has been observed in the negative campaign literature. Specifically, following our hypothesis in chapter 2, we expect that accusations of scandalous behaviour will heighten interest during a campaign, similar to what has been observed when studying the impact of negative campaigning on the information search (see also Daignault, Soroka, and Giasson 2013; Lau, Sigelman, and Brown Rovner 2007; Roy and Alcantara 2016; Soroka and McAdams 2015). However, while accusations of scandalous behaviour may heighten interest in an election, we expect that, all else being equal, the net impact of a scandal will lower vote share for the accused candidate. These assumptions form the basis of our first two hypotheses:

H1: The amount of attention a candidate receives will be greater when he or she is involved in a scandal relative to the attention received absent a scandal.

H2: The vote share a candidate receives will be lower when he or she is involved in a scandal relative to the vote share received absent a scandal.

We further theorize that the effects of a scandal will be strongest when it is of a financial nature relative to a sexual one. While recent work by Barnes et al. (2018) has demonstrated that sex scandals may have considerable impact on the vote, depending on both the sex of the candidate and the individual-level traits (namely, benevolent or hostile sexism), the bulk of the research tends to favour financial over sex scandals when it comes to influencing political behaviour (see Carlson, Ganiel, and Hyde 2000; Doherty, Dowling, and Miller 2014; Funk 1996; but see Brown 2006; Welch and Hibbing 1997). Thus, we expect that:

H3: The amount of attention a candidate receives will be greater when he or she is involved in a financial scandal relative to the attention received when involved in a sex scandal.

H4: The vote share a candidate receives will be lower when he or she is involved in a financial scandal relative to the attention received when involved in a sex scandal.

---

2 There are studies that examine the effects of different amounts of information about a scandal on vote choice and public opinion but virtually nothing on how scandals affect the behaviour of voters – that is, whether they search for more or less information (Blais et al. 2010; Funk 1996).

Our final set of expectations considers the domain of the scandal: whether the scandal takes place in the public or private life of a candidate. Journalists and commentators assume that Canadians are not interested in political scandals involving the private lives of their national politicians (Cohen 2014; Mancuso et al. 2006; Renzetti 2011; Williams 2014). But is this assertion true? Based on the arguments above, we expect that financial scandals, regardless of domain, will have a stronger influence than sex scandals. However, we expect that, scandal type being equal, public scandals will have a stronger effect than private-life scandals. Accordingly, we assume that financial scandals involving public institutions and figures (e.g., taking money from one's constituency office) will have a stronger effect relative to scandals involving private institutions and figures (e.g., taking money from family members). Similarly, we assume that sex scandals that occur in the public domain (e.g., having an extramarital affair with an MP) will yield stronger effects than a private sex scandal (e.g., having an extramarital affair with a neighbour). These assumptions form the basis of our final two hypotheses:

H5: The amount of attention a candidate receives will be greatest when he or she is involved in a financial scandal that takes place in the public sphere, followed by a financial scandal in the private sphere, followed by a moral scandal in the public sphere, with the weakest effects observed for a moral scandal that takes place in the private sphere.

H6: The vote share a candidate receives will be lowest when he or she is involved in a financial scandal that takes place in the public sphere, followed by a financial scandal in the private sphere, followed by a moral scandal in the public sphere, with the weakest effects observed for a moral scandal that takes place in the private sphere.

For all six hypotheses, we control for the influence of PID. As noted above, partisans may assess the accusation of scandalous behaviour differently when it is their party's candidate being accused as opposed to one in an opposition party.[3]

Methodology

To test our hypotheses, we employed a web-based experiment restricted to Canadian respondents living outside Quebec (see chapter 1

---

3 Ideally, we would estimate different treatment effects according to partisanship. However, as is the case in the other studies reported in this book, the number of partisans in each group is too small to accurately assess such effects.

Table 3.1. Political scandal treatments

Treatment	CPC	LIB	NDP	N
Control	Control	Control	Control	108
1	Sex personal	Neutral	Neutral	105
2	Sex public	Neutral	Neutral	88
3	Finance personal	Neutral	Neutral	95
4	Finance public	Neutral	Neutral	109
5	Neutral	Sex personal	Neutral	96
6	Neutral	Sex public	Neutral	97
7	Neutral	Finance personal	Neutral	109
8	Neutral	Finance public	Neutral	92
9	Neutral	Neutral	Sex personal	107
10	Neutral	Neutral	Sex public	109
11	Neutral	Neutral	Finance personal	115
12	Neutral	Neutral	Finance public	104
Total				1334

Note: The cells indicate the presence and type of scandal for each candidate by treatment. The number of participants in each group is listed in the last column.

for additional sample information and study dates). After consenting to participate in our study, the respondents completed a brief survey that allowed us to capture a host of individual-level characteristics, including socio-demographic information, PID, political interest, ideology, and so forth. Following the pre-survey, the participants were randomly assigned to one of twelve experimental conditions or to a control group that did not refer to any scandal (see table 3.1 for treatments and appendix 3.1 for summary statistics). We modelled assignment to treatment groups as a function of socio-demographic characteristics, ideology, political knowledge (a scale based on their responses to five factual, political-knowledge questions), satisfaction with the way democracy works in Canada, political interest, PID (strong or very strong partisans), and the participant's response to an attention-check question, included in the pre-survey, to test whether random assignment to our treatments produced similar samples. Our likelihood ratio statistic (χ^2 statistic, 219.36) indicated that assignment to treatment condition was independent of the respondents' characteristics, suggesting balance on observables between conditions ($p = 0.22$; see appendix 3.2). In other words, the random assignment process generated groups that were similar to one another. Therefore, with the exception of PID, we excluded any controls in the models that follow.

The twelve treatments allowed us to assess each type of scandal, in both public and private life, for each of the three main Canadian political parties outside Quebec. We included actual party labels with

Figure 3.1. Election campaign information screen

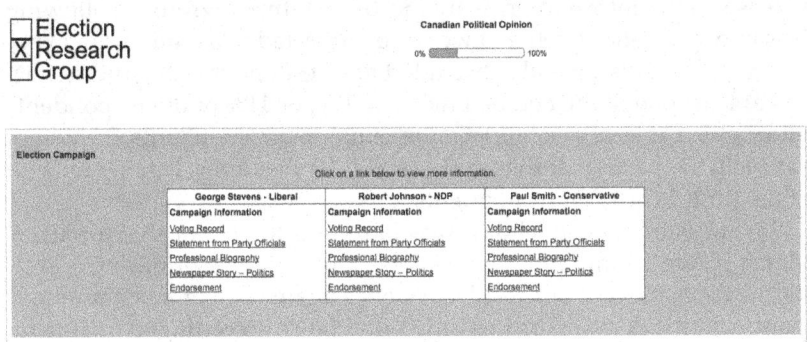

☐ Election
☒ Research
☐ Group

Canadian Political Opinion

0% [========] 100%

Election Campaign			
	Click on a link below to view more information.		
	George Stevens - Liberal	Robert Johnson - NDP	Paul Smith - Conservative
	Campaign Information	Campaign Information	Campaign Information
	Voting Record	Voting Record	Voting Record
	Statement from Party Officials	Statement from Party Officials	Statement from Party Officials
	Professional Biography	Professional Biography	Professional Biography
	Newspaper Story – Politics	Newspaper Story – Politics	Newspaper Story – Politics
	Endorsement	Endorsement	Endorsement

fictional candidates. To control for any potential candidate gender or ethnicity effects, all candidates were male, with names that suggested Anglo-Saxon heritage (see chapter 1 for the discussion of our choice to use homogeneous candidates). After reviewing the instructions (see appendix 3.3), the participants were presented with the Election campaign information screen, similar to that used in our negative campaign study (see figure 3.1). In this experiment, instead of learning of the tone (negative or positive, see chapter 2) of the candidates' campaign, they learned of a scandal through three cueing links: a newspaper story, a statement from a party official, and an endorsement (see appendix 3.4 for text). All newspaper stories and party statement links cued the scandal, regardless of the candidates' party affiliation, with the endorsement for the non-treatment candidates and the control stating: "There have been no endorsements to date." For the candidate involved in the scandal, the endorsement text was altered to emphasize that there was no endorsement due to the scandal. We once again included two non-cueing links, the candidate's biography and voting record, which were identical in all treatments and the control.

Given that it was impossible to assume a causal relationship between the scandal and changes in the information search if a participant was not aware of the scandal, we measured the information search as a count of the number of links that the individuals accessed, beginning with the first cueing link that they viewed in the treatment groups or the similar link in the control. The study began with 2,154 individuals. However, we excluded respondents who did not view any information links from all groups ($n = 620$, or 29%) to ensure that we were not biasing the results by comparing treatment groups, in which the minimum number of links was one, with a control group that would have included all participants who viewed zero links (e.g., an artificial increase in the information search in the treatment group). Following the same logic, and given that we were interested in the impact of exposure to the scandal, we also excluded any respondent who did not access at least one of the cueing links ($n = 174$, or 11% of the respondents who viewed at least one link). Of the remaining respondents, 26 did not complete the partisanship questions on the pre-survey, leaving us with a final sample of 1,334 respondents.

Our measure of vote choice was based on the ballot that a participant cast after completing the information search. As a means of testing the robustness of our results, we once again tested for within-party changes in the decision process and vote choice according to treatment. In all models, we controlled for PID (individuals who identify strongly or very strongly with a political party).[4] We turn now to the results of our analyses.

Results

We begin by considering the overall change in the information search when the scandal stimulus is present relative to the effort allotted to the decision-making process in the control. Given that this measure is a count of the number of links the participants viewed before casting their ballot, we employ a Poisson regression specification. We include a dichotomous measure of scandal that takes the value of "1" if the participants were exposed to any of the treatments and "0" if they were part of the control. A positive coefficient on our measure of exposure will support our assumption that the effort allotted to the information search will increase when there are reports of a scandal relative to the amount of information that individuals consider without the scandal cue.[5] To simplify interpretation, we display the results graphically.[6] The

---

4 As noted in chap. 2, it would also be interesting to consider PID as a mediating variable. However, due to the low number of partisans in each of the groups, we are unable to estimate reliable conditional effects. As such, we include PID only as a control.
5 Similar to the test we used in chap. 2 and again in chap. 4, we included a count of the information links accessed before the first cuing link as a control in all information search models (see chap. 2 for further explanation). The results were once again nearly identical to those without this control. Thus, we maintain the more parsimonious model specification.
6 See chap. 1 for an overview of how to read the results reported in the tables and graphs. See appendix 3.5 for full results for all models. We wish to thank Patrick Fournier and Shane Singh for their contribution to the graphing syntax used throughout this book.

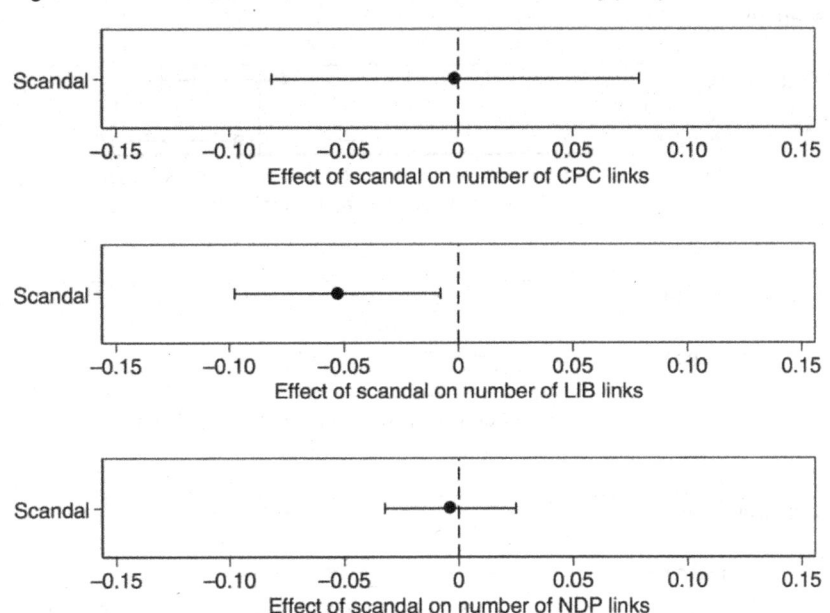

Figure 3.2. Treatment effects on the information search by party

[Forest plot: Effect of scandal on number of CPC links — point near 0, CI approximately −0.06 to 0.10]

[Forest plot: Effect of scandal on number of LIB links — point near −0.04, CI approximately −0.09 to 0.01]

[Forest plot: Effect of scandal on number of NDP links — point near −0.02, CI approximately −0.05 to 0.04]

point estimates report the change in the number of information links accessed when a participant is exposed to scandal information relative to the control group for each party separately. We also include 90% confidence intervals for each estimate. Figure 3.2 presents the results from this first model.

Contrary to expectations, exposure to a scandal did not lead to a more detailed information search. In fact, we find the exact opposite: exposure to a scandal treatment led the individuals to decrease the amount of information they accessed before voting, although this negative effect is only significant ($p < 0.10$) in the Liberal (LIB) model (see figure 3.2). It would seem that exposure to accusations of a scandal does little to alter the information search that individuals undertake before voting. Do these results hold if we account for the type of scandal? Our expectation is that financial scandals will have a stronger effect on the information relative to a sex scandal. To test this assumption, we rerun our models, this time taking into account the type of scandal (financial versus sexual). The results from these models are displayed in figure 3.3.

Our results once again contradict expectations. In all cases, we find virtually no difference between sex and financial scandals. As with

Figure 3.3. Treatment effects on the information search by party and type of scandal

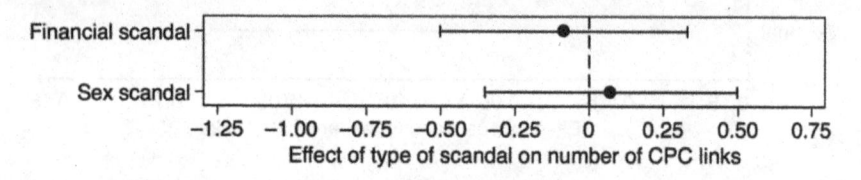

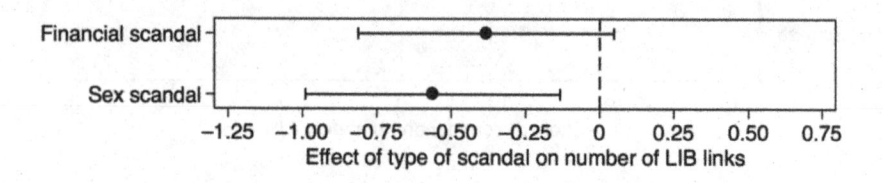

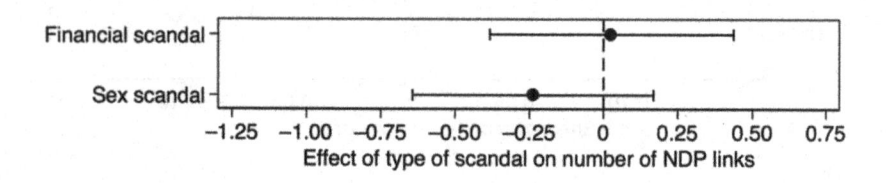

scandals in general, we continue to observe significant effects for the LIB sex scandal, but the opposite of what we anticipated. The one possible exception is the case of the New Democratic Party (NDP). Here we find that the change in the information search according to the type of scandal approaches significance ($p = 0.11$), with the financial scandal having a slightly positive effect on the number of information links accessed relative to the sex scandal (an increase of 0.03 links compared with a decrease of 0.24 links, respectively). For the CPC and the LIB, the amount of attention the candidates receive is no different, regardless of the type of scandal.

Do these findings hold when we consider whether the scandal took place in the public or private realm? To answer this question, we run a final Poisson model to estimate the change in the information search for each party according to the type of scandal and whether it occurs in the private or public sphere. We report these results in figure 3.4.

Once again, we find little support for our hypothesis: interest in a political party does not significantly increase when a candidate is involved in a scandal, regardless of scandal type or whether it takes

Figure 3.4. Treatment effects on the information search by party and by type and sphere of scandal

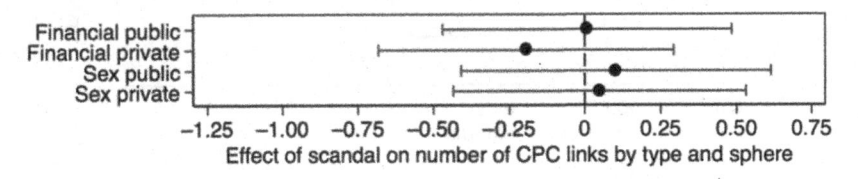

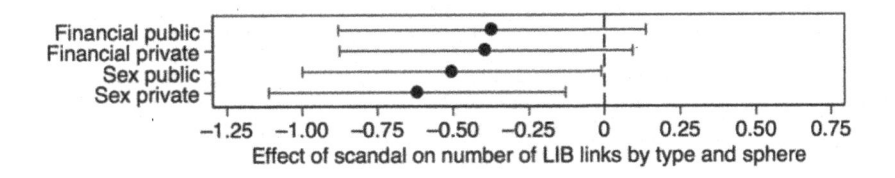

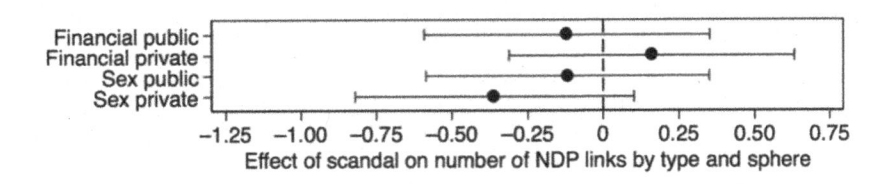

Effect of scandal on number of CPC links by type and sphere

Effect of scandal on number of LIB links by type and sphere

Effect of scandal on number of NDP links by type and sphere

place in public or private life. In fact, for the LIB, all four treatments led to a reduction in the attention the candidate received, albeit only the sex scandal results are found to be statistically significant ($p < 0.10$). In contrast with the results from our negative campaign experiment (see chapter 2), reports of scandalous behaviour do not significantly increase the pre-vote information search, as we had expected.

What are the implications of scandal accusations for the vote? To answer this question, we use logistic regression to estimate changes in vote share as a function of the reported scandal. We once again present the results graphically.[7] The point estimates report the change in the probability of voting for a candidate accused of a scandal relative to the probability of voting for that candidate in the control group, with 90% confidence intervals for each estimate. Results are presented separately for each party. Our first set of results (see figure 3.5) shows the change in vote probability, regardless of scandal type or sphere.

---

7 See appendix 3.5 for full results.

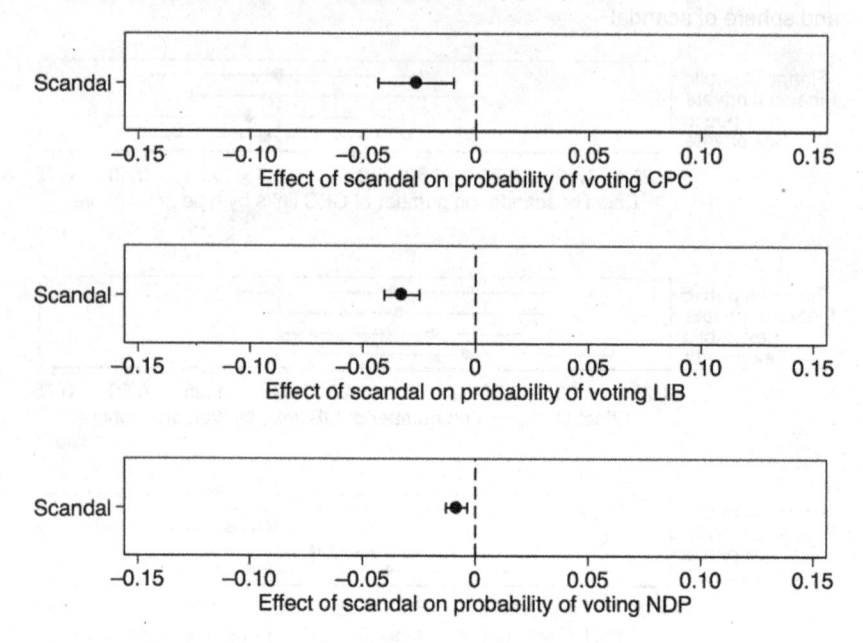

Figure 3.5. Treatment effects on vote choice by party

[Three forest plots showing treatment effects. Top: Effect of scandal on probability of voting CPC, point estimate near -0.03. Middle: Effect of scandal on probability of voting LIB, point estimate near -0.03. Bottom: Effect of scandal on probability of voting NDP, point estimate near -0.01.]

Parties pay a price at the ballot box when candidates are involved in scandalous behaviour. Our results suggest that such behaviour translates to as much as a 3-percentage-point decrease in the probability of voting for either the CPC or the LIB, while the NDP suffer a 1-percentage-point penalty when its candidate is embroiled in scandal. We dissect these effects further by isolating two types of scandal, as reported in figure 3.6.

Accounting for scandal types reveals some cross-party differences as well as partial support for our hypothesis. We had expected financial scandals to have a greater impact on the vote than sex scandals. For all three parties, we find that this expectation is true, although the difference fails to meet conventional levels of statistical significance in the LIB model ($p = 0.26$). Do these findings hold when we account for the domain in which the sex or financial scandal took place? Figure 3.7 reports the results from our final analysis, which estimates changes in vote share according to the type of scandal as well as the sphere in which the scandal took place.

Contrary to our expectations, voters did not view financial scandals in the public sphere as most serious. For all parties, it is the scandal involving personal finances that has the strongest effect – in the case

Political Scandals 59

Figure 3.6. Treatment effects on vote choice by party and type of scandal

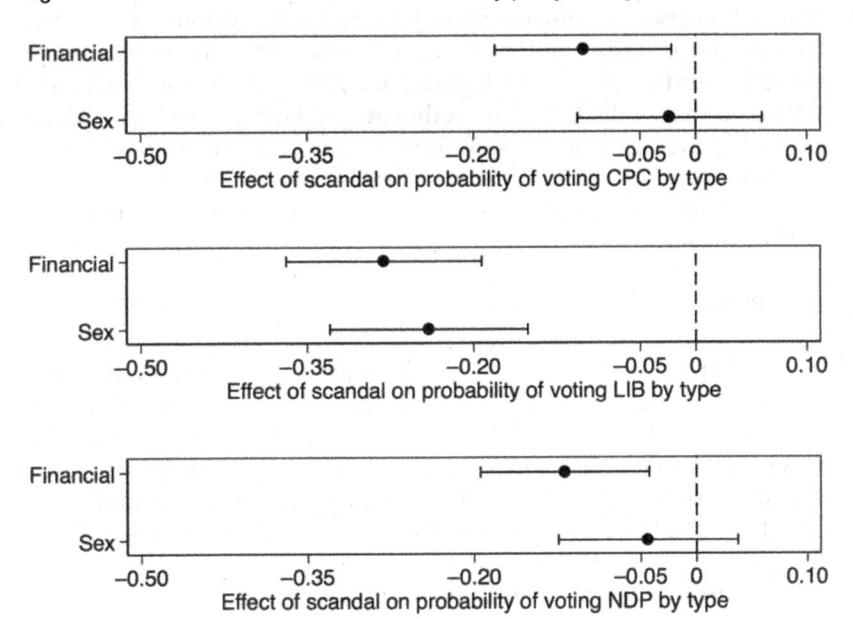

Effect of scandal on probability of voting CPC by type

Effect of scandal on probability of voting LIB by type

Effect of scandal on probability of voting NDP by type

Figure 3.7. Treatment effects on vote choice by party and by type and sphere of scandal

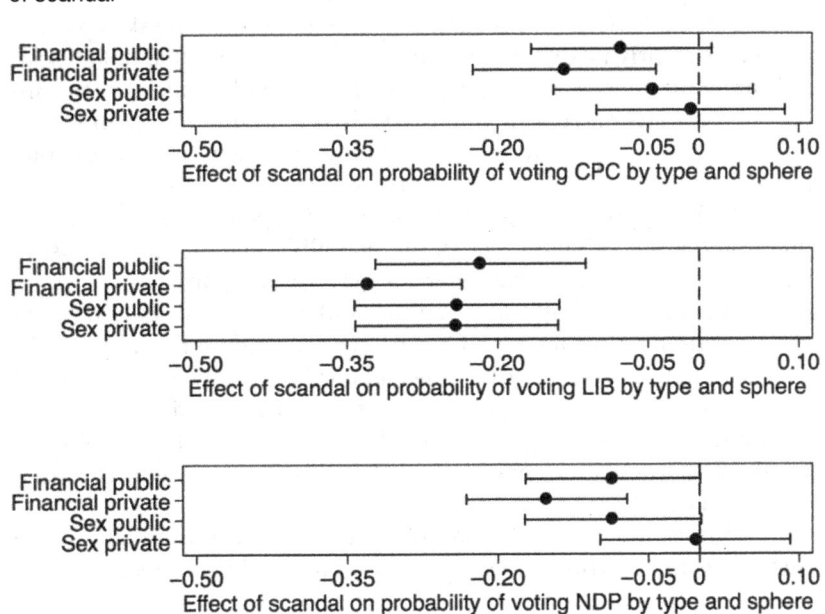

Effect of scandal on probability of voting CPC by type and sphere

Effect of scandal on probability of voting LIB by type and sphere

Effect of scandal on probability of voting NDP by type and sphere

of the LIB, decreasing the vote probability by more than 30 percentage points. It is also the personal financial scandal that is found to produce the only statistically significant effect for the CPC, although public financial scandal approaches significance. The pattern for the NDP is similar to that of the CPC, but in this model, both public financial and sex treatments are found to significantly ($p < 0.10$) reduce vote share. In the case of the LIB, there is little difference across scandal treatments: all four scandal scenarios produce a sizeable and significant reduction in LIB vote support.

Discussion and Conclusion

In this chapter, we set out to assess the impact of scandals on the information that voters seek out before voting and the vote they ultimately cast. We found that scandals can affect the information search that voters undertake. However, contrary to our expectations, the effect is negative. When exposed to accusations of scandalous behaviour, an accused candidate tends to receive less attention relative to the attention that the same candidate receives in the control group, net of partisanship. Contrary to expectations, these results tend to hold regardless of the type of scandal or sphere in which the scandal takes place.

We do find some evidence that the type of scandal can impact the vote. Sex scandals tend to have a weaker effect than financial scandals, failing to significantly reduce the vote for the CPC and NDP candidates (see figure 3.6). When we control for whether a scandal takes place in the public or private domain, we find further evidence that not all scandals are equal: the private financial treatment had a much greater impact on vote share, regardless of party, than our other treatments.

What are the implications of these findings for winning and keeping power? Given that the effects of scandals on vote choice are relatively small at the aggregate (e.g., between 1 and 3 percentage points) and that scandalous behaviour does not actually generate an increase in information-seeking among voters, it may be that parties could spend less time, money, and effort on vetting candidates for past scandals and their potential for future ones. Our results also suggest that not all scandals are equal, nor do scandals affect all parties equally. We certainly do not endorse the idea that political strategists dismiss the vetting process, but one potential implication of our research findings is that the cost-benefit calculation may be more heavily skewed towards caution than need be.

Of course, some readers may question how well the results from this experiment would hold up in the real world. For example, our treatments do not consider how a scandal may fuel opposition parties to shift their campaigns to focus on the scandalous behaviour and prime voters to consider how such behaviour may be representative of what to expect from the candidate if he or she were to win. Our work also does not account for the increased media scrutiny that may follow accusations of scandalous behaviour. These considerations certainly suggest areas for future work to build upon our efforts. However, at a minimum, our findings indicate that the impact of scandals on voting behaviour may be much more nuanced than we realize. Future work that adds to our research by considering various types of financial and sexual scandal (e.g., tax evasion, sex with an employee, etc.), media coverage and framing of various scandals, as well as the public's response to how accusations of scandalous behaviour are dealt with by party elites, would provide further insight into how scandals affect winning and keeping power in Canadian politics. We hope that our study serves as the catalyst for such future efforts.

REFERENCES

Anduiza, Eva, Aina Gallego, and Jordi Muñoz. 2013. "Turning a Blind Eye: Experimental Evidence of Partisan Bias in Attitudes toward Corruption." *Comparative Political Studies* 46 (12): 1664–92. https://doi.org/10.1177/0010414013489081.

Barnes, Tiffany D., Emily Beaulieu, and Gregory W. Saxton. 2018. "Sex and Corruption: How Sexism Shapes Voters' Responses to Scandal." *Politics, Groups, and Identities*. https://doi.org/10.1080/21565503.2018.1441725.

Blais, André, Elisabeth Gidengil, Patrick Fournier, Neil Nevitte, Joanna Everitt, and Jiyoon Kim. 2010. "Political Judgments, Perceptions of Facts, and Partisan Effects." *Electoral Studies* 29 (1): 1–12. https://doi.org/10.1016/j.electstud.2009.07.001.

Brown, Laura. 2006. "Revisiting the Character of Congress: Scandals in the U.S. House of Representatives, 1966–2002." *Journal of Political Marketing* 5 (1–2): 149–72. https://doi.org/10.1300/J199v05n01_08.

Canadian Encyclopedia. 2013. "Saskatchewan Tories in Fraud Scandal." 17 March 2003. Originally written by Brian Bergman and Dale Eisler for *Maclean's*, 18 November 1996. http://www.thecanadianencyclopedia.ca/en/article/saskatchewan-tories-in-fraud-scandal/.

Carlson, James, Gladys Ganiel, and Mark S. Hyde. 2000. "Scandal and Political Candidate Image." *Southeastern Political Review* 28 (4): 747–57. https://doi.org/10.1111/j.1747-1346.2000.tb00798.x.

CBC News. 2000. "Clark Charged in Casino Scandal." *CBC News*, 20 October 2000. http://www.cbc.ca/news/canada/clark-charged-in-casino-scandal -1.250439.
– 2015. "List of Candidates, Party Officials Who Have Made Headlines for Various Gaffes." Canadian Press, 16 September 2015. https://www.cbc.ca /news/politics/canada-election-2015-candidates-dropped-gaffes-in -trouble-1.3231366.
– 2016. "London Mayor Matt Brown Separates with Wife after Affair." *CBC News*, 29 September 2016. http://www.cbc.ca/news/canada/windsor /london-mayor-wife-separation-1.3783962.
Choi, Eunjung, and Jongseok Woo. 2010. "Political Corruption, Economic Performance, and Electoral Outcomes: A Cross-National Analysis." *Contemporary Politics* 16 (3): 249–62. https://doi.org/10.1080/13569775.2010 .501636.
Cohen, Andrew. 2014. "Cohen: The Private Lives of Politicians." *Ottawa Citizen*, 23 September 2014. http://ottawacitizen.com/news/national /private-lives.
Daignault, Pénélope, Stuart Soroka, and Thierry Giasson. 2013. "The Perception of Political Advertising during an Election Campaign: A Measure of Cognitive and Emotional Effects." *Canadian Journal of Communication* 38 (2): 167–86. https://doi.org/10.22230/cjc.2013v38n2a2566.
Dimock, Michael, and Gary Jacobson. 1995. "Checks and Choices: The House Bank Scandal's Impact on Voters in 1992." *Journal of Politics* 57 (4): 1143–59. https://doi.org/10.2307/2960406.
Doherty, David, Conor M. Dowling, and Michael G. Miller. 2011. "Are Financial or Moral Scandals Worse? It Depends." *PS: Political Science & Politics* 44 (4): 749–57. https://doi.org/10.1017/ S1049096511001247.
– 2014. "Does Time Heal All Wounds? Sex Scandals, Tax Evasion, and the Passage of Time." *PS: Political Science & Politics* 47 (2): 357–66. https://doi .org/10.1017/S1049096514000213.
Eggers, Andrew C. 2013. "Partisanship and Electoral Accountability: Evidence from the UK Expenses Scandal." *Quarterly Journal of Political Science* 9 (4): 441–72. https://doi.org/10.1561/100.00013140.
Flanagan, Thomas. 2007. *Harper's Team: Behind the Scenes in the Conservative Rise to Power*. Montreal and Kingston: McGill-Queen's University Press.
Funk, Carolyn. 1996. "The Impact of Scandal on Candidate Evaluations: An Experimental Test of the Role of Candidate Traits." *Political Behaviour* 18 (1): 1–24. https://doi.org/10.1007/BF01498658.
Hall, Chris. 2013. "Senate Expense Scandal: The Mike Duffy–Harper Credibility War." *CBC News*, 23 October 2013. http://www.cbc.ca/news

/politics/senate-expense-scandal-the-mike-duffy-stephen-harper-credibility-war-1.2159732.

Hazan, Reuven Y., and Gideon Rahat. 2010. *Democracies with Parties: Candidate Selection Methods and Their Political Consequences*. Oxford: Oxford University Press.

Hirano, Shigeo, and James Snyder. 2012. "What Happens to Incumbents in Scandals?" *Quarterly Journal of Political Science* 7 (4): 447–56. https://doi.org/10.1561/100.00012039.

Hume, Mark. 2004. "Charges Laid in B.C. Legislature Raid." *Globe and Mail*, 22 December 2004. https://www.theglobeandmail.com/news/national/charges-laid-in-bc-legislature-raid/article22733177/.

Lau, Richard R., Lee Sigelman, and Ivy Brown Rovner. 2007. "The Effects of Negative Political Campaigns: A Meta-analytic Reassessment." *Journal of Politics* 69 (4): 1176—209. https://doi.org/10.1111/j.1468-2508.2007.00618.x.

Maclean's. 2012. "8 Canadian Political Sex Scandals – and One Maybe." 29 August 2012. http://www.macleans.ca/society/life/8-canadian-political-sex-scandals-and-one-maybe/.

Maier, Jürgen. 2011. "The Impact of Political Scandals on Political Support: An Experimental Test of Two Theories." *International Political Science Review* 32 (3): 283–302. https://doi.org/10.1177/0192512110378056.

Mancuso, Maureen, Michael M. Atkinson, André Blais, Ian Greene, and Neil Nevitte. 2006. *A Question of Ethics: Canadians Speak Out*. Toronto: Oxford University Press.

National Post. 2013. "Stephen Harper's Conservative Party Tilts Right While He Faces Slow-Burning Scandal." Postmedia News, 3 November 2013. http://nationalpost.com/news/politics/stephen-harpers-conservative-party-tilts-right-while-he-faces-slow-burning-scandal/wcm/c2ab3e51-82fe-4b0e-92a8-07b2951221b0.

Pammett, Jon H., and Christopher Dornan, eds. 2016. *The Canadian Federal Election of 2015*. Toronto: Dundurn Press.

Pattie, Charles, and Ron Johnston. 2012. "The Electoral Impact of the UK 2009 MPs' Expenses Scandal." *Political Studies* 60 (4): 730–50. https://doi.org/10.1111/j.1467-9248.2011.00943.x.

Peters, John G., and Susan Welch. 1980. "The Effects of Charges of Corruption on Voting Behavior in Congressional Elections." *American Political Science Review* 74 (3): 697–708. https://doi.org/10.2307/1958151.

Praino, Rodrigo, Daniel Stockemer, and Vincent G. Moscardelli. 2013. "The Lingering Effect of Scandals in Congressional Elections: Incumbents, Challengers, and Voters." *Social Science Quarterly* 94 (4): 1045–61. https://doi.org/10.1111/ssqu.12046.

Redlawsk, David P., and James A. McCann. 2005. "Popular Interpretations of 'Corruption' and Their Partisan Consequences." *Political Behavior* 27 (3): 261–83. https://doi.org/10.1007/s11109-005-4469-3.

Renzetti, Elizabeth. 2011. "Why Are Canadian Sex Scandals So Boring?" *Globe and Mail*, 16 September 2011. https://www.theglobeandmail.com/arts/why-are-canadian-sex-scandals-so-boring/article594709/.

Roy, Jason, and Christopher Alcantara. 2016. "Fighting Fire with Fire: The Implications of (Not) Going Negative in a Multiparty Election Campaign." *Canadian Journal of Political Science* 49 (3): 473–97. https://doi.org/10.1017/S0008423916000548.

Soroka, Stuart, and Stephen McAdams. 2015. "News, Politics, and Negativity." *Political Communication* 32 (1): 1–22. https://doi.org/10.1080/10584609.2014.881942.

Tasker, John Paul. 2018. "Woman Who Accused Trudeau of Groping Breaks Her Silence." *CBC News*, 6 July 2018. https://www.cbc.ca/news/politics/woman-accused-trudeau-breaks-silence-1.4737511.

Thompson, John B. 2000. *Political Scandal: Power and Visibility in the Media Age*. Cambridge: Polity.

Welch, Susan, and John R. Hibbing. 1997. "The Effects of Charges of Corruption on Voting Behavior in Congressional Elections, 1982–1990." *Journal of Politics* 59 (1): 226–39. https://doi.org/10.2307/2998224.

Williams, Mimi. 2014. "Oh Canada, You're So Vanilla." *Vue Weekly*, 11 September 2014. http://www.vueweekly.com/political-sex-scandals-ring-around-world-canada-bit-quiet/.

Appendix 3.1. Summary statistics

	Control	Treatment 1	Treatment 2	Treatment 3	Treatment 4	Treatment 5	Treatment 6
Age	47.94 (16.86)	47.31 (16.02)	45.28 (15.74)	45.77 (15.99)	47.24 (17.06)	49.85 (16.04)	51.26 (18.19)
Female	0.50 (0.50)	0.63 (0.48)	0.56 (0.50)	0.55 (0.50)	0.51 (0.50)	0.41 (0.50)	0.50 (0.50)
No high school	0.07 (0.25)	0.05 (0.22)	0.02 (0.15)	0.03 (0.17)	0.03 (0.17)	0.05 (0.23)	0.03 (0.17)
University graduate	0.35 (0.48)	0.36 (0.48)	0.34 (0.48)	0.21 (0.41)	0.35 (0.48)	0.28 (0.45)	0.32 (0.47)
Income	3.86 (1.90)	3.72 (1.79)	3.57 (1.93)	3.66 (1.66)	3.72 (1.79)	3.84 (1.73)	3.44 (1.67)
Prairies	0.28 (0.45)	0.24 (0.43)	0.18 (0.39)	0.23 (0.42)	0.22 (0.41)	0.31 (0.47)	0.31 (0.47)
Ontario	0.48 (0.50)	0.54 (0.50)	0.49 (0.50)	0.52 (0.50)	0.50 (0.50)	0.43 (0.50)	0.45 (0.50)
Atlantic	0.07 (0.26)	0.01 (0.10)	0.15 (0.36)	0.15 (0.36)	0.13 (0.34)	0.11 (0.31)	0.07 (0.26)
Satisfaction	0.87 (0.34)	0.84 (0.37)	0.80 (0.40)	0.80 (0.41)	0.80 (0.40)	0.78 (0.42)	0.82 (0.39)
Political interest	6.61 (2.24)	5.94 (2.41)	6.19 (2.44)	6.32 (2.40)	6.76 (2.25)	6.77 (2.20)	6.70 (2.46)
Political knowledge	0.61 (0.29)	0.60 (0.32)	0.55 (0.32)	0.60 (0.28)	0.54 (0.31)	0.52 (0.33)	0.56 (0.30)
Political ideology	4.88 (2.23)	4.87 (1.94)	4.59 (2.24)	4.82 (2.33)	4.75 (2.34)	4.95 (2.23)	5.06 (2.30)
CPC PID	0.19 (0.39)	0.24 (0.43)	0.14 (0.35)	0.17 (0.38)	0.21 (0.41)	0.27 (0.45)	0.27 (0.45)
GRN PID	0.05 (0.21)	0.02 (0.14)	0.07 (0.25)	0.01 (0.10)	0.01 (0.10)	0.02 (0.14)	0.04 (0.20)
LIB PID	0.26 (0.44)	0.19 (0.39)	0.24 (0.43)	0.27 (0.45)	0.20 (0.40)	0.24 (0.43)	0.23 (0.42)
NDP PID	0.06 (0.25)	0.09 (0.28)	0.09 (0.29)	0.14 (0.35)	0.12 (0.33)	0.07 (0.26)	0.09 (0.29)
Response check	0.95 (0.21)	0.96 (0.19)	0.92 (0.27)	0.96 (0.20)	0.93 (0.26)	0.93 (0.26)	0.95 (0.22)
N	108	105	88	95	109	96	97

Note: The cells report averages, with standard deviations in parentheses. Age is the respondents' age in years. Female, no high school, university graduate, regional variables, PID, and response check are dichotomous measures, coded "1" in correspondence with the variable name. Political interest and political ideology are self-reported positions on an eleven-point scale running from "No interest" to "Great deal of interest" and "Left–Right," respectively. Political knowledge is an index (alpha = 0.60) based on five factual questions: the name of the British prime minister, the level of government that has primary responsibility for education and health care in Canada, the name of the federal finance minister, the name of the governor general, and the number of seats in the House of Commons. The respondents received one point for each correct response. The variable was then rescaled to fit between 0 and 1. N = number of usable cases in each treatment.

Appendix 3.1. Summary statistics (Continued)

	Treatment 7	Treatment 8	Treatment 9	Treatment 10	Treatment 11	Treatment 12
Age	48.05 (15.48)	46.44 (15.92)	45.67 (15.71)	46.80 (15.99)	47.24 (15.63)	47.07 (17.28)
Female	0.49 (0.50)	0.43 (0.50)	0.59 (0.49)	0.56 (0.50)	0.54 (0.50)	0.51 (0.50)
No high school	0.02 (0.14)	0.09 (0.29)	0.01 (0.10)	0.03 (0.16)	0.03 (0.16)	0.03 (0.17)
University graduate	0.44 (0.50)	0.39 (0.49)	0.31 (0.47)	0.36 (0.48)	0.28 (0.45)	0.35 (0.48)
Income	3.52 (1.78)	3.79 (1.95)	3.38 (1.84)	3.87 (1.88)	4.02 (1.83)	3.90 (1.81)
Prairies	0.22 (0.42)	0.18 (0.39)	0.21 (0.41)	0.23 (0.42)	0.29 (0.46)	0.20 (0.40)
Ontario	0.49 (0.50)	0.54 (0.50)	0.48 (0.50)	0.52 (0.50)	0.46 (0.50)	0.59 (0.49)
Atlantic	0.08 (0.28)	0.11 (0.32)	0.11 (0.32)	0.12 (0.32)	0.11 (0.31)	0.06 (0.24)
Satisfaction	0.77 (0.43)	0.77 (0.42)	0.74 (0.44)	0.75 (0.43)	0.72 (0.45)	0.81 (0.40)
Political interest	6.76 (2.25)	6.15 (2.53)	6.18 (2.36)	6.30 (2.54)	6.43 (2.48)	6.62 (2.39)
Political knowledge	0.60 (0.28)	0.60 (0.31)	0.54 (0.30)	0.56 (0.32)	0.54 (0.31)	0.55 (0.29)
Political ideology	5.21 (2.20)	5.26 (2.32)	4.76 (2.34)	4.73 (2.15)	4.90 (2.12)	5.05 (2.04)
CPC PID	0.27 (0.44)	0.27 (0.45)	0.15 (0.36)	0.18 (0.39)	0.27 (0.45)	0.19 (0.40)
GRN PID	0.03 (0.16)	0.02 (0.15)	0.04 (0.19)	0.03 (0.16)	0.03 (0.16)	0.00 (0.00)
LIB PID	0.23 (0.42)	0.14 (0.35)	0.25 (0.44)	0.28 (0.45)	0.16 (0.36)	0.21 (0.41)
NDP PID	0.08 (0.28)	0.10 (0.30)	0.14 (0.35)	0.11 (0.31)	0.10 (0.30)	0.13 (0.33)
Response check	0.91 (0.29)	0.96 (0.21)	0.93 (0.26)	0.95 (0.22)	0.91 (0.28)	0.92 (0.27)
N	109	92	107	109	115	104

Note: The cells report averages, with standard deviations in parentheses. Age is the respondents' age in years. Female, no high school, university graduate, regional variables, PID, and response check are dichotomous measures, coded "1" in correspondence with the variable name. Political interest and political ideology are self-reported positions on an eleven-point scale running from "No interest" to "Great deal of interest" and "Left–Right," respectively. Political knowledge is an index (alpha = 0.60) based on five factual questions: the name of the British prime minister, the level of government that has primary responsibility for education and health care in Canada, the name of the federal finance minister, the name of the governor general, and the number of seats in the House of Commons. The respondents received one point for each correct response. The variable was then rescaled to fit between 0 and 1. N = number of usable cases in each treatment.

Appendix 3.2. Multinomial logistic regression results for test of random assignment to treatments

	Treatment 1	Treatment 2	Treatment 3	Treatment 4	Treatment 5	Treatment 6	Election 8
Age	−0.00 (0.01)	−0.01 (0.01)	−0.01 (0.01)	−0.00 (0.01)	0.00 (0.01)	0.00 (0.01)	0.01 (0.01)
Female	0.55a 0.31)	0.07 (0.33)	0.09 (0.31)	0.06 (0.30)	−0.30 (0.31)	0.09 (0.31)	0.00 (0.32)
No high school	0.28 (0.72)	−1.18 (1.15)	−0.40 (0.81)	−0.96 (0.90)	−0.02 (0.72)	−0.91 (0.90)	−0.16 (0.96)
University graduate	0.17 (0.33)	0.15 (0.35)	−0.94* (0.37)	−0.01 (0.33)	−0.33 (0.35)	0.05 (0.33)	0.15 (0.34)
Income	−0.07 (0.09)	−0.04 (0.09)	−0.05 (0.09)	−0.04 (0.08)	0.02 (0.09)	−0.13 (0.09)	0.06 (0.09)
Prairies	−0.16 (0.46)	−0.62 (0.54)	0.16 (0.54)	−0.12 (0.47)	0.53 (0.48)	0.11 (0.46)	0.72 (0.60)
Ontario	−0.14 (0.41)	−0.03 (0.45)	0.46 (0.48)	0.06 (0.42)	0.19 (0.45)	−0.04 (0.42)	0.47 (0.56)
Atlantic	−1.96a (1.14)	0.75 (0.65)	1.24a (0.66)	0.83 (0.62)	0.88 (0.66)	0.03 (0.69)	0.40 (0.73)
Satisfaction	−0.04 (0.42)	−0.43 (0.43)	−0.07 (0.43)	−0.23 (0.40)	−0.30 (0.40)	−0.17 (0.41)	0.05 (0.42)
Political interest	−0.08 (0.07)	−0.02 (0.07)	0.02 (0.07)	0.06 (0.07)	0.07 (0.07)	0.04 (0.07)	0.04 (0.08)
Political knowledge	0.09 (0.53)	−0.56 (0.56)	0.24 (0.54)	−0.86a (0.52)	−1.09* (0.53)	−0.40 (0.53)	−0.09 (0.55)
Political ideology	−0.04 (0.08)	−0.07 (0.08)	−0.06 (0.08)	−0.07 (0.07)	−0.09 (0.08)	−0.02 (0.07)	0.10 (0.08)
CPC PID	0.43 (0.43)	−0.55 (0.57)	0.13 (0.47)	0.31 (0.43)	0.57 (0.43)	0.45 (0.43)	−0.55 (0.48)
GRN PID	−0.86 (0.91)	0.09 (0.78)	−16.56 (1937.31)	−16.75 (1873.59)	−0.86 (0.92)	−0.11 (0.77)	0.25 (0.82)
LIB PID	−0.33 (0.40)	−0.13 (0.41)	−0.04 (0.39)	−0.39 (0.39)	−0.04 (0.39)	−0.11 (0.39)	−0.59 (0.42)
NDP PID	0.56 (0.61)	0.63 (0.63)	0.92 (0.60)	0.80 (0.58)	0.39 (0.64)	0.58 (0.62)	−0.39 (0.59)
Response check	0.17 (0.79)	−0.83 (0.68)	−0.18 (0.73)	−0.57 (0.65)	−0.62 (0.65)	−0.22 (0.69)	−1.73 (1.11)
Constant	0.75 (1.21)	2.30a (1.20)	0.75 (1.22)	1.42 (1.13)	1.05 (1.15)	0.49 (1.17)	−0.08 (1.53)

Note: The cells report multinomial logistic regression coefficients, with standard errors in parentheses. The control group is set as the base outcome. Age is the respondents' age in years. Female, no high school, university graduate, regional variables, PID, and response check are dichotomous measures, coded "1" in correspondence with the variable name. Political interest and political ideology are self-reported positions on an eleven-point scale running from "No interest" to "Great deal of interest" and "Left–Right," respectively. Political knowledge is an index (alpha = 0.61) based on five factual questions: the name of the British prime minister, the level of government that has primary responsibility for education and health care in Canada, the name of the federal finance minister, the name of the governor general, and the number of seats in the House of Commons. The respondents received one point for each correct response. The variable was then rescaled to fit between 0 and 1. N = number of cases with full response set.

*** $p < 0.001$; ** $p < 0.01$; * $p < 0.05$; [a] $p < 0.10$.

Appendix 3.2. Multinomial logistic regression results for test of random assignment to treatments (Continued)

	Treatment 7	Treatment 8	Treatment 9	Treatment 10	Treatment 11	Treatment 12	Election 8
Age	−0.00 (0.01)	−0.01 (0.01)	−0.01 (0.01)	−0.00 (0.01)	−0.00 (0.01)	−0.00 (0.01)	0.01 (0.01)
Female	0.08 (0.30)	−0.30 (0.32)	0.26 (0.31)	0.25 (0.30)	0.27 (0.30)	0.16 (0.30)	0.00 (0.32)
No high school	−1.52 (1.15)	0.62 (0.68)	−1.56 (1.15)	−1.53 (1.14)	−0.53 (0.80)	−0.82 (0.90)	−0.16 (0.96)
University graduate	0.51 (0.32)	0.21 (0.34)	−0.06 (0.34)	0.05 (0.33)	−0.36 (0.33)	−0.06 (0.33)	0.15 (0.34)
Income	−0.15[a] (0.09)	−0.03 (0.09)	−0.14 (0.09)	0.03 (0.08)	0.08 (0.08)	0.02 (0.08)	0.06 (0.09)
Prairies	−0.11 (0.46)	−0.18 (0.52)	−0.60 (0.48)	−0.10 (0.50)	0.41 (0.47)	−0.24 (0.49)	0.72 (0.60)
Ontario	0.00 (0.41)	0.30 (0.45)	−0.35 (0.42)	0.32 (0.43)	0.31 (0.43)	0.27 (0.42)	0.47 (0.56)
Atlantic	0.32 (0.66)	0.96 (0.66)	0.27 (0.63)	0.95 (0.64)	0.94 (0.65)	−0.18 (0.72)	0.40 (0.73)
Satisfaction	−0.42 (0.39)	−0.52 (0.40)	−0.53 (0.40)	−0.59 (0.39)	−0.66[+] (0.38)	−0.15 (0.41)	0.05 (0.42)
Political interest	0.02 (0.07)	−0.07 (0.07)	−0.03 (0.07)	−0.03 (0.07)	0.02 (0.07)	0.06 (0.07)	0.04 (0.08)
Political knowledge	−0.06 (0.52)	0.09 (0.55)	−0.50 (0.53)	−0.53 (0.52)	−0.57 (0.51)	−0.83 (0.52)	−0.09 (0.55)
Political ideology	−0.01 (0.07)	0.02 (0.08)	−0.02 (0.07)	−0.08 (0.07)	−0.07 (0.07)	−0.03 (0.07)	0.10 (0.08)
CPC PID	0.71[a] (0.43)	0.35 (0.45)	0.05 (0.47)	0.50 (0.44)	0.62 (0.42)	−0.15 (0.45)	−0.55 (0.48)
GRN PID	−0.26 (0.82)	−0.45 (0.92)	−0.47 (0.82)	−0.30 (0.83)	−1.03 (0.92)	−16.71 (1866.65)	0.25 (0.82)
LIB PID	−0.06 (0.39)	−0.46 (0.43)	0.15 (0.39)	0.17 (0.38)	−0.35 (0.40)	−0.40 (0.38)	−0.59 (0.42)
NDP PID	0.53 (0.62)	0.64 (0.62)	1.03[a] (0.59)	0.63 (0.61)	0.58 (0.60)	0.68 (0.58)	−0.39 (0.59)
Response check	−0.70 (0.64)	−0.21 (0.73)	−0.89 (0.64)	0.22 (0.78)	−0.73 (0.64)	−0.78 (0.64)	−1.73 (1.11)
Constant	1.45 (1.12)	1.06 (1.20)	2.84[*] (1.13)	0.67 (1.21)	1.29 (1.12)	1.24 (1.13)	−0.08 (1.53)

N = 1,181
χ^2 (df = 204) = 219.36
Pseudo R^2 = 0.04

Note: The cells report multinomial logistic regression coefficients, with standard errors in parentheses. The control group is set as the base outcome. Age is the respondents' age in years. Female, no high school, university graduate, regional variables, PID, and response check are dichotomous measures, coded "1" in correspondence with the variable name. Political interest and political ideology are self-reported positions on an eleven-point scale running from "No interest" to "Great deal of interest" and "Left–Right," respectively. Political knowledge is an index (alpha = 0.61) based on five factual questions: the name of the British prime minister, the level of government that has primary responsibility for education and health care in Canada, the name of the federal finance minister, the name of the governor general, and the number of seats in the House of Commons. The respondents received one point for each correct response. The variable was then rescaled to fit between 0 and 1. N = number of cases with full response set.

*** $p < 0.001$; ** $p < 0.01$; * $p < 0.05$; [a] $p < 0.10$.

Political Scandals   69

Appendix 3.3. Election instructions

> **Instructions**
>
> Welcome to our online election. You will be presented with a list of information on THREE candidates competing in this election (NOTE: all candidates are fictional):
>
> - Paul Smith - Conservative
> - George Stevens - Liberal
> - Robert Johnson - NDP
>
> You may view information for each candidate by clicking on the title of the information you wish to see. Once you are finished viewing the information, you can return to the main page by clicking "Close" at the bottom of the information window.
>
> Once you have viewed enough information to make your decision, click on the "Next" button located on the bottom of the election campaign screen to cast your ballot.

Appendix 3.4. Sample cueing links

Newspaper story:

> **NEWSPAPER STORY**
>
> **Conservative Candidate Paul Smith faces allegations of extra-marital affair with neighbour**
>
> METCALF – Paul Smith of the Conservatives spent the day meeting with reporters about an extra-marital affair that he allegedly had with a neighbour. Speaking by phone from Townsville last night, he gave the following response to the allegations:
>
> "Right now, I'm trying to meet with as many voters as possible to hear their views and talk about my plans for improving the community."
>
> Smith is scheduled to speak at a community event in Metcalf later this week. His campaign tour will soon take him to a number of neighbouring communities.

Statement from a party official:

> **George Stevens**
> **Liberal**
>
> **Statement from Party Officials**
>
> Party officials have offered their full support to George Stevens, candidate for the Liberals in this month's election. They offered no comment regarding the allegations that the Conservative candidate, Paul Smith, has been having an extra-marital affair with a neighbour.

Endorsement:

> **Paul Smith**
> **Conservative**
>
> **Endorsement**
>
> Given the current allegations involving an extra-marital affair with a neighbour, Paul Smith of the Conservatives has received no endorsements to date.

Appendix 3.5. Full results for figures 3.2 to 3.7
Results for figure 3.2: Treatment effects on the information search by party

	CPC	LIB	NDP
Scandal	−0.00 (0.02)	−0.02 (0.01)	−0.00 (0.01)
	[−0.00]	[−0.05]	[−0.00]
Accused PID	0.09 (0.07)	0.05 (0.06)	0.18 (0.08)*
Other PID	−0.17 (0.06)***	−0.08 (0.06)	−0.21 (0.05)***
Constant	1.09 (0.19)***	1.40 (0.13)***	1.20 (0.11)***
Pseudo R^2	0.01	0.00	0.01
N	505	502	543

Note: The cells report Poisson regression coefficients, with standard errors in parentheses and marginal effects/discrete changes reported in square brackets. PID is included in the model as a control, with no or weak PID set as the reference category.
***$p < 0.001$; **$p < 0.01$; *$p < 0.05$; ª$p < 0.10$.

Results for figure 3.3: Treatment effects on the information search by party and type of scandal

	CPC	LIB	NDP
Sex scandal	0.02 (0.07)	−0.17 (0.07)**	−0.08 (0.07)
	[0.07]	[−0.56]	[−0.24]
Finance scandal	−0.03 (0.07)	−0.12 (0.07)ª	0.01 (0.07)
	[−0.09]	[−0.38]	[0.03]
Accused PID	0.03 (0.07)	0.06 (0.06)	0.18 (0.08)*
Other PID	−0.20 (0.06)***	−0.07 (0.06)	−0.20 (0.05)***
Constant	1.23 (0.06)***	1.23 (0.06)***	1.20 (0.07)***
Pseudo R^2	0.01	0.01	0.01
N	505	502	543

Note: The cells report Poisson regression coefficients, with standard errors in parentheses and marginal effects/discrete changes reported in square brackets. PID is included in the model as a control, with no or weak PID set as the reference category.
***$p < 0.001$; **$p < 0.01$; *$p < 0.05$; ª$p < 0.10$.

Results for figure 3.4: Treatment effects on the information search by party and by type and sphere of scandal

	CPC	LIB	NDP
Sex: private scandal	0.02 (0.08)	−0.19 (0.08)*	−0.12 (0.08)
	[0.05]	[−0.62]	[−0.36]
Sex: public scandal	0.03 (0.08)	−0.16 (0.08)*	−0.04 (0.08)
	[0.10]	[−0.50]	[−0.12]
Finance: private scandal	−0.06 (0.08)	−0.12 (0.07)	0.05 (0.08)
	[−0.19]	[−0.39]	[0.16]

(Continued)

Political Scandals 71

	CPC	LIB	NDP
Finance: public scandal	0.00 (0.08) [0.01]	−0.11 (0.08) [−0.37]	−0.04 (0.08) [0.12]
Accused PID	0.03 (0.07)	0.06 (0.06)	0.19 (0.08)*
Other PID	−0.20 (0.06)***	−0.07 (0.06)	−0.21 (0.05)***
Constant	1.23 (0.06)***	1.27 (0.06)***	1.20 (0.06)***
Pseudo R^2	0.01	0.01	0.02
N	505	502	543

Note: The cells report Poisson regression coefficients, with standard errors in parentheses and marginal effects/discrete changes reported in square brackets. PID is included in the model as a control, with no or weak PID set as the reference category.
***$p < 0.001$; **$p < 0.01$; *$p < 0.05$; ª$p < 0.10$.

Results for figure 3.5: Treatment effects on vote choice by party

	CPC	LIB	NDP
Scandal	−0.24 (0.09)** [−0.03]	−0.26 (0.04)*** [−0.03]	−0.09 (0.03)** [−0.01]
Accused PID	2.49 (0.29)***	2.10 (0.28)***	2.51 (0.34)***
Other PID	−2.03 (0.49)***	−2.35 (0.43)***	−1.67 (0.39)***
Constant	1.03 (1.00)	2.59 (0.61)***	0.22 (0.52)
Pseudo R^2	0.32	0.34	0.26
N	505	502	543

Note: The cells report logistic regression coefficients, with standard errors in parentheses and marginal effects/discrete changes reported in square brackets. PID is included in the model as a control, with no or weak PID set as the reference category.
***$p < 0.001$; **$p < 0.01$; *$p < 0.05$; ª$p < 0.10$.

Results for figure 3.6: Treatment effects on vote choice by party and type of scandal

	CPC	LIB	NDP
Sex scandal	−0.19 (0.34) [−0.02]	−1.67 (0.33)*** [−0.24]	−0.38 (0.35) [−0.04]
Finance scandal	−0.92 (0.36)* [−0.10]	−2.01 (0.34)*** [−0.28]	−1.24 (0.39)*** [−0.12]
Accused PID	2.52 (0.29)***	2.16 (0.29)***	2.53 (0.35)***
Other PID	−2.03 (0.49)***	−2.37 (0.43)***	−1.68 (0.39)***
Constant	−1.16 (0.29)***	0.36 (0.26)	−1.08 (0.29)***
Pseudo R^2	0.32	0.35	0.27
N	505	502	543

Note: The cells report logistic regression coefficients, with standard errors in parentheses and marginal effects/discrete changes reported in square brackets. PID is included in the model as a control, with no or weak PID set as the reference category.
***$p < 0.001$; **$p < 0.01$; *$p < 0.05$; ª$p < 0.10$.

Results for figure 3.7: Treatment effects on vote choice by party and by type and sphere of scandal

	CPC	LIB	NDP
Sex: private scandal	−0.06 (0.38) [−0.01]	−1.70 (0.39)*** [−0.24]	−0.03 (0.39) [−0.00]
Sex: public scandal	−0.37 (0.43) [−0.04]	−1.70 (0.40)*** [−0.24]	−0.83 (0.44)[a] [−0.09]
Finance: private scandal	−1.27 (0.47)** [−0.13]	−2.51 (0.42)*** [−0.33]	−1.79 (0.51)*** [−0.15]
Finance: public scandal	−0.67 (0.40)[a] [−0.08]	−1.51 (0.39)*** [−0.22]	−0.83 (0.43)[a] [−0.09]
Accused PID	2.52 (0.30)***	2.26 (0.30)***	2.57 (0.36)***
Other PID	−2.01 (0.49)***	−2.36 (0.43)***	−1.67 (0.39)***
Constant	−1.16 (0.29)***	0.35 (0.26)	−1.08 (0.29)***
Pseudo R^2	0.32	0.36	0.28
N	505	502	543

Note: The cells report logistic regression coefficients, with standard errors in parentheses and marginal effects/discrete changes reported in square brackets. PID is included in the model as a control, with no or weak PID set as the reference category.
***$p < 0.001$; **$p < 0.01$; *$p < 0.05$; [a]$p < 0.10$.

Chapter Four

Candidate Endorsements

I have known Patrick Brown for a number of years now. Hard working and dedicated, Patrick is a strong Conservative. He has the passion and vision to lead Ontario. (Hockey star Wayne Gretzky, quoted in *CBC News* 2015)

Put in Mulcair ... or if you can't put in Mulcair put in Trudeau's son, Justin. (Canadian actor Donald Sutherland, *CBC News* 2015)

Do endorsements help candidates and political parties win power? Or is soliciting endorsements a waste of time and energy? Candidates and campaign staff seem to think that they are valuable for generating interest and garnering votes, while the media uses them to gauge which candidates and parties are the front-runners and most likely to win the election or leadership race. During the 2017 leadership contest for the Conservative Party of Canada (CPC), for instance, all the candidates had eagerly sought out the support of current and former politicians at all levels to boost their chances of leading the party. According to the CBC, Andrew Scheer was the clear front-runner in January 2017, with fifty-eight endorsements, followed by Erin O'Toole at twenty-three, Maxime Bernier at sixteen, Lisa Raitt at thirteen, Michael Chong at nine, and Kellie Leitch at five. Endorsers included MPs Scott Reid, Tony Clement, Peter Kent, and Peter Van Loan; former MPs John Duncan, John Reynolds, Ed Holder, and Peter Penashue; senators Dennis Patterson and Nicole Eaton; and provincial MPPs or MLAs Ted Arnott, Alfie MacLeod, and Christine Tell (Grenier 2017; see also Sayers 1999, 72–3).

The race for endorsements is not limited to leadership races. Candidates and political parties at all levels have long courted the support of prominent individuals and organizations during general and local elections (Sayers 1999, 132). During the 2015 federal election, for instance, all the political parties vied for endorsements from Canada's major newspapers; by the time election day arrived, the *Toronto Star*, *La Presse*, the *Hamilton Spectator*, and a number of other regional newspapers had endorsed the Liberals (LIB) and Justin Trudeau; the *National Post*, the *Ottawa Citizen*, and the Sun chain of newspapers had endorsed the CPC and Stephen Harper, while the *Globe and Mail* had endorsed the CPC but not Stephen Harper; and the *Prince Arthur Herald* and *NOW Magazine* had thrown their support behind the New Democratic Party (NDP) and Thomas Mulcair (Kohut 2015; Winseck 2015). Newspapers also endorse local candidates. The *Ottawa Citizen*, for instance, endorsed David McGuinty in the 2011 federal election over CPC candidate Elie Salibi and NDP candidate James McLaren, citing McGuinty's "depth," "roots in Ottawa South," and "richness of experience ... from his early training in agriculture to his education in literature and law, from his work for UNICEF in West Africa to his contributions to environmental policy" (*Ottawa Citizen* 2011).

In addition to political and media endorsements, candidates and party officials seek out expressions of support from prominent citizens and non-governmental associations and groups. During the 2015 federal election, party officials widely promoted endorsements from celebrities such as hockey star Wayne Gretzky and singer Chantal Kreviazuk, each of whom supported Stephen Harper and Justin Trudeau, respectively. Some political parties and their leaders also received endorsements from civil society groups such as the College of Family Physicians of Canada, the Campaign Life Coalition, the Assembly of First Nations, and the Canadian Arab Federation, among others. During the 2015 federal election, LIB candidate Anita Vandenbeld in Ottawa West–Nepean received an endorsement from the grassroots "Anybody-But-Conservative movement," which concluded "that Vandenbeld has the best chance of snatching the riding ... from the Conservatives" (Butler 2015). Similarly, Victoria MP Murray Rankin had maintained a long list of endorsements from community leaders on his website, including former politicians but also civil society leaders from local, regional, and provincial organizations such as Kelly Newhook, executive director of Together Against Poverty Society; Michael Eso, president of the Victoria Labour Council; and Miles Richardson, past president of the Haida Nation and former chief commissioner of the BC Treaty Commission (Rankin 2019).

In short, candidates, parties, and campaign staff believe that endorsements from public and private actors are instrumental in convincing voters to pay more attention to their campaigns and ultimately support them on election day. In this chapter, we consider whether these assumptions about the impact of political endorsements on voting behaviour hold true. Specifically, we consider whether endorsements affect the information search that voters undertake before casting their ballots and how they vote on election day. We also consider the impact of the endorser by assessing how the decision-making process and vote choice change according to whether an endorsement is from a national or local civil society leader.

The chapter begins by surveying the academic literature on endorsements and voting behaviour and notes that much of that literature is based on empirical evidence gathered from elections in the United States. To our knowledge, there have not been any empirical studies published that assess whether and/or how endorsements matter in the Canadian context. The chapter then constructs and tests a number of hypotheses before ending with a discussion about the impact of endorsements and what they mean for political campaigning and vote choice in Canada.

Background, Theory, and Expectations

Fundamentally, endorsements are a type of cognitive heuristic that humans use to process information, deal with complexity, and ultimately make decisions. Heuristics are important because a large body of literature has found that most people have difficulty processing information efficiently. As well, in many situations, individuals frequently lack the requisite knowledge to make judgments that are consistent with their true preferences, and sometimes the cost of gathering that requisite knowledge is far too high (Downs 1957). In "Competing for Endorsements," in the June 1999 issue of *American Economic Review*, Grossman and Helpman say that, in the political arena, it is frequently the case that "the cost of gathering information can easily exceed the private gains they [voters] might expect to achieve with their single votes" (quoted in Neddenriep and Nownes 2014, 618). As a result, most citizens rely heavily on various "information shortcuts" to quickly make a variety of decisions affecting most aspects of their lives (Fiske and Taylor 1991; Kahneman, Slovic, and Tversky 1982).

When it comes to elections, voters commonly rely on one or more of the following heuristics: party identification or affiliation (Bittner 2011; Merolla, Stephenson, and Zechmeister 2008; Popkin 1994), political ideology (Conover and Feldman 1989), public opinion polls (Mutz 1992; Singh, Roy, and Fournier 2016), candidate appearance (Cutler 2002; Rosenberg et al. 1986; Rosenberg and McCafferty 1987), and endorsements (Williams, Gulati, and Foxman 2009; Grossman and Helpman 1999). According to Lau and Redlawsk (2001, 958), "virtually all voters employ cognitive heuristics at least some of the time in making their vote decision."

An endorsement is particularly valuable as a cognitive heuristic because it can help an individual more efficiently sort through situations in which the relationship between individual preferences and candidate and party positions on various issues is muddy or unknown. An environmentally minded voter, for instance, may not know, and may not be able or willing to expend sufficient cognitive effort to find out, which party prioritizes environmental protection, and so he or she may rely on an endorsement from a national or local environmental interest group to figure out which party is aligned with his or her preferences. In short, as Neddenriep and Nownes (2014, 617) observe, "interest-group endorsements help people sort themselves out – that is, they provide information that moves many people away from candidates with whom they disagree on important policy issues and toward candidates with whom they agree."

The precise effect of endorsements, however, varies depending on the level of political knowledge and awareness of voters, factors that are often combined as a measure of political sophistication (e.g., Fiske, Kinder, and Larter 1983; Miller 2011; Zaller 1990). A number of studies have found that endorsements tend to have stronger effects on individuals with lower levels of political sophistication relative to their more sophisticated counterparts. The reasons for these effects are fairly straightforward. Individuals with higher levels of political interest and knowledge typically have more stable and well-developed preferences, which are less likely to change as a result of exposure to such heuristics (Converse 1964; Lau and Redlawsk 2006; Zaller 1992). Conversely, individuals with lower levels of political information and awareness are more apt to be swayed by such a cue, relying more heavily on endorsements because of the high costs of acquiring the full information they need to cast their vote (Arceneaux and Kolodny 2009; Downs 1957; Lupia 1994; Neddenriep and Nownes 2014, 628; Veer, Becirovic, and Martin 2010).

One consequence of these relationships is that individuals who rely on endorsements and have lower levels of political sophistication are more likely to be misaligned from the parties and candidates that best match their interests. Lau and Redlawsk (2001, 966), for instance, found that "heavy reliance on political heuristics actually made decision making less accurate among those low in political sophistication" (see also Merolla, Stephenson, and Zechmeister 2008; Roy 2011; Singh and Roy 2014). In contrast, endorsements can help political sophisticates align or confirm their preferences with the correct candidates and parties.

As Lau and Redlawsk (2001, 967) note, "Ironically, heuristics are most valuable to those who might in fact need them the least."

Generally speaking, endorsements seem to have a positive effect on the recipients, encouraging voters to support and take an interest in them. Pease and Brewer (2008, 395), for instance, found that celebrity endorsements had a positive impact on Barack Obama's campaign for the presidency in 2008. In their study of the Oprah effect on Barack Obama's candidacy for the Democratic nomination, they found that voters were more likely to view him as a viable candidate and "to say that they would be more likely to vote for him" as a result of Oprah's endorsement. Similarly, Garthwaite and Moore (2012) found that Oprah's endorsement increased financial contributions and provided approximately one million additional votes to the Obama campaign. The profile of Oprah, a national celebrity, was likely an important factor in influencing voter interest and support. Mishra and Mishra (2014, 421) investigated whether the profile of an endorser mattered and found "that local celebrities can also be used to build political brand equity, though not as effectively as a national celebrity." On the other hand, using an experimental design to study the impact of endorsements, Wood and Herbst (2007, 154) found that celebrity endorsements seemed to have little effect on voter behaviour, leading the authors to conclude that "it would appear that the money and time invested in celebrity support is wasteful."

In this chapter, we rely on empirical findings from the United States to guide our expectations given, as noted above, the limited empirical work that looks at the effects of endorsements on voting behaviour in Canada. As such, we expect that endorsements, in general, will have a positive effect on a candidate's vote share (Lau and Redlawsk 2001; Neddenriep and Nownes 2014; Pease and Brewer 2008). As well, if endorsements are cognitive heuristics, then voters will be less likely to undertake an exhaustive search of information about a candidate when an endorsement is available relative to the effort absent an endorsement. We make this assumption based on the fact that acquiring full or sufficient information about parties, candidates, and their positions on issues as they relate to one's own preferences during elections is costly, and so endorsements serve as cost-effective information cues to simplify decision-making (Grossman and Helpman 1999, 501; Neddenriep and Nownes 2014, 618). More formally, we expect the following:

> H1: When a candidate receives an endorsement, it will decrease the overall information search that individuals undertake relative to the information search when there is no endorsement.

H2: Receiving an endorsement will increase a candidate's vote share relative to the vote share that he or she receives without an endorsement.

Does the profile (national versus local recognition) of the endorser matter? The literature suggests that national endorsements will have a stronger impact relative to local and no endorsements (Mishra and Mishra 2014). As such, we expect the following:

H3: When a candidate receives a national-level endorsement, it will decrease the overall information search that individuals undertake towards the recipient relative to a local-level or no endorsement.

H4: A national-level endorsement will yield a greater increase in vote share relative to a local-level or no endorsement.

As a final assessment of endorsement effects, we consider how the relation between endorsements and the information search and/or vote choice varies according to level of political sophistication. Based on the literature discussed above, we expect that endorsement effects will be stronger for low sophisticates relative to their more sophisticated counterparts. Adding political sophistication to the hypotheses already stated, we expect the following:

H5: Low sophisticates will be more apt to decrease their overall information search when presented with an endorsement compared with their more sophisticated counterparts.

H6: Low sophisticates will be more apt to vote for the endorsed candidate compared with their more sophisticated counterparts.

H7: Low sophisticates, relative to their more sophisticated counterparts, will be more apt to decrease their overall information search when the endorsement is at the national level over a local-level or no endorsement.

H8: Low sophisticates, relative to their more sophisticated counterparts, will be more apt to vote for an endorsed candidate when the endorsement is at the national level compared with a local-level or no endorsement.

Methodology

To test our assumptions, we employed a web-based experiment restricted to Canadian respondents living outside Quebec (see chapter 1 for additional sample information and study dates). After completing a pre-survey, the participants were randomly assigned to one of six possible treatments or a control group (see table 4.1 for treatment groups and the number of participants in each). Information for each

Table 4.1. Political endorsement treatments

Treatment	CPC	LIB	NDP	N
Control	Neutral	Neutral	Neutral	108
1	Local	Neutral	Neutral	99
2	National	Neutral	Neutral	108
3	Neutral	Local	Neutral	90
4	Neutral	National	Neutral	115
5	Neutral	Neutral	Local	101
6	Neutral	Neutral	National	99
Total				720

Note: The cells indicate the endorsement for each candidate by treatment. The number of participants in each group is listed in the last column.

fictional candidate contesting the election for the CPC, LIB, and NDP was presented using an Election campaign information screen (see figure 4.1). The order of the candidates and the list of links were randomized for each individual to account for potential ordering effects. For all conditions, the participants were offered five information links: the candidate's biography, his voting record, a newspaper story, a statement from a party official, and an endorsement.

The manipulation was to alter the newspaper story, party official statements, and endorsement to reflect one of: no endorsement, an endorsement from a local chapter president of Water First (a fictional organization), or an endorsement from the national director of the same fictional organization (see appendix 4.1 for the content of the information link).[1] The newspaper story cueing the endorsement was identical for all candidates. The statement from party officials also cued the endorsement, either noting the endorsement for their candidate or stating that they had no comment on the endorsement for a competing candidate. The biographies for each candidate were identical across all treatments, designed to make the candidates as similar as possible. (For example, all were married men with similar family situations, education, and experience. Their names reflected Anglo-Saxon descent. See

---

[1] Participants were not told that the organization was fictional. We chose Water First as our fictional organization in an effort to present an endorsement from a non-controversial organization that would appeal to all voters. However, it is possible that the name of the organization cued different sentiments across the sample, depending on the position and salience that individuals placed upon water conservation issues. While we believe that any such difference should cancel out with random assignment to treatment groups, we note this possibility and potential for partisan differences.

Figure 4.1. Election campaign information screen

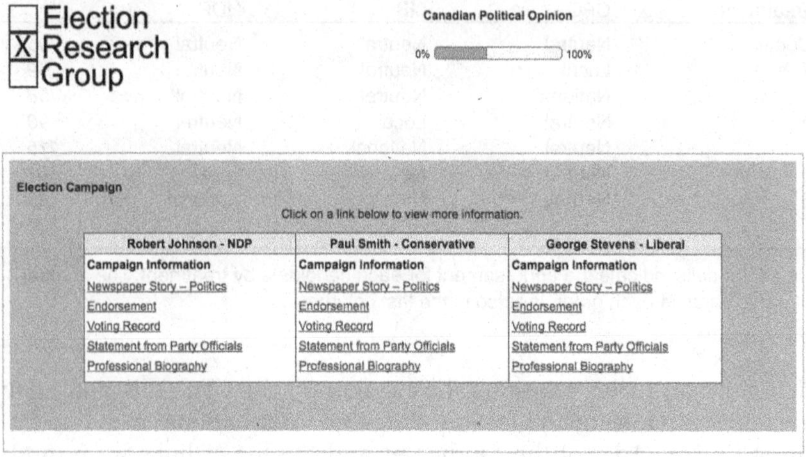

☐ Election
☒ Research
☐ Group

Canadian Political Opinion

0% ▬▬▬▬▬ 100%

Election Campaign		
Click on a link below to view more information.		
Robert Johnson - NDP	Paul Smith - Conservative	George Stevens - Liberal
Campaign Information	Campaign Information	Campaign Information
Newspaper Story – Politics	Newspaper Story – Politics	Newspaper Story – Politics
Endorsement	Endorsement	Endorsement
Voting Record	Voting Record	Voting Record
Statement from Party Officials	Statement from Party Officials	Statement from Party Officials
Professional Biography	Professional Biography	Professional Biography

Note: Party placement and link order randomized by respondent.

chapter 1 for a discussion of the homogeneity of the candidates.) The participants were instructed to view as many of the information links as they wished and then cast their ballot.

Unbeknown to the participants, we recorded the information links they accessed on the campaign screen before voting. We also recorded their vote choice. Based on this design, we could test the impact of the endorsements, distinguishing between local and national endorsers, and their effects on both the information search and the vote that was cast. To assess the former, we compared the number of information links accessed on the campaign screen according to treatment. We assessed the number of links accessed for each of the three political parties separately to identify any within-party differences across treatments. Given this set-up, any difference in the number of information links accessed can be attributable only to exposure to the stimulus: an endorsement. Similarly, the differences in vote share across groups allowed us to assess the magnitude of the endorsement's impact on vote choice.[2]

We drew from the information collected in our pre-survey to test political sophistication (a combined measure of political knowledge and

---

[2] See chap. 1 for further discussion of the strength of experimental designs to isolate causal relationships.

interest) as a conditional factor. In addition, we included controls for partisanship (PID: strong or very strong party identifiers). We included these controls to account for the use of actual party labels in our study, based on the assumption that partisan behaviour may vary, regardless of treatment, according to whether the endorsement was for a respondent's own or an opposition party as well as to account for the potential impact of our fictional endorser (Water First).

Results

Our initial sample for this study consists of 1,150 respondents. However, 319 (27.7%) did not view any information from the campaign screen and instead proceeded straight to the vote screen. Of the remaining 831 respondents, 94 (11.3%) did not view any of the information links cueing the endorsement (or similar link in the control group), and an additional 17 respondents did not complete the survey questions pertaining to political sophistication and/or partisanship. Given our interest in how exposure to a stimulus changes behaviour, we include only those individuals who viewed at least one of the cueing information links with complete responses to the political sophistication and partisanship questions. This procedure leaves us with a final sample of 720 respondents.

Our two dependent variables are information search and vote choice. The former is operationalized as a count of all information links that a participant accessed after being exposed to a cueing link; we cannot assume that exposure to the cue changed the participant's behaviour if the change in behaviour preceded exposure to the stimulus. Thus, we estimate changes in the information search following exposure to the cueing link. Vote choice is a dichotomous measure that takes the value of "1" if a respondent voted for the candidate who received the endorsement and "0" otherwise. All models set the control group as the reference.

We begin by testing for random assignment to the treatments according to socio-demographic characteristics, a respondent's level of satisfaction with the way democracy works in Canada, ideology, political knowledge (a scale based on the participants' responses to five factual, political-knowledge questions), political interest, and PID (strong or very strong partisans) as well as whether the respondent correctly answered a careless-response question administered during the survey (see appendix 4.2 for summary statistics). The results of our estimate of multinomial logistic regression confirm that the groups do not include any systematic differences (χ^2 = 104.60; p = 0.241; see appendix 4.3).

Given these results, we are confident that the randomization process created similar groups of respondents across treatments. On this basis, we proceed with our assessment controlling only for PID.[3]

Our first hypothesis states that exposure to an endorsement will decrease the overall information search. To estimate this effect, we set the number of information links accessed overall as the dependent variable, with a dichotomous measure of exposure to an endorsement (treatments 1 to 6, coded as "1") compared with the control group (coded as "0"). Given that our dependent variable is based on a count of the number of links accessed, we use a Poisson regression specification. To simplify the interpretation of the results, we report a graphical representation of the marginal effects/discrete changes in the text, with the full table of results reported in appendix 4.3.[4] The graphs include tails that represent a 90% confidence interval. Results with both tails on either side of the "0" indicate a statistically significant finding. A negative coefficient for our dichotomous measure will indicate that the individuals viewed less information when exposed to the endorsement stimulus relative to the participants who were assigned to the control group.

The results from our first estimate show that exposure to an endorsement did reduce the number of links accessed by 0.09 links and 0.15 links for the CPC and LIB, respectively (see appendix 4.4); however, neither meets conventional levels of statistical significance (figure 4.2). The results for the NDP indicate no difference between the experimental groups and the control group. Given these results, we find little support for our assumption that exposure to an endorsement would lead to a reduction in the information search undertaken before casting a ballot.

Do the results change if we consider the type of endorsement? To answer this question, we rerun our models, this time including two measures of endorsement – local and national level – setting the control group as the reference category and producing separate results for each party, with controls for PID. These results are reported in figure 4.3.

Once again, we find little support for our assumption that exposure to an endorsement, regardless of the level of the endorser, reduces the

---

[3] Similar to the procedure outlined in chaps. 2 and 3, we also tested the models with a control variable that takes into account the number of links a respondent accessed before viewing the first cueing link. The reason for testing with this control is to assess whether the results differ due to fatigue (e.g., viewing a larger number of non-cueing links before the first cueing link) as opposed to a treatment effect. Once again, the results with and without the inclusion of this control are nearly identical. Thus, we report only the latter.

[4] See chap. 1 for an overview of how to read the results reported in the tables and graphs.

Candidate Endorsements 83

Figure 4.2. Treatment effects on the information search by party

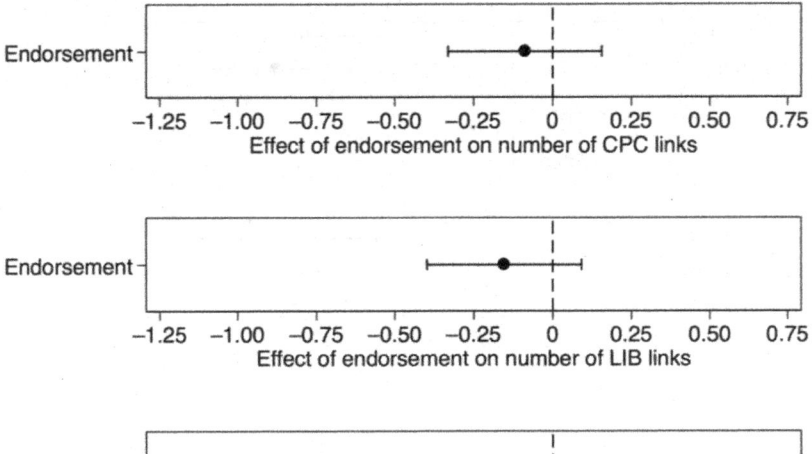

Figure 4.3: Treatment effects on the information search by party and level of endorsement

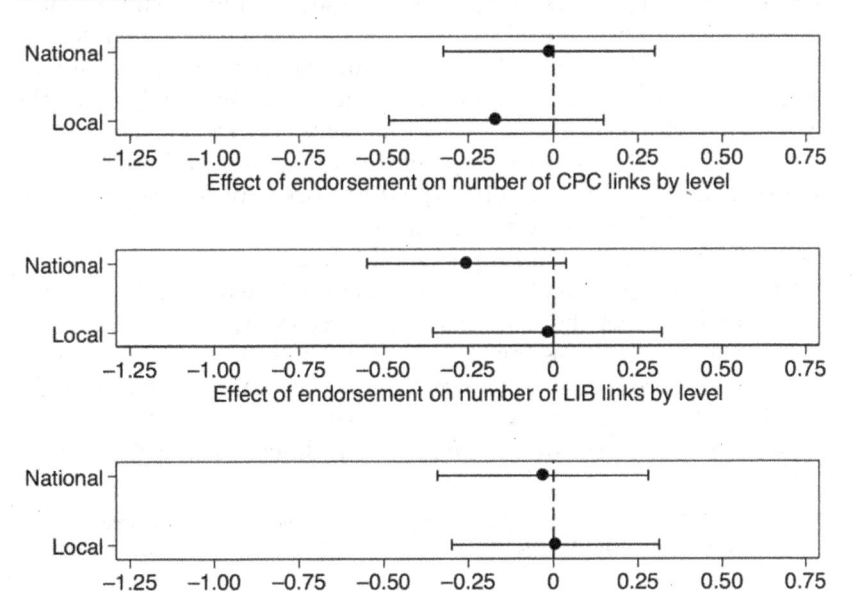

Figure 4.4. Treatment effects on the information search by party and level of political sophistication (PS)

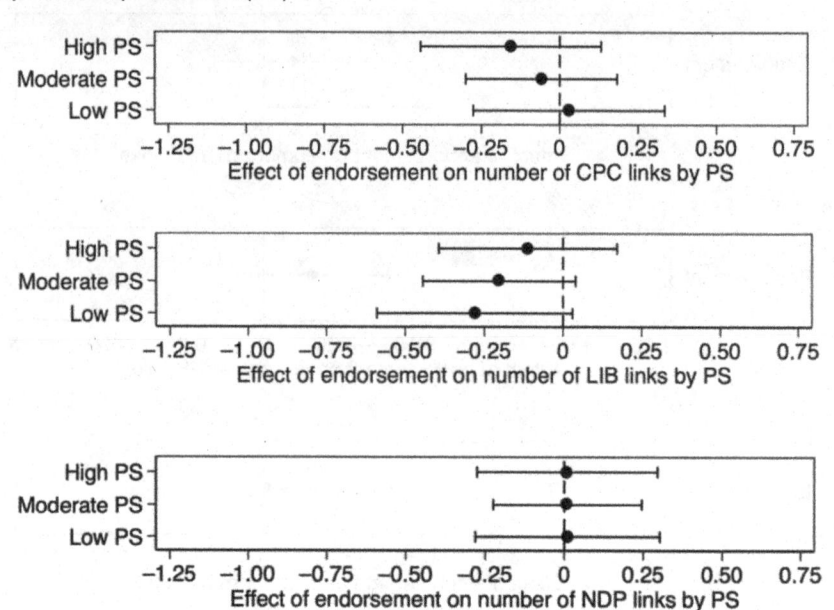

[Forest plot: Effect of endorsement on number of CPC links by PS, with High PS, Moderate PS, and Low PS on the y-axis and values from −1.25 to 0.75 on the x-axis]

[Forest plot: Effect of endorsement on number of LIB links by PS, with High PS, Moderate PS, and Low PS on the y-axis and values from −1.25 to 0.75 on the x-axis]

[Forest plot: Effect of endorsement on number of NDP links by PS, with High PS, Moderate PS, and Low PS on the y-axis and values from −1.25 to 0.75 on the x-axis]

information search. In no case is the change in the number of links viewed following exposure to a local versus a national endorsement statistically significant. In the case of the national endorsement for the LIB candidate, the results do fit with our expectation that a national endorsement would yield a greater reduction in the number of links considered. However, the observed difference between the national endorsement and the control group fails to achieve conventional levels of statistical significance ($p = 0.16$). The difference between the local- and national-level LIB endorsements is also not found to be statistically significant. Thus, we find no support for this hypothesis.

Our final assessment of the impact of endorsements on the information search considers how the effects vary according to level of political sophistication. To assess this argument, we interact political sophistication with exposure to an endorsement to estimate the change in the number of links accessed according to low, moderate, and high levels of sophistication.[5] We do so, first without differentiating the level of

---

5 Political sophistication is treated as a continuous variable, with low, moderate, and high levels of sophistication estimated at the 25th-, 50th-, and 75th-percentile values.

Figure 4.5. Treatment effects on the information search by party, level of political sophistication, and level of endorsement

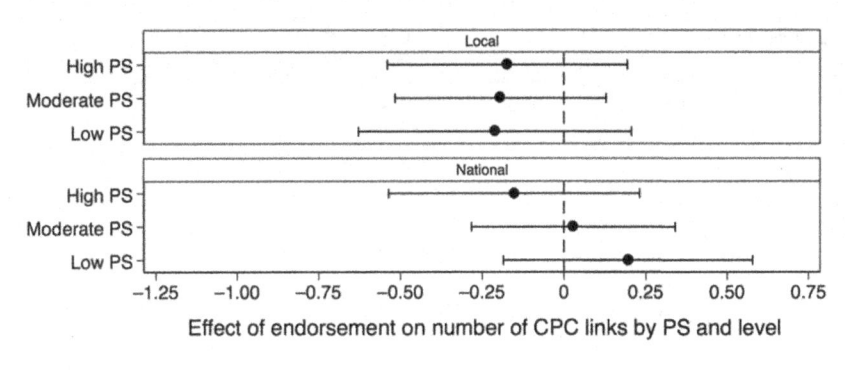

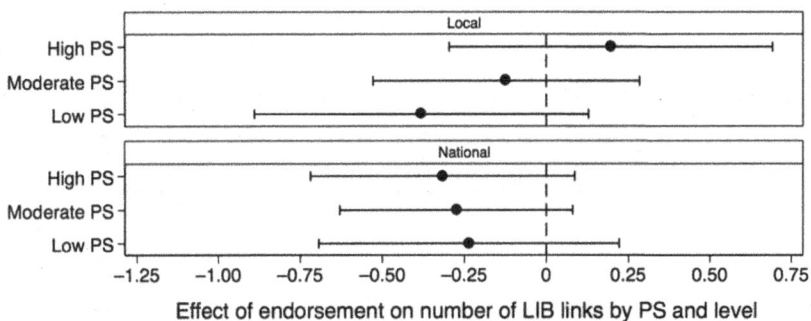

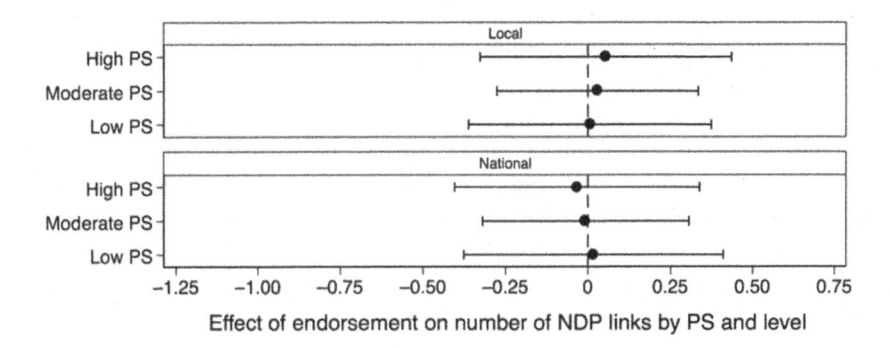

Effect of endorsement on number of CPC links by PS and level

Effect of endorsement on number of LIB links by PS and level

Effect of endorsement on number of NDP links by PS and level

endorsement and then with separate measures for local and national endorsers. The results from these assessments are reported in figures 4.4 and 4.5.

As indicated by our results, there is practically no evidence that political sophistication mediates the relationship between exposure to

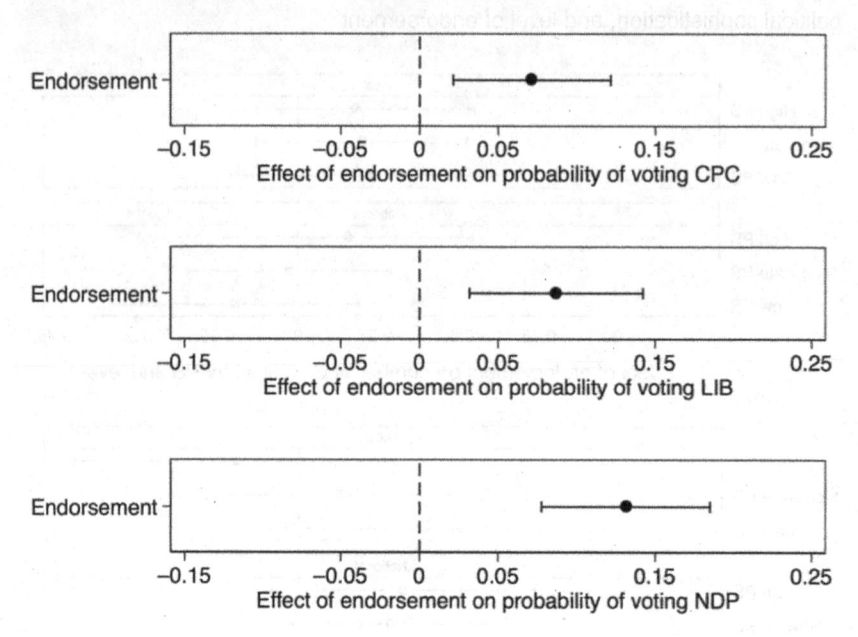

Figure 4.6. Treatment effects on vote choice by party

[Figure 4.6: Three coefficient plots showing the effect of endorsement on the probability of voting CPC, LIB, and NDP, respectively. X-axis ranges from −0.15 to 0.25 in each panel.]

political endorsements and the information search, regardless of the level of endorsement (see figures 4.4 and 4.5). The one exception is the local-level endorsement for the LIB candidate, where we observe a significant ($p < 0.10$) 0.25-link difference between low and high sophisticates, which is consistent with our expectations (figure 4.5). However, this appears to be the exception, with no discernible or consistent pattern in any of the other models.

Do endorsements affect vote choice? To assess the impact of endorsements on the vote, we use logistic regression to estimate the probability of voting for each party. We once again begin by considering endorsement effects in general, controlling for partisanship. The results for each party are presented in figure 4.6.

Clearly, political endorsements affect the vote. For all three parties, we find a positive and statistically significant ($p < 0.05$) relationship between receiving an endorsement and the likelihood of an individual voting for the party, net of PID. For example, in the case of the NDP, we find a 13-percentage-point increase in the probability of an individual casting a vote for the party when exposed to an endorsement relative to the probability of voting for the same party absent an endorsement. The

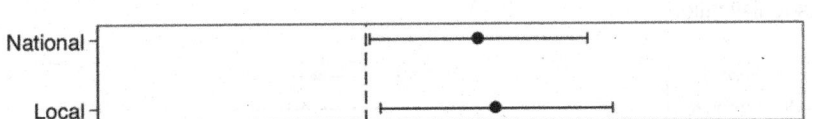

Figure 4.7. Treatment effects on vote choice by party and level of endorsement

[Forest plot: Effect of endorsement on probability of voting CPC by level, with National and Local estimates, x-axis from -0.15 to 0.25]

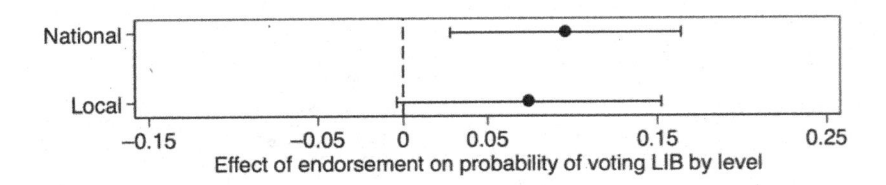

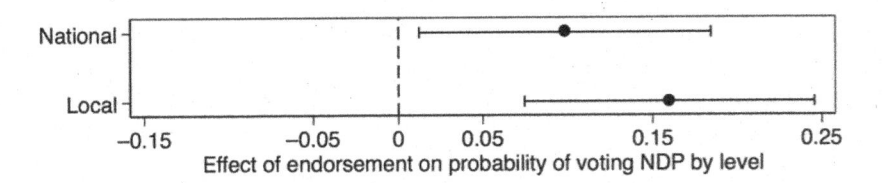

[Forest plot: Effect of endorsement on probability of voting LIB by level, with National and Local estimates, x-axis from -0.15 to 0.25]

[Forest plot: Effect of endorsement on probability of voting NDP by level, with National and Local estimates, x-axis from -0.15 to 0.25]

increase in the probability of voting for the LIB and CPC when the participants are exposed to an endorsement relative to the control group is 9 and 7 percentage points, respectively. These results fully support our expectations: endorsements do increase vote share.

But are all endorsements equal? Hypothesis 4 contends that national endorsements will have a greater impact on vote share than local-level endorsements or no endorsements. We test this argument by separating the level of endorsement and re-estimating the vote models. The results are presented in figure 4.7.

While there is some hint that local endorsements may have a slightly greater impact than national-level endorsements for the NDP (6 percentage points; $p = 0.30$), the results overall suggest little difference according to the level of endorsement and party. Thus, we find no support for this hypothesis: national-level endorsements do not have a greater impact compared with local-level endorsements when it comes to the vote.

Does the relationship between political endorsements and vote share vary according to political sophistication? As with the information search, we expect that those with lower levels of political sophistication will be more apt to be influenced by endorsements relative to their

Figure 4.8. Treatment effects on vote choice by party and level of political sophistication

Effect of endorsement on probability of voting CPC by PS

Effect of endorsement on probability of voting LIB by PS

Effect of endorsement on probability of voting NDP by PS

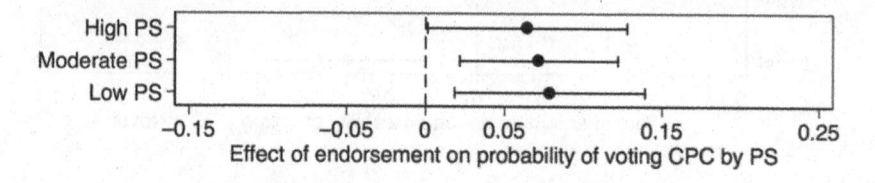

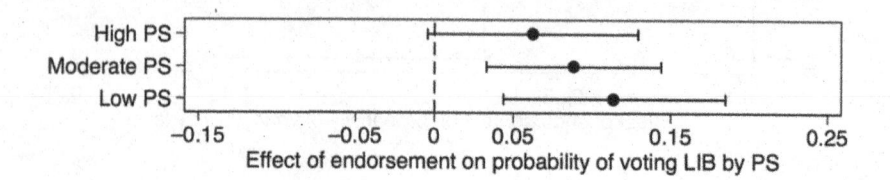

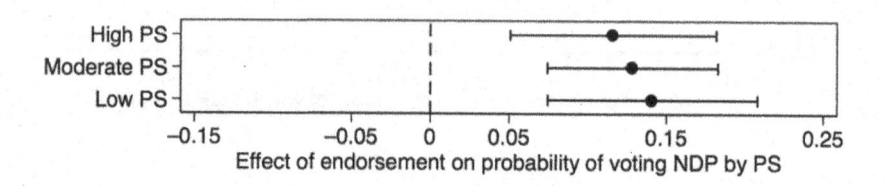

more sophisticated counterparts. To assess this argument, we interact political sophistication, first with endorsements in general and then according to the level of endorsement. We do this separately for each party and once again estimate sophistication at the 25th, 50th, and 75th percentiles to represent low, moderate, and high sophisticates. The results from these analyses are presented in figure 4.8 for endorsements in general and figure 4.9 for endorsements by level of endorser.

As was the case with the information search, we find little evidence to support our assumption that political sophistication conditions the relationship between endorsements and vote choice. While there is evidence of some small differences according to level of sophistication – for example, for the LIB candidate with a local-level endorsement – the magnitude of the difference is negligible. Put simply, political endorsement increases the probability of an individual supporting the recipient of the endorsement, regardless of the level of endorsement or the individual's level of political sophistication. Net of PID, the increased probability of voting for an endorsed candidate ranged from a low of

Figure 4.9. Treatment effects on vote choice by party, level of political sophistication, and level of endorsement

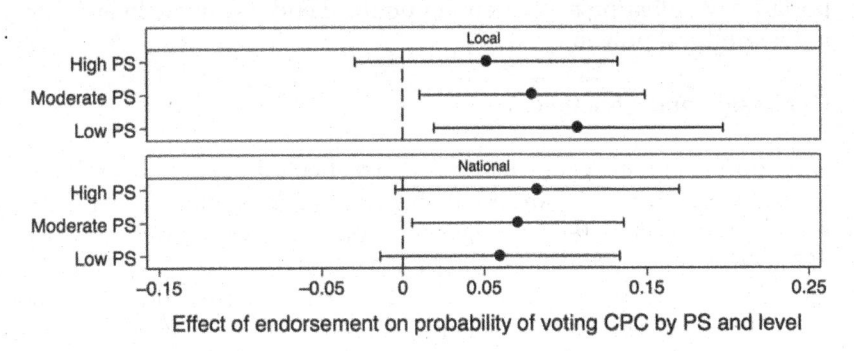

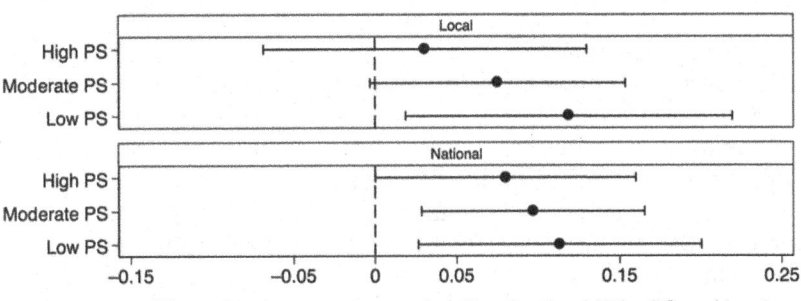

Effect of endorsement on probability of voting CPC by PS and level

Effect of endorsement on probability of voting LIB by PS and level

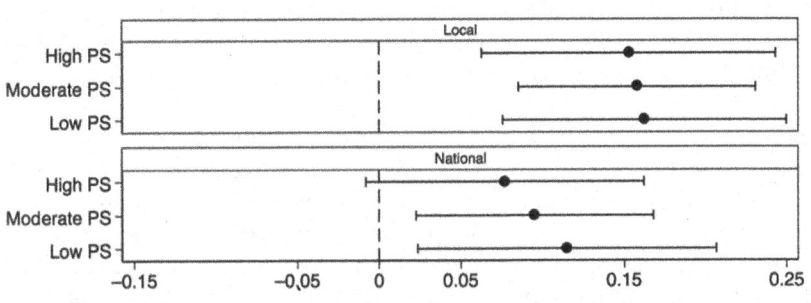

Effect of endorsement on probability of voting NDP by PS and level

3 percentage points (the LIB candidate with a local endorsement among high-sophisticate voters) to a high of 16 points (low-sophisticate voters when the NDP candidate was endorsed at the local level). While political endorsements seem to have little influence on the vote-decision process, the impact on vote share is notable. The fact that this effect is

observed regardless of the level of endorsement and individual levels of political sophistication is both unexpected and exemplary of the importance of soliciting and receiving political endorsements in an effort to win political power.

Discussion and Conclusion

Our efforts to identify information-search effects as a result of endorsement proved futile. Regardless of the level of the endorser or the sophistication of the voter, endorsements had little impact on the amount of information that the individuals engaged in before casting their ballot. Of course, it could be that the treatment stimulus employed in this study, an endorsement from a fictional organization, explains the limited treatment effects. Future work should consider such a possibility, altering the endorser across treatments, to test this possibility directly.

While our treatment appears to have had limited impact on the decision-making process, it clearly affected the vote that was cast. For all three parties, exposure to an endorsement increased the likelihood of an individual supporting the candidate relative to the probability of supporting the same candidate absent the stimulus. Contrary to expectations, there is little evidence to suggest that the level of the endorsement or the sophistication of the voter conditions this relationship. Candidate endorsements increase vote shares. However, given that our fictional organization provided the endorsement, we are not able to explore how individual-level recognition and the opinion of the endorser may alter this relationship. It certainly seems plausible that an endorser that is respected by one voter may increase support for a candidate, while the same endorser who is less popular with another voter could have the opposite effect. This second area of future research would build upon the results reported here and provide more clarity on the value of soliciting and receiving public endorsements.

What are the implications of these research findings for winning and keeping power in Canada? The big takeaway is that there is significant value in seeking out endorsements from prominent individuals and organizations, whether they are at the local or national level. While there are differences in endorser effects by party – for example, the stronger influence of local-level endorsements for the NDP relative to the CPC and the LIB – overall, the effects are remarkably similar across party lines. Ultimately, our results leave us to conclude that, as many observers have noted, endorsements do help candidates win elections. For individual political candidates, seeking out support from prominent individuals in the local community should be an important part of the election campaign. At the national level, endorsements from individuals with national profiles can not only be leveraged to increase the vote shares of the party leader and the party more generally, but may also be used strategically to strengthen voter support for candidates in key ridings. What our study does not tell us is what kinds of endorsement parties and candidates should seek out. We look forward to doing future work in this area so that we can extend this analysis to include variations according to *who* is offering the endorsement and how that person or group might alter the conclusions drawn here.

REFERENCES

Arceneaux, Kevin, and Robin Kolodny. 2009. "Educating the Least Informed: Group Endorsements in a Grassroots Campaign." *American Journal of Political Science* 53 (4): 755–70. https://doi.org/10.1111/j.1540-5907.2009.00399.x.

Bittner, Amanda. 2011. *Platform or Personality? The Role of Party Leaders in Elections.* Toronto: Oxford University Press.

Butler, Don. 2015. "Vandenbeld gets Leadnow's Anybody-but-Conservative Endorsement in Ottawa West–Nepean." *Ottawa Citizen*, 16 October. https://ottawacitizen.com/news/politics/vandenbeld-gets-leadnows-anybody-but-conservative-endorsement-in-ottawa-west-nepean.

CBC News. 2015. "Wayne Gretzky Endorses Harper despite Not Being Allowed to Vote." *CBC News*, 18 September 2015. http://www.cbc.ca/news/politics/gretzky-harper-1.3234136.

Conover, Pamela Johnston, and Stanley Feldman. 1989. "Candidate Perception in an Ambiguous World: Campaigns, Cues, and Inference Processes." *American Journal of Political Science* 33 (4): 912–40. https://doi.org/10.2307/2111115.

Converse, Philip E. 1964. "The Nature of Belief Systems in Mass Publics." In *Ideology and Discontent*, edited by D.E. Apter. New York: Free Press.

Cutler, Fred. 2002. "The Simplest Shortcut of All: Sociodemographic Characteristics and Electoral Choice." *Journal of Politics* 6 (2): 466–90. https://doi.org/10.1111/1468-2508.00135.

Downs, Anthony. 1957. *An Economic Theory of Democracy.* New York: Harper and Row.

Fiske, Susan T., Donald R. Kinder, and W. Michael Larter. 1983. "The Novice and the Expert: Knowledge-Based Strategies in Political Cognition." *Journal of Experimental Social Psychology* 19 (4): 381–400. https://doi.org/10.1016/0022-1031(83)90029-X.

Fiske, Susan T., and Shelley E. Taylor. 1991. *Social Cognition.* 2nd ed. New York: McGraw-Hill.

Garthwaite, Craig, and Timothy J. Moore. 2012. "Can Celebrity Endorsements Affect Political Outcomes? Evidence from the 2008 US Democratic Presidential Primary." *Journal of Law, Economics, and Organization* 29 (2): 355–84. https://doi.org/10.1093/jleo/ewr031.

Grenier, Eric. 2017. "Andrew Scheer Leads Endorsement Race in Conservative Leadership Campaign." *CBC News*, 17 January 2017. http://www.cbc.ca/news/politics/grenier-conservatives-endorsements-1.3931211.

Grossman, Gene M., and Elhanan Helpman. 1999. "Competing for Endorsements." *American Economic Review* 89 (3): 501–24. https://doi.org/10.1257/aer.89.3.501.

Kahneman, Daniel, Paul Slovic, and Amos Tversky, eds. 1982. *Judgment under Uncertainty: Heuristics and Biases*. New York: Cambridge University Press.

Kohut, Tania. 2015. "Who's Endorsing Whom: Newspaper Editorial Boards Pick Their Parties." *Global News*, 16 October 2015. http://globalnews.ca/news/2281623/whos-endorsing-whom-newspaper-editorial-boards-pick-their-parties/.

Lau, Richard R., and David P. Redlawsk. 2001. "Advantages and Disadvantages of Cognitive Heuristics in Political Decision Making." *American Journal of Political Science* 45 (4): 951–71. https://doi.org/10.2307/2669334.

– 2006. *How Voters Decide: Information Processing during Election Campaigns*. Cambridge Studies in Public Opinion and Political Psychology. New York: Cambridge University Press.

Lupia, Arthur. 1994. "Shortcuts versus Encyclopedias: Information and Voting Behavior in California Insurance Reform Elections." *American Political Science Review* 88 (1): 63–76. https://doi.org/10.2307/2944882.

Merolla, Jennifer L., Laura B. Stephenson, and Elizabeth J. Zechmeister. 2008. "Can Canadians Take a Hint? The (In)Effectiveness of Party Labels as Information Shortcuts in Canada." *Canadian Journal of Political Science* 41 (3): 673–96. https://doi.org/10.1017/S0008423908080797.

Miller, Patrick R. 2011. "The Emotional Citizen: Emotion as a Function of Political Sophistication." *Political Psychology* 32 (4): 575–600. https://doi.org/10.1111/j.1467-9221.2011.00824.x.

Mishra, Anubhav A., and Abhinav Mishra. 2014. "National vs. Local Celebrity Endorsement and Politics." *International Journal of Politics, Culture, and Society* 27 (4): 409–425. 10.1007/s10767-014-9174-y.

Mutz, Diana C. 1992. "Impersonal Influence: Effects of Representations of Public Opinion on Political Attitudes." *Political Behavior* 14 (2): 89–122. https://doi.org/10.1007/BF00992237.

Neddenriep, Gregory, and Anthony J. Nownes. 2014. "An Experimental Investigation of the Effects of Interest-Group Endorsements on Poorly Aligned Partisans in the 2008 Presidential Election." *Party Politics* 20 (4): 617–31. https://doi.org/10.1177/1354068811436067.

Ottawa Citizen. 2011. "Endorsement: Ottawa South Riding – McGuinty Is an MP with Depth." 27 April 2011. https://ottawacitizen.com/news/endorsement-ottawa-south-riding-mcguinty-is-an-mp-with-depth/wcm/e751e7a0-c1e5-41a1-8319-20b5131b52eb.

Pease, Andrew, and Paul R. Brewer. 2008. "The Oprah Factor: The Effects of a Celebrity Endorsement in a Presidential Primary Campaign." *Harvard International Journal of Press/Politics* 13 (4): 386–400. https://doi.org/10.1177/1940161208321948.

Popkin, Samuel L. 1994. *The Reasoning Voter.* 2nd ed. Chicago: University of Chicago Press.

Rankin, Murray. 2019. "Supporters and Endorsements." *Murray Rankin* (website). Accessed spring 2019. http://murrayrankin.ndp.ca/supporters-and-endorsements.

Rosenberg, Shawn W., Lisa Bohan, Patrick McCafferty, and Kevin Harris. 1986. "The Image and the Vote: The Effect of Candidate Presentation on Voter Preference." *American Journal of Political Science* 30 (1): 108–27. https://doi.org/10.2307/2111296.

Rosenberg, Shawn W., and Patrick McCafferty. 1987. "The Image and the Vote: Manipulating Voters' Preferences." *Public Opinion Quarterly* 51 (1): 31–47. https://doi.org/10.1086/269012.

Roy, Jason. 2011. "Information Heterogeneity, Complexity and the Vote Calculus." *Journal of Elections, Public Opinion and Parties* 21 (1): 29–56. https://doi.org/10.1080/17457289.2010.537342.

Sayers, Anthony. 1999. *Parties, Candidates, and Constituency Campaigns in Canadian Elections.* Vancouver: UBC Press.

Singh, Shane, and Jason Roy. 2014. "Political Knowledge, the Decision Calculus, and Proximity Voting. *Electoral Studies* 34 (3): 89–99. https://doi.org/10.1177/2053168017751993.

Singh, Shane, Jason Roy, and Patrick Fournier. 2016. "Polls, Partisanship, and Voter Decision-Making: An Experimental Analysis." In *Voting Experiments*, edited by André Blais, Jean-François Laslier, and Karine Van der Straeten. Cham, Switzerland: Springer, 171–89.

Veer, Ekant, Ilda Becirovic, and Brett A.S. Martin. 2010. "If Kate Voted Conservative, Would You? The Role of Celebrity Endorsements in Political Party Advertising." *European Journal of Marketing* 44 (3–4): 436–50. https://doi.org/10.1108/03090561011020516.

Williams, Christine B., Girish J. Gulati, and Ellen R. Foxman. 2009. "What's in an Endorsement? An Analysis of Web-Based Marketing in the 2004 Presidential Campaign." *Journal of Political Marketing* 8 (3): 173–89. https://doi.org/10.1080/15377850903048214.

Winseck, Dwayne. 2015. "Canadian Newspaper Editorial Election Endorsements: Elite and out of Sync." *Policy Options.* 3 November. http://

policyoptions.irpp.org/2015/11/03/canadian-newspaper-editorial-endorsements-in-the-2015-federal-election-elite-and-out-of-sync/.
Wood, Natalie T., and Kenneth C. Herbst. 2007. "Political Star Power and Political Parties." *Journal of Political Marketing* 6 (2–3): 141–58. https://doi.org/10.1300/J199v06n02_08.
Zaller, John. 1990. "Political Awareness, Elite Opinion Leadership, and the Mass Survey Response." *Social Cognition*, 8 (1): 125–53. https://doi.org/10.1521/soco.1990.8.1.125.
– 1992. *The Nature and Origins of Mass Opinion*. New York: Cambridge University Press.

Appendix 4.1. Political-endorsement cueing links

Endorsement

1 **Endorsement (control):** "There have been no endorsements for Robert Johnson of the NDP to date."
2 **Endorsement (national):** "Paul Smith, the Conservative candidate, is the best person to represent this riding in the House of Commons. On election day, I hope all voters will cast their ballots in support of Paul."

Larry Watson, president of Water First, a national organization dedicated to the long-term health of Canada's water supply.

3 **Endorsement (local):** "Paul Smith, the Conservative candidate, is the best person to represent this riding in the House of Commons. On election day, I hope all voters will cast their ballots in support of Paul."

Larry Watson, local chapter president of Water First, a national organization dedicated to the long-term health of Canada's water supply.

Statement from Party Officials

1 **Statement from party officials about non-endorsed candidate (national):** Party officials have offered their full support to Robert Johnson, candidate for the NDP in this month's election. They have no comment on Larry Watson, president of Water First, a national organization dedicated to the long-term health of Canada's water supply, endorsing the Conservative candidate, Paul Smith.

2. **Statement from party officials about non-endorsed candidate (local):** Party officials have offered their full support to Robert Johnson, candidate for the NDP in this month's election. They have no comment on Larry Watson, local chapter president of Water First, a national organization dedicated to the long-term health of Canada's water supply, endorsing the Conservative candidate, Paul Smith.
3. **Statement from party officials about endorsed candidate (national):** Party officials are pleased that Larry Watson, president of Water First, a national organization dedicated to the long-term health of Canada's water supply, has endorsed Paul Smith, candidate for the Conservatives in this month's election.
4. **Statement from party officials about endorsed candidate (local):** Party officials are pleased that Larry Watson, local chapter president of Water First, a national organization dedicated to the long-term health of Canada's water supply, has endorsed Paul Smith, candidate for the Conservatives in this month's election.

Newspaper Story

1. Newspaper Story (Control):

CANDIDATES REACH OUT TO PUBLIC IN CAMPAIGN PUSH
METCALF – Candidates from this month's election are inviting voters to meet them "on the town." As part of their continuing outreach efforts, all three candidates will make numerous public appearances to solicit suggestions as to how to best meet the needs of local residents.

Speaking to voters in Metcalf, event organizer Larry Watson noted that "being out in the community is the only way to get a sense of the challenges that voters face." The next all-candidates meeting will be held in neighbouring Townsville later this week.

2. Newspaper Story (National):

CONSERVATIVE CANDIDATE PAUL SMITH RECEIVES ENDORSEMENT FROM NATIONAL LEADER
METCALF – Paul Smith of the Conservatives spent the day meeting with reporters about the endorsement he had received from Larry Watson, president of Water First, a national organization dedicated to the long-term health of Canada's water supply.

"It was a real honour to receive this endorsement today. Mr. Watson is one of Canada's most celebrated leaders, and to receive his support during this campaign was very unexpected but most welcome."

Smith is scheduled to speak at a community event in Metcalf later this week. His campaign tour will soon take him to a number of neighbouring communities.

3. Newspaper Story (Local):

CONSERVATIVE CANDIDATE PAUL SMITH RECEIVES ENDORSEMENT FROM LOCAL LEADER

METCALF – Paul Smith of the Conservatives spent the day meeting with reporters about the endorsement he had received from Larry Watson, local chapter president of Water First, a national organization dedicated to the long-term health of Canada's water supply.

"It was a real honour to receive this endorsement today. Mr. Watson is one of our community's most celebrated leaders, and to receive his support during this campaign was very unexpected but most welcome."

Smith is scheduled to speak at a community event in Metcalf later this week. His campaign tour will soon take him to a number of neighbouring communities.

Appendix 4.2. Summary statistics

	Control	Treatment 1	Treatment 2	Treatment 3	Treatment 4	Treatment 5	Treatment 6
Age	47.94 (16.86)	47.81 (17.18)	50.60 (17.05)	46.61 (18.49)	46.72 (17.65)	47.45 (16.01)	47.61 (16.94)
Female	0.50 (0.50)	0.48 (0.50)	0.59 (0.49)	0.64 (0.48)	0.53 (0.50)	0.56 (0.50)	0.53 (0.50)
No high school	0.07 (0.25)	0.03 (0.17)	0.04 (0.19)	0.04 (0.21)	0.06 (0.24)	0.01 (0.10)	0.04 (0.20)
University graduate	0.35 (0.48)	0.37 (0.48)	0.32 (0.47)	0.31 (0.47)	0.36 (0.48)	0.42 (0.50)	0.37 (0.48)
Income	3.86 (1.90)	3.89 (1.85)	3.91 (1.86)	3.95 (1.86)	3.66 (1.71)	3.75 (1.87)	3.55 (1.65)
Prairies	0.28 (0.45)	0.26 (0.44)	0.27 (0.45)	0.22 (0.41)	0.19 (0.40)	0.18 (0.39)	0.27 (0.45)
Ontario	0.48 (0.50)	0.49 (0.50)	0.47 (0.50)	0.59 (0.49)	0.59 (0.49)	0.56 (0.50)	0.51 (0.50)
Atlantic	0.07 (0.26)	0.08 (0.28)	0.08 (0.28)	0.10 (0.30)	0.15 (0.36)	0.09 (0.28)	0.10 (0.30)
Satisfaction	0.87 (0.34)	0.81 (0.39)	0.81 (0.39)	0.83 (0.38)	0.74 (0.44)	0.80 (0.40)	0.79 (0.41)
Political interest	6.61 (2.24)	6.67 (2.45)	6.36 (2.57)	6.36 (2.44)	6.47 (2.72)	6.15 (2.38)	6.60 (2.41)
Political knowledge	0.61 (0.29)	0.58 (0.32)	0.53 (0.30)	0.59 (0.30)	0.62 (0.30)	0.54 (0.33)	0.55 (0.31)
Political ideology	4.88 (2.23)	4.74 (2.09)	5.01 (2.06)	5.21 (2.10)	4.97 (2.34)	4.82 (1.90)	4.81 (2.18)
CPC PID	0.19 (0.39)	0.16 (0.37)	0.15 (0.36)	0.23 (0.43)	0.17 (0.38)	0.19 (0.39)	0.30 (0.46)
GRN PID	0.05 (0.21)	0.02 (0.14)	0.04 (0.19)	0.00 (0.00)	0.03 (0.18)	0.02 (0.14)	0.02 (0.14)
LIB PID	0.26 (0.44)	0.27 (0.45)	0.29 (0.45)	0.27 (0.44)	0.23 (0.42)	0.19 (0.39)	0.22 (0.42)
NDP PID	0.06 (0.25)	0.13 (0.34)	0.07 (0.26)	0.09 (0.29)	0.05 (0.22)	0.08 (0.27)	0.09 (0.29)
Response check	0.95 (0.21)	0.97 (0.17)	0.97 (0.16)	0.96 (0.21)	0.97 (0.18)	0.90 (0.30)	0.92 (0.27)
N	108	99	108	90	115	101	99

Note: The cells report averages, with standard deviations in parentheses. Age is the respondents' age in years. Female, no high school, university graduate, regional variables, PID, and response check are dichotomous measures, coded "1" in correspondence with the variable name. Political interest and political ideology are self-reported positions on an eleven-point scale running from "No interest" to "Great deal of interest" and "Left–Right," respectively. Political knowledge is an index (alpha = 0.61) based on five factual questions: the name of the British prime minister, the name of the governor general, and the number of seats in the House of Commons. The respondents received one point for each correct response. The variable was then rescaled to fit between 0 and 1. N = number of usable cases in each treatment.

Appendix 4.3. Multinomial logistic regression results for test of random assignment to treatments

	Treatment 1	Treatment 2	Treatment 3	Treatment 4	Treatment 5	Election 6
Age	-0.00 (0.01)	0.01 (0.01)	-0.00 (0.01)	-0.00 (0.01)	0.00 (0.01)	-0.00 (0.01)
Female	-0.03 (0.31)	0.31 (0.31)	0.67 (0.33)[*]	0.07 (0.30)	0.35 (0.31)	0.06 (0.31)
No high school	-0.37 (0.81)	-0.53 (0.81)	-0.32 (0.81)	-0.16 (0.73)	-1.49 (1.15)	-0.46 (0.82)
University graduate	-0.03 (0.33)	-0.14 (0.33)	-0.25 (0.35)	0.03 (0.32)	0.36 (0.32)	0.14 (0.33)
Income	-0.02 (0.09)	0.07 (0.08)	0.04 (0.09)	-0.04 (0.09)	-0.07 (0.09)	-0.08 (0.09)
Prairies	-0.01 (0.47)	0.12 (0.46)	0.82 (0.58)	0.65 (0.55)	-0.40 (0.48)	0.30 (0.50)
Ontario	-0.10 (0.42)	0.08 (0.42)	1.09 (0.53)[*]	1.09 (0.50)[*]	0.07 (0.41)	0.30 (0.45)
Atlantic	0.33 (0.67)	0.44 (0.65)	1.56 (0.73)[*]	1.69 (0.68)[*]	-0.10 (0.70)	0.79 (0.69)
Satisfaction	-0.31 (0.41)	-0.24 (0.41)	-0.20 (0.43)	-0.47 (0.40)	-0.16 (0.41)	-0.30 (0.41)
Political interest	0.03 (0.07)	-0.02 (0.07)	-0.05 (0.07)	-0.02 (0.07)	-0.06 (0.07)	0.00 (0.07)
Political knowledge	-0.29 (0.52)	-0.86 (0.51)[a]	0.01 (0.54)	0.30 (0.51)	-0.74 (0.51)	-0.63 (0.52)
Political ideology	-0.03 (0.08)	0.03 (0.08)	0.04 (0.09)	-0.01 (0.08)	-0.11 (0.08)	-0.15 (0.08)[a]
CPC PID	0.16 (0.47)	-0.31 (0.47)	0.37 (0.47)	0.12 (0.46)	0.12 (0.46)	1.22 (0.45)[**]
GRN PID	-1.31 (1.15)	-0.10 (0.76)	-14.02 (605.03)	-0.47 (0.82)	-1.04 (0.91)	-1.29 (1.17)
LIB PID	0.09 (0.39)	0.11 (0.37)	0.11 (0.40)	-0.22 (0.38)	-0.60 (0.40)	-0.10 (0.41)
NDP PID	1.02 (0.60)[a]	0.15 (0.66)	0.59 (0.66)	-0.20 (0.69)	-0.04 (0.65)	0.46 (0.65)
Response check	0.30 (0.79)	0.36 (0.79)	0.01 (0.74)	0.48 (0.79)	-1.05 (0.63)[a]	-0.82 (0.65)
Constant	0.30 (1.23)	-0.53 (1.23)	-1.21 (1.28)	-0.48 (1.25)	2.38 (1.11)	1.96 (1.14)[a]

$N = 649$
χ^2 (df = 102) = 104.60
Pseudo R^2 = 0.04

Note: The cells report multinomial logistic regression coefficients, with standard errors in parentheses. The control group is set as the base outcome. Age is the respondents' age in years. Female, no high school, university graduate, regional variables, PID, and response check are dichotomous measures, coded "1" in correspondence with the variable name. Political interest and political ideology are self-reported positions on an eleven-point scale running from "No interest" to "Great deal of interest" and "Left–Right," respectively. Political knowledge is an index (alpha = 0.61) based on five factual questions: the name of the British prime minister, the level of government that has primary responsibility for education and health care in Canada, the name of the federal finance minister, the name of the governor general, and the number of seats in the House of Commons. The respondents received one point for each correct response. The variable was then rescaled to fit between 0 and 1. N = number of cases with full response set.
[***] $p < 0.001$; [**] $p < 0.01$; [*] $p < 0.05$; [a] $p < 0.10$.

Appendix 4.4. Full results for figures 4.2 to 4.9

Results for figure 4.2. Treatment effects on the information search by party

	CPC	LIB	NDP
Endorsement	−0.03 (0.05) [−0.09]	−0.05 (0.05) [−0.15]	−0.00 (0.05) [−0.01]
Same PID	−0.00 (0.06)	−0.06 (0.05)	0.08 (0.08)
Other PID	−0.18 (0.05)***	−0.13 (0.05)**	−0.20 (0.05 ***
Constant	1.22 (0.03)***	1.22 (0.03)***	1.16 (0.03)***
Pseudo R^2	0.01	0.00	0.01
N	720	720	720

Note: The cells report Poisson regression coefficients, with standard errors in parentheses and marginal effects/discrete changes reported in square brackets. PID is included in the model as a control, with no or weak PID set as the reference category.
***$p < 0.001$; **$p < 0.01$; *$p < 0.05$; a$p < 0.10$.

Results for figure 4.3: Treatment effects on the information search by party and level of endorsement

	CPC	LIB	NDP
Local endorsement	−0.05 (0.06) [−0.17]	−0.01 (0.06) [−0.02]	−0.00 (0.06) [0.01]
National endorsement	−0.00 (0.06) [−0.01]	−0.08 (0.06) [−0.26]	−0.01 (0.06) [−0.03]
Same PID	−0.00 (0.06)	−0.06 (0.05)	0.08 (0.08)
Other PID	−0.18 (0.05 ***	−0.14 (0.05)**	−0.20 (0.05)***
Constant	1.22 (0.03)***	1.22 (0.03)***	1.16 (0.03)***
Pseudo R^2	0.01	0.00	0.01
N	720	720	720

Note: The cells report Poisson regression coefficients, with standard errors in parentheses and marginal effects/discrete changes reported in square brackets. PID is included in the model as a control, with no or weak PID set as the reference category.
***$p < 0.001$; **$p < 0.01$; *$p < 0.05$; a$p < 0.10$.

Results for figure 4.4: Treatment effects on the information search by party and level of political sophistication

	CPC	LIB	NDP
Endorsement	−0.02 (0.05)	−0.07 (0.05)	0.00 (0.05)
Political sophistication	0.10 (0.03)**	0.08 (0.03)**	0.09 (0.03)**
Endorsement × Political sophistication	−0.05 (0.06)	0.05 (0.06)	−0.00 (0.06)
Same PID	−0.04 (0.06)	−0.10 (0.05)a	0.04 (0.08)
Other PID	−0.21 (0.05)***	−0.17 (0.05)***	−0.24 (0.05)***
Constant	1.22 (0.03)***	1.23 (0.03)***	1.16 (0.03)***
Pseudo R^2	0.01	0.01	0.01
N	720	720	720

Note: The cells report Poisson regression coefficients, with standard errors in parentheses. PID is included in the model as a control, with no or weak PID set as the reference category.
***$p < 0.001$; **$p < 0.01$; *$p < 0.05$; a$p < 0.10$.

Results for figure 4.5: Treatment effects on the information search by party, level of political sophistication, and level of endorsement

	CPC	LIB	NDP
Local endorsement	−0.06 (0.07)	−0.04 (0.07)	0.01 (0.06)
National endorsement	0.01 (0.06)	−0.09 (0.06)	−0.00 (0.07)
Political sophistication	0.10 (0.03)**	0.08 (0.03)**	0.09 (0.03)*
Local endorsement × Political sophistication	−0.02 (0.08)	0.16 (0.09)a	0.01 (0.08)
National endorsement × Political sophistication	−0.10 (0.07)	−0.02 (0.07)	−0.01 (0.08)
Same PID	−0.04 (0.06)	−0.11 (0.05)*	0.04 (0.08)
Other PID	−0.21 (0.03)***	−0.18 (0.05)***	−0.24 (0.05)***
Constant	1.22 (0.03)***	1.24 (0.03)***	1.16 (0.03)***
Pseudo R^2	0.01	0.01	0.01
N	720	720	720

Note: The cells report Poisson regression coefficients, with standard errors in parentheses. PID is included in the model as a control, with no or weak PID set as the reference category.
***$p < 0.001$; **$p < 0.01$; *$p < 0.05$; a$p < 0.10$.

Results for figure 4.6: Treatment effects on vote choice by party

	CPC	LIB	NDP
Endorsement	0.54 (0.23)*	0.52 (0.20)**	0.94 (0.22)***
	[0.07]	[0.09]	[0.13]
Same PID	3.53 (0.35)***	1.99 (0.24)***	2.85 (0.39)***
Other PID	−1.80 (0.28)***	−2.10 (0.26)***	−1.44 (0.24)***
Constant	−1.05 (0.14)***	−0.36 (0.13)**	−1.34 (0.15)***
Pseudo R^2	0.37	0.27	0.23
N	720	720	720

Note: The cells report logistic regression coefficients, with standard errors in parentheses and marginal effects/discrete changes reported in square brackets. PID is included in the model as a control, with no or weak PID set as the reference category.
***$p < 0.001$; **$p < 0.01$; *$p < 0.05$; [a]$p < 0.10$.

Results for figure 4.7: Treatment effects on vote choice by party and level of endorsement

	CPC	LIB	NDP
Local endorsement	0.58 (0.30)[a]	0.45 (0.28)	1.10 (0.27)***
	[0.08]	[0.07]	[0.16]
National endorsement	0.51 (0.29)[a]	0.58 (0.25)*	0.73 (0.30)*
	[0.07]	[0.10]	[0.10]
Same PID	3.53 (0.35)***	2.00 (0.24)***	2.86 (0.39)***
Other PID	−1.80 (0.28)***	−2.10 (0.26)***	−1.42 (0.24)***
Constant	−1.05 (0.14)***	−0.36 (0.13)**	−1.35 (0.15)***
Pseudo R^2	0.37	0.27	0.23
N	720	720	720

Note: The cells report logistic regression coefficients, with standard errors in parentheses and marginal effects/discrete changes reported in square brackets. PID is included in the model as a control, with no or weak PID set as the reference category.
***$p < 0.001$; **$p < 0.01$; *$p < 0.05$; [a]$p < 0.10$.

Results for figure 4.8: Treatment effects on vote choice by party and level of political sophistication

	CPC	LIB	NDP
Endorsement	0.55 (0.23)*	0.54 (0.20)**	0.92 (0.22)***
Political sophistication	0.12 (0.16)	0.13 (0.14)	−0.21 (0.17)
Endorsement × Political sophistication	−0.11 (0.28)	−0.27 (0.26)	−0.05 (0.27)
Same PID	3.49 (0.36)***	1.97 (0.25)***	2.94 (0.40)***
Other PID	−1.82 (0.29)***	−2.13 (0.27)***	−1.36 (0.25)***
Constant	−1.05 (0.14)***	−0.36 (0.13)***	−1.37 (0.15)***
Pseudo R^2	0.37	0.27	0.23
N	720	720	720

Note: The cells report logistic regression coefficients, with standard errors in parentheses. PID is included in the model as a control, with no or weak PID set as the reference category.
*** $p < 0.001$; ** $p < 0.01$; * $p < 0.05$; [a] $p < 0.10$.

Results for figure 4.9: Treatment effects on vote choice by party, level of political sophistication, and level of endorsement

	CPC	LIB	NDP
Local endorsement	0.61 (0.30)*	0.46 (0.29)	1.09 (0.27)***
National endorsement	0.54 (0.29)[a]	0.59 (0.25)*	0.72 (0.30)*
Political sophistication	0.13 (0.16)	0.13 (0.14)	−0.22 (0.17)
Local endorsement × Political sophistication	−0.36 (0.37)	−0.46 (0.39)	0.03 (0.33)
National endorsement × Political sophistication	0.12 (0.36)	−0.17 (0.30)	−0.15 (0.36)
Same PID	3.49 (0.36)***	1.99 (0.25)***	2.96 (0.40)***
Other PID	−1.84 (0.29)***	−2.12 (0.27)***	−1.34 (0.25)***
Constant	−1.05 (0.14)***	−0.36 (0.13)***	−1.37 (0.15)***
Pseudo R^2	0.37	0.27	0.23
N	720	720	720

Note: The cells report logistic regression coefficients, with standard errors in parentheses. PID is included in the model as a control, with no or weak PID set as the reference category.
*** $p < 0.001$; ** $p < 0.01$; * $p < 0.05$; [a] $p < 0.10$.

Chapter Five

The Quality of Local Candidates[1]

"We have as a Liberal candidate a great Canadian hero," Dion said Friday at a news conference in Montreal. "[Garneau] is a hero of our history, he will be an architect of his future." (*CTV News* 2007)

Local candidates matter. Not in every instance and not in every place, of course, but they remain an important element in our elections. Their importance is probably related, and strongly so, to how much voters decide to learn about them and to base their decisions on their judgment of those candidates. (Loewen 2015)

Canadian political parties have long believed that recruiting local candidates with desirable qualities is a crucial part of winning elections. Party elites assume that voters are more apt to support a candidate who has a strong set of skills and experiences relative to a candidate whose résumé is less impressive on those dimensions. In the 2015 federal election, for instance, the Conservative Party of Canada (CPC) spent considerable time recruiting highly experienced candidates in Quebec who could help them increase their support in that province. To that end, party officials were able to convince and/or help nominate candidates such as Alain Rayes, a popular mayor; Gérard Deltell, a former member of the provincial legislative assembly; and Jean Pelletier, "who for years ran Quebec City's winter carnival" (*CBC News* 2015). Similarly, Justin Trudeau in 2014 brought with him to the leadership convention a number of star candidates whom he had recruited to run under his

---

1 This chapter has been adapted from work originally published in the *Journal of Elections, Public Opinion and Parties* (Roy and Alcantara 2015).

leadership in the 2015 general election. These individuals included "Jim Carr, president of the Business Council of Manitoba; Bill Morneau, head of the country's largest human resources consulting company and chairman of a respected think-tank; and Jody Wilson-Raybould, British Columbia regional chief for the Assembly of First Nations." His team also included a retired general, Andrew Leslie, and former journalist Chrystia Freeland (*National Post* 2014).

How does the quality of a local candidate influence vote choice? Do voters care about the qualifications of their local candidates when they are at the ballot box? Generally speaking, existing research on this topic has tended to focus on two areas. One group of scholars has directed their efforts towards examining the particular traits of local candidates that seem to matter (Arzheimer and Evans 2012; Campbell and Cowley 2013; Glasgow and Alvarez 2000; Górecki and Marsh 2012; Heixweg 1979; Irvine 1982; Schoen and Schumann 2007), while others have estimated the percentage of voters in a particular election whose vote choice was influenced by the local candidate (Blais et al. 2003; Daoust and Blais 2018; Marsh 2007; Tavits 2010).

We add to the existing literature by directly assessing the way in which individual-level characteristics of voters, such as partisanship (PID) and political awareness, mediate local candidate effects. To do so, we draw upon original data collected from an online voting experiment to answer the following questions: Does the quality of the local candidate influence vote choice? What impact do individual-level differences, such as awareness and PID, have on the relationship between vote choice and local candidates? Finally, what is the potential magnitude of candidate effects in relation to change in vote support?

As in the other chapters in this book, we begin with a brief review of the literature and a set of assumptions and hypotheses that guide our analysis. We then discuss the data and methods used to explore these hypotheses before presenting our results. We conclude by arguing that there is considerable merit in the belief that running a strong local candidate can boost vote shares, but there are also some limits to applying this assumption equally across the electorate.

Background, Theory, and Expectations

Much of the early literature on voting behaviour paid little attention to the quality of a local candidate. What little work there was on local candidate effects focused mainly on exploring incumbency effects (Irvine 1982; Krashinsky and Milne 1986; see also Blais et al. 2003, 657–8; Marsh 2007, 500–1). It was not until the late 1980s and then again during the

2000s that scholars began to look comprehensively at the saliency of local candidates on vote choice (Arter 2006; Gallagher and Mitchell 2005; Górecki and Marsh 2012; Moser and Scheiner 2005).

One body of literature has assessed the extent to which voters pay attention to local candidates when casting their ballot. André Blais and his colleagues (2003, 662) analysed data from the 2000 Canadian Election Study and found that "the local candidate was a decisive consideration for 5 percent of Canadian voters" (6% outside and 2% inside Quebec). They also found that rural voters and highly sophisticated voters were more likely to vote for a local candidate than urban and less sophisticated voters. Michael Marsh (2007, 520–1) conducted a somewhat similar study of the 2002 Irish election and found that 20% of all Irish voters and 40% of voters who supported three particular parties – Labour, Progressive Democrats, and Fine Gael – were candidate-centred at the ballot box. Ian McAllister's (2013) study of Australian elections from 1996 to 2010 found that political parties in that country tended to have a stronger effect on vote choice than candidates.

In contrast to this literature, other scholars have focused on identifying specific candidate characteristics that might increase a party's vote share. Margit Tavits (2010, 216–17), for instance, found that candidates with prior local-level political experience tended to garner more electoral support than those candidates who lacked such experience. This local-level experience is important because it signals to voters that a candidate understands local needs and contexts (Marsh 1987; Shugart et al. 2005). Other scholars have focused on different types of prior elected political experience (Squire 1991), different candidate occupations and places of residence (Campbell and Cowley 2013; Arzheimer and Evans 2012; Górecki and Marsh 2012), and a variety of personal qualities (Krebs 2001; Keeter 1987; Schoen and Schumann 2007). We draw upon this scholarship in designing our own study, emphasizing these candidate qualities to present voters with a strong local candidate. We describe these characteristics in detail below.

We set out to test four hypotheses. The first considers whether fielding a *strong* candidate – defined broadly as one who has exhibited a high level of community involvement and awareness, and exceptional qualifications and experience (see detailed description below) – improves a party's relative vote share. Our assumption is that a local candidate will matter, yielding a larger percentage of the vote than the percentage that would be realized given an average candidate under similar circumstances. We base this assumption largely upon rational choice theory. Quite simply, we assume that, all else being equal, individuals will view a strong candidate as more likely to yield the greatest benefit. As such, our first hypothesis can be stated as:

> H1: A strong candidate will yield a larger relative vote share than an average candidate.

Our second hypothesis considers the conditional effect of political awareness. Our assumption is that individuals who engage in a more detailed information search before casting their ballot will be more apt to support a strong candidate. This assumption is based on the logic that voters with more information about the candidates will be more likely to vote for the strong candidate. Indeed, we would not expect the quality of a candidate to affect vote choice if an individual was not aware of these candidate differences (see Zaller 1992). Formally, we expect that:

> H2: Individuals who engage in a more detailed campaign-information search will be more likely to vote for the strong candidate than those who pursue a less detailed search.

Our third hypothesis addresses the relationship between partisan attachment and candidate effects. Here we are interested in the interactive and counteractive effects between partisan preferences and candidate strength. To assess this relationship, we divided our sample into groups based on a partisanship strength continuum that ranges from strong to no attachment. Our groups consisted of those with strong or very strong partisan attachments (partisans), those with only weak or very weak party ties (leaners), and individuals who claim no party affiliation (non-partisans). Our assumption is that an inverse relationship will be observed between how strongly one identifies with a political party and the effect that the quality of the party's candidate has on vote choice. Strong partisans will support their party regardless of the candidate, while non-partisans are more apt to be influenced by the quality of the candidates. Formally, we expect:

> H3: The stronger an individual's partisan attachment, the lower the candidate effect.

A final consideration examines the combined effect of partisanship and candidate quality. While we expect partisans in general to be less swayed by the strength of a local candidate, we recognize that this effect may vary depending on whether the strong candidate is running for their party or a rival one. Our assumption is that individuals who identify with the party fielding the strong candidate will be more likely to support this party than their non-partisan counterparts. We expect a similar effect when we compare individuals who identify with the party fielding the strong candidate with partisans in elections in which the strong candidate is running for a rival party. In this instance, we expect the middle group, leaners, to yield the largest change in vote probability when the party to which they are weakly attached fields the strong candidate. Our reasoning here is that strong partisans will likely support their party regardless of the candidate. Leaners, however, given an additional reason (e.g., a strong candidate) to support the party to which they are weakly attached, should be more strongly influenced by the combined effect of weak partisan ties with a high-quality candidate to boost support. If our assumption is correct, we should observe the largest candidate effect on leaners under conditions in which their party is fielding the strong candidate. Formally, we state this as:

> H4: Candidate effects will be strongest for leaners when the strong candidate is running for the leaner's preferred party.

Methodology

To test these hypotheses, we employed an experimental design using an online election platform.[2] This platform allowed us to collect individual-level information (e.g., measures of PID, political ideology, and political knowledge, among others) on each of the participants in a pre-survey, randomly assign the respondents to one of four election conditions, record the decision-making process that a participant undertook before casting his or her ballot, and record the vote that was cast (see below). To populate our study, we sent an email invitation to the entire student population at Wilfrid Laurier University (see chapter 1 for additional sample information and study dates). After removing cases with missing information on key variables, the final count was 552 usable observations.[3]

To assess the impact of a strong candidate, we created a profile of a fictitious candidate who embodied community awareness and

---

2   See chap. 1 for a discussion of the strength of experimental designs to isolate causal relationships.
3   This number includes the 27 individuals who were removed in our original publication (Roy and Alcantara 2015) because of changes in our approach to assessing random distribution across treatments.

involvement. We highlighted this fact by reporting the candidate's previous experience serving on a number of business, environmental, and culturally oriented local associations; creating school programs to aid children; and devoting extensive volunteer hours to the community. This candidate was also presented as being well educated and having an extensive employment history that included high-profile positions, both nationally and internationally (see appendix 5.1). In addition, we included a newspaper story covering a local event, where the candidate was largely credited with reopening two local factories, bringing thousands of lost jobs back to the community (see appendix 5.2). To emphasize the strength of this candidate further, we included three opposition candidates, all of whom paled in comparison when it came to community involvement and had relatively limited professional experience.

Our design consisted of four election conditions in which we used actual Canadian federal party labels for each of the candidates (see figure 5.1).[4] Upon completing a pre-survey, the participants were randomly assigned to one of these four treatments.[5] The introductory screen informed them that they were being asked to vote in a mock Canadian federal election. The four fictional candidates, along with their corresponding political party, were listed on the Introduction screen. As a control, all candidates were men with Anglo-Saxon names (see chapter 1 for a discussion of the homogeneity of the candidates). Once the participants had reviewed the instructions, they could advance to the Election campaign information screen to begin. This screen listed all four candidates along with their party affiliation, followed by a list of information links that the participants could click to access information on each candidate (see figure 5.1). We also included links that provided information about the four parties, drawing statements from each of their official websites. The individuals could access as many links as they wished and could vote at any time by clicking the Vote Now button, located at the bottom of the screen. We recorded each link that a participant accessed as a measure of the information search that he or she had engaged in before voting.

The manipulation in this experiment was to alter the party affiliation of the strong candidate in each of the four elections. In election 1, the

---

[4] We included four Canadian federal political parties that were represented in Parliament at the time of the study (2012): CPC (government), LIB, NDP (official Opposition), and GRN. A fifth party, the BQ, was excluded from our study because it fields candidates only in the province of Quebec, thus making it inapplicable to members of our sample.

[5] Note that each participant took part in only one election.

Figure 5.1. Election campaign information screen

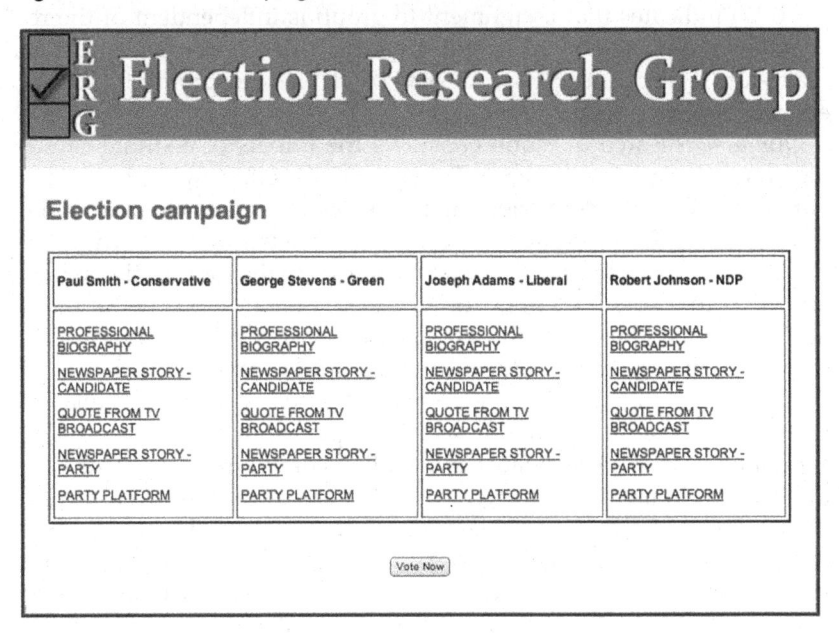

CPC fielded the strong candidate. In election 2, the strong candidate ran for the GRN. Elections 3 and 4 placed the strong candidate under the Liberal (LIB) and New Democratic Party (NDP) labels, respectively. The other three candidates (average candidates) were assigned to each of the parties in turn to ensure that unintended candidate effects were not at play. In all elections, the information for a given candidate (strong or otherwise) remained the same, with only the party affiliation altered. Thus, we can estimate the candidate effect by comparing the vote share of the party when fielding the strong candidate against the conditions when a relatively weaker candidate is offered. Given the inclusion of real party labels, we control for PID in all models.

Results

To confirm the absence of systematic differences in the distribution of the sample in each treatment, we model assignment to treatment as a function of socio-demographic characteristics, satisfaction with the way democracy works in Canada, political interest, political knowledge (a scale based on the participants' responses to five factual, political-knowledge questions), political ideology, and PID (strong or very strong partisans).[6] Our likelihood ratio statistic (χ^2 statistic, 37.43; $p = 0.17$) indicates that assignment to group is independent of the respondents' characteristics: in other words, the groups are similar in make-up (see appendix 5.4). As such, with the exception of PID, we exclude any controls in the models that follow.

Our first research question considers the impact of a strong candidate on the relative vote share. To estimate this effect, we compare the vote share that each party fielding the strong candidate received in the election with the vote share that it received when fielding a weaker candidate. We run a separate analysis for each of the four parties, which allows us to assess the impact of candidate qualifications net of party affiliation. The change in the vote shares is presented graphically in figure 5.2, and the full set of results is reported in appendix 5.5.[7]

As expected, the results show a clear increase in each party's relative vote share in the competition in which the party ran a strong candidate compared with its performance in the other competitions: a strong candidate does, indeed, yield a larger relative vote share than a weaker candidate. For the CPC, this translates to a 7-percentage-point boost, while the other three parties receive more than a 10-percentage-point increase in their respective vote shares when fielding a strong candidate (see appendix 5.5).[8] While we cannot be sure that effects of this magnitude would be observed in real elections, our experimental results certainly suggest the potential for a sizeable and positive candidate effect: voters appear to be more apt to support a strong local candidate than a relatively weaker candidate. To further explore the impact of a local candidate on vote choice, we turn to our second hypothesis, which considers the impact of the information search that individuals engage in before voting as a conditioning factor for candidate effects.

To isolate the impact of the information search on the probability of supporting a higher-quality candidate, we employ logistic regression. We model a dichotomous dependent variable coded "1" if an individual voted for a strong candidate and "0" otherwise. For the models that follow, we estimate the effects for all parties combined.[9] Our first model

---

6   See appendix 5.3 for summary statistics.
7   See chap. 1 for an overview of how to read the results reported in the tables and graphs.
8   Note that the method we used here has been modified from that employed in our original work (Roy and Alcantara 2015). However, the substantive results are the same, with only minor differences in the estimated values reported in each study.
9   Unlike the approach applied in earlier chapters, this model uses a larger sample, so estimating the models for all parties combined allows us to test for partisan effects (see below).

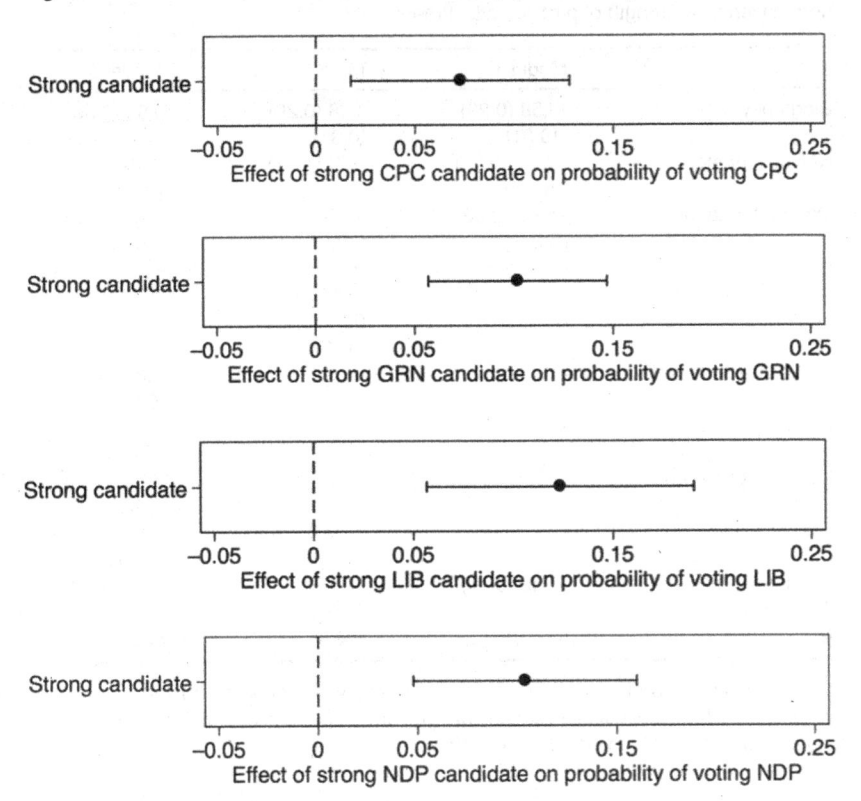

Figure 5.2. Treatment effects on vote choice by partisanship

[Strong candidate — Effect of strong CPC candidate on probability of voting CPC]

[Strong candidate — Effect of strong GRN candidate on probability of voting GRN]

[Strong candidate — Effect of strong LIB candidate on probability of voting LIB]

[Strong candidate — Effect of strong NDP candidate on probability of voting NDP]

considers how individual-level differences in the campaign-information search influence the effect that a candidate has on the vote. To measure the campaign-information search, we include three measures of the links accessed: a dichotomous variable measuring whether a participant viewed the strong candidate's biography (viewed biography = 1), a dichotomous variable measuring whether the participant viewed the newspaper story about the strong candidate (viewed story = 1), and a raw count of the number of "other" information links that each participant accessed before casting their ballot.[10]

Recall that our expectation is that individuals who allotted more time to learning about the candidates will be more likely to vote for a strong

---

10 We wish to thank one of the anonymous reviewers of the journal article from which this chapter was adapted for suggesting this line of enquiry.

Table 5.1. Support for a strong local candidate according to information search undertaken and strength of partisan attachment

	Model 1	Model 2	Model 3
Biography	1.58 (0.29)*** [0.31]	1.58 (0.29)*** [0.31]	1.56 (0.36)*** [0.20]
Newspaper story	0.71 (0.27)** [0.14]	0.74 (0.27)** [0.14]	0.19 (0.33) [0.02]
Other information	−0.06 (0.03)* [−0.01]	−0.06 (0.03)* [−0.01]	0.01 (0.03)** [0.00]
Partisan	-	0.71 (0.40)[a] [0.14]	-
Leaner	-	0.87 (0.40)* [0.17]	-
Partisan – preferred	-	-	3.89 (0.47)*** [0.51]
Partisan – rival	-	-	−0.80 (0.39)* [−0.10]
Leaner – preferred	-	-	2.50 (0.47)*** [0.33]
Leaner – rival	-	-	−0.28 (0.36) [−0.04]
Constant	−1.32 (0.15)***	−2.06 (0.39)***	−2.00 (0.36)***
Pseudo R^2	0.09	0.09	0.34
N	552	552	552

Note: The cells report logistic regression coefficients, with standard errors in parentheses. Marginal effects/discrete changes are reported in square brackets.
***$p < 0.001$; **$p < 0.01$; *$p < 0.05$; [a]$p < 0.10$.

candidate. Our logic is straightforward: those who are more aware of candidate differences are most apt to be influenced by such differences. As such, isolating the types of link that each respondent considered is important for capturing the impact of a candidate's strength: if a respondent failed to access information regarding the strong candidate, then suggesting that viewing more links would increase the probability of voting for the strong candidate is nonsensical. Furthermore, separating the candidate information provided in the candidate's biography from that offered in the newspaper story allows us to assess the impact of each independently. The results from this analysis are presented as model 1 in table 5.1.

As expected, the amount of effort allotted to information gathering did indeed affect the probability of voting for the strong candidate, but only when this information cued that candidate's qualities. It is also evident that the candidate's biography had a much stronger effect than the candidate information presented in the newspaper story (model 1). Our results show that viewing the biography of the strong candidate increased the probability of supporting the candidate by 31 percentage points ($p < 0.001$), more than double the effect of viewing the newspaper story (14 percentage points). However, while viewing information highlighting the strength of the candidate increased the probability of voting for that candidate, we observe a negative and statistically significant coefficient for other types of information. Here we find that every additional information link pertaining to the other candidates or parties that an individual accessed *decreased* the probability of voting for the strong candidate by 1 percentage point ($p < 0.05$), net of information pertaining to the strong candidate. Taken together, we believe that these results offer insight into what we might expect in non-experimental settings: while a strong candidate has the potential to boost electoral support, this potential can be realized only if the electorate is aware of the candidate's strength.

Our third hypothesis contends that the strength of an individual's partisan attachment will condition the effect of candidate quality. As explained above, we consider three types of voter according to partisan attachment, ranging from strong to no party ties: partisans (those with strong or very strong partisan attachments), leaners (those with only weak or very weak party ties), and non-partisans (individuals who claim no party affiliation). Individuals were assigned to the groups based on their response to a question that asked, "In federal politics, do you usually think of yourself as a: Liberal, Conservative, NDP, Green, Other, or none of these?" Voters indicating a party affiliation were then asked a follow-up question that tapped the strength of this identification (see Johnston 1992). As we have explained above, we expect the relationship between strength of partisanship and candidate effects to be inversely related: the stronger an individual's partisan attachment, the lower the candidate effect. To assess this expectation, we add a dichotomous variable for partisans (partisan = 1) and leaners (leaner = 1) to our model, setting non-partisans as the reference category (see table 5.1, model 2).

Clearly, partisanship mattered when it came to candidate effects, but not in the way we had anticipated. We had expected an inverse relationship between partisanship and candidate effects. However, the results indicate that this is not the case; relative to the probability for their non-partisan counterparts, the probability of leaners supporting the strong candidate is 17 percentage points greater and 14 points greater for partisans (see table 5.1, model 2). We believe that these results reflect the election treatment in which these individuals participated. If our assumption is correct, the explanation for the unanticipated result here reflects partisans and leaners overwhelmingly supporting the strong candidate in competitions in which that candidate is competing for their preferred party. To test this assumption, we split our leaners and partisans variables into two subgroups according to whether an individual's preferred party is fielding the strong candidate (preferred) or whether the strong candidate is running for a rival party (rival). The results from this analysis are presented as table 5.1, model 3.

Controlling for the election context helps explain the results from model 2. While we still do not find support for our third hypothesis, the additional consideration helps identify the relationship between having at least some sense of attachment towards a party and that party fielding a strong candidate.[11] For partisans, a strong candidate competing for *their* party boosts the probability of voting for the candidate by 51 points ($p < 0.001$) relative to their non-partisan counterparts. Similarly, leaners are significantly (33 percentage points) more likely to support a strong candidate relative to non-partisans when the strong candidate is running for the leaner's preferred party. However, when the strong candidate is competing for a party other than the one to which an individual has some ties, we find no difference between leaners and non-partisans and a relatively small and negative impact for partisans. As one might expect, strong or very strong partisans are less likely to support a rival party's candidate, and even more so when that candidate is exceptionally strong. Taken together, these findings highlight both the potential benefits as well as the limitations of fielding a strong local candidate. While a strong candidate is likely to generate votes, these votes are most likely to come from individuals predisposed to support the party anyway (e.g., partisans).

We can explore these results further and estimate the magnitude of candidate effects according to the type of individual (partisan, leaner, non-partisan). Recall that we have hypothesized that candidate effects will be stronger for leaners compared with partisans and non-partisans when the strong candidate is running for the leaners' preferred party (see hypothesis 4 above). To assess the validity of this assumption, we estimate the change in the probability of voting for each party in elections in which all parties field an average candidate compared with elections where they run a strong candidate. We estimate these effects by type of voter (partisan, leaner, non-partisan). As is depicted in figure 5.3,

---

11 Note that these results do not reflect differences across partisans, leaners, and non-partisans in the amount or type of information that each individual accessed. A comparison of the number and type of links accessed shows no significant difference across individuals.

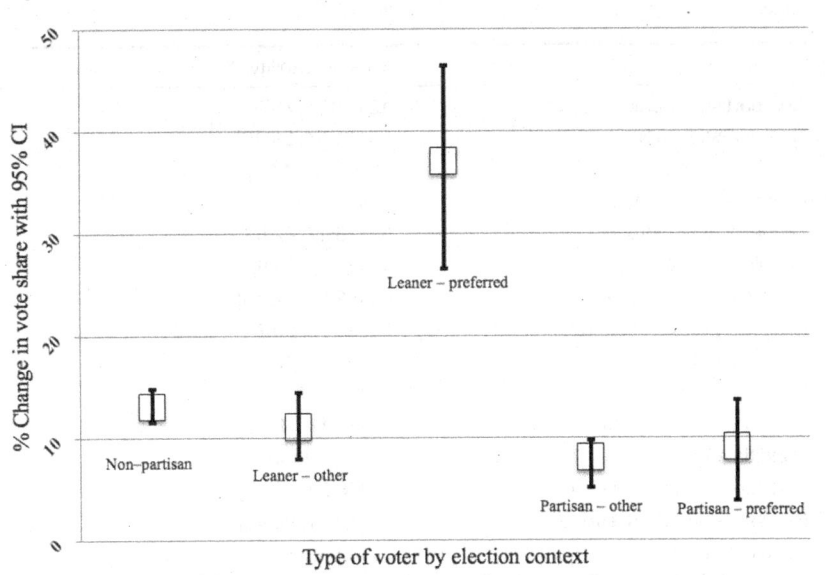

Figure 5.3. Candidate effect by voter type and election context

[Figure: bar chart with 95% confidence intervals showing % Change in vote share by Type of voter by election context. Categories: Non-partisan, Leaner – other, Leaner – preferred, Partisan – other, Partisan – preferred. The Leaner – preferred category shows the largest effect, around 36 percentage points.]

the candidate effect is sizeable for all types of voters.[12] However, the largest effect is clearly observed in the case of leaners in competitions in which the party they prefer is fielding the strong candidate.

Based on the results presented in figure 5.3, we find that the candidate effect for non-partisans and leaners – other is very similar (a 13- compared with a 12-percentage-point change in vote probability for non-partisans and leaners – other, respectively).[13] Partisans – other and partisans – preferred yield similar results, with 7- and 9-point candidate effects, respectively. The clear outlier is observed in the leaner – preferred result. Here we find a 36-percentage-point increase in the

---

12 Note that this graph differs from others presented in this book. However, the interpretation is similar to that outlined in chap. 1. Here we report the change in a candidate's vote share when the candidate is presented as a strong candidate compared with the treatments when the candidate is average. We report the change according to the type of partisan, as indicated by the respondent in the pre-survey. The 95% confidence intervals indicate the range of values between which the population from which the sample was drawn value falls, with only a 5% chance that the population value lies outside this interval.

13 To estimate this effect, we subtracted the average predicted vote probability when a party fields a relatively weak candidate from the average vote probability observed for a strong candidate.

Table 5.2. Average vote probability by type of candidate and strength of partisan attachment

	Vote probability, %
Non-partisan: weak	12 [6.13; 17.37]
Non-partisan: strong	25 [20.54; 29.46]
Candidate effect	13 [11.58; 14.92]
Leaner – other: weak	9 [6.67; 11.83]
Leaner – other: strong	21 [18.17; 22.83]
Candidate effect	12 [8.01; 14.49]
Leaner – preferred: weak	63 [52.94; 72.56]
Leaner – preferred: strong	99 [98.76; 99.74
Candidate effect	36 [26.59; 46.41]
Partisan – other: weak	6 [3.46; 7.54]
Partisan – other: strong	13 [10.12; 15.88]
Candidate effect	7 [5.17; 9.83]
Partisan – preferred: weak	84 [76.23; 92.27]
Partisan – preferred: strong	93 [89.51; 96.49]
Candidate effect	9 [3.86; 13.64]

Note: Column 2 reports average vote probability, with 95% confidence intervals in square brackets. The candidate effect is the difference between the probability of voting for a party offering a relatively weak candidate ("weak") and the probability of voting for the same party fielding a strong candidate ("strong").

probability of voting for the party that the leaner supports when the party fields a strong local candidate compared with the vote share the party would receive when offering an average candidate. We can understand this result more clearly by examining the change in the average vote probability for the parties when offering a relatively weak versus strong candidate according to the strength of an individual's partisan attachment. These results are presented in table 5.2.

A number of important points can be drawn from the results reported in this table. First, the results highlight the relationship between PID and vote choice. In the case of partisans, we find an 84% probability of support for their party, even when faced with a weaker candidate. On the one hand, this result may be surprising to some insomuch as it suggests a 16% probability that partisans moved to another party when faced with a weaker option. Clearly, PID affects vote choice (with an 84% probability of partisans voting for their party regardless of the candidate quality), but it is not a perfect predictor of vote choice.

As indicated above, the strongest candidate effect is shown in the case of leaners. Our results indicate a 63% probability of a leaner voting for his or her preferred party, even when the local candidate is relatively weak. However, the combined effect of a predisposition to support a party mixed with a strong local candidate yields nearly a 100% probability of vote support. Our results show that the type of individual most susceptible to candidate effects (a 36-percentage-point increase in vote probability) is one who claims weak party ties. While strong partisans are likely to support their party regardless of candidate strength, it is the leaners who appear most energized by the presence of a strong local candidate. Non-partisans can be moved by candidate effects (a 13-percentage-point increase in the probability of voting for the strong candidate), but the size of this effect pales in comparison to that observed in the case of leaners.[14]

Of course, we must consider the relative proportions of each type of voter within the electorate before making our claims too strongly. For example, an electoral district consisting of 20% leaners, 30% partisans, and 50% non-identifiers is less susceptible to candidate effects than one in which the majority of the population consider themselves leaners. Furthermore, we must heed the results of other researchers, such as André Blais and his colleagues (2003), who have found that a mere 5% of the voting population in Canada takes a local candidate into account when formulating its vote decision. Indeed, both these factors could limit the magnitude of the results we have offered here. However, while these factors may constrain the effect of a local candidate on vote choice, they do not eliminate it. Understanding how a local candidate influences vote choice is an important consideration in our broader efforts towards explaining voting behaviour. We have provided clear, empirical evidence that the strength of a local candidate matters and have identified the individual-level characteristics that mediate these effects.

---

14 We might also consider these results in light of potential "ceiling effects" (Górecki 2013). Given non-partisans' relatively strong support of their candidate to begin with (84%), only a 16-percentage-point increase is possible. In the case of leaners, the difference between the support observed for an average candidate and full support is 37 percentage points. In other words, there is a much larger gap between initial support and full support in the case of weak partisans. To account for these differences, we can consider the relative increase in vote probability for each type of voter. To do so, we divide the change in vote probability by 100% minus the vote probability obtained for the weak candidate. This yields a relative candidate effect of 15% for non-partisans, 13% for leaners – other, 97% for leaners – preferred, 7% for partisans – other, and 56% for partisans – preferred. While these relative changes differ from the raw changes reported, especially in the case of leaners – preferred and partisans – preferred, the substantive interpretation remains the same: the strongest candidate effect is clearly observed for leaners – preferred.

Discussion and Conclusion

Overall, the results from our online experiment provide considerable support for the existence of candidate effects. First and foremost, we have shown that the strength of a local candidate can make a difference: strong candidates increase a party's vote share, all else being equal. However, we have identified two important factors that can influence the size of the candidate effect. First, voters who are more aware of the candidate offerings – those paying more attention to the campaign – are more likely to support a strong candidate. As we have argued above, one can be expected to support a strong candidate only if one is aware of the differences across the field of contestants. Second, and perhaps the more important contribution from this work, we have found that it is partisan leaners who are most affected by a strong local candidate, at least when that candidate is representing his or her preferred party.

So what are the practical implications of our findings? Generally speaking, it pays for political parties to try and attract as many high-quality local candidates to run in as many ridings as they can, especially if those candidates are superior (at least on paper) to the candidates fielded by the other parties. If possible, it is also helpful to field high-quality candidates who already have some sort of public profile in their riding. Without this profile, party officials will likely have to spend significant resources to draw attention to their candidates. A surprising finding from our study was the large difference in effects between information about a candidate presented in a newspaper article versus accessing the candidate's biography directly. The fact that accessing the biography had a much stronger effect on vote choice suggests that not all information sources are equal, and it may be more effective to invest in strategies that provide candidate information directly to voters rather than through third parties like the media.

Finally, if party recruitment resources are finite (which they almost always are), party officials should be strategic in how they spend them. They should identify ridings with high numbers of partisan leaners and focus their efforts on recruiting high-profile and high-quality candidates for those ridings, since local candidate effects are highest among those voters. In short, our findings support the long-standing practice of recruiting star candidates to contest local elections as an effective strategy for winning power. However, the evidence marshalled here suggests that while such a practice is effective, the impact is by no means equal across the electorate.

REFERENCES

Arter, David. 2006. *Democracy in Scandinavia: Consensual, Majoritarian or Mixed?* Manchester: Manchester University Press.

Arzheimer, Kai, and Jocelyn Evans. 2012. "Geolocation and Voting: Candidate–Voter Distance Effects on Party Choice in the 2010 UK General Election in England." *Political Geography*. 31 (5): 301–10. https://doi.org/10.1016/j.polgeo.2012.04.006.

Blais, André, Elisabeth Gidgengil, Agnieszka Dobrzynska, Neil Nevitte, and Richard Nadeau. 2003. "Does the Local Candidate Matter? Candidate Effects in the Canadian Election of 2000." *Canadian Journal of Political Science* 36 (3): 657–64. https://doi.org/10.1017/S0008423903778810.

Campbell, Rosie, and Philip Cowley. 2013. "What Voters Want: Reactions to Candidate Characteristics in a Survey Experiment." *Political Studies* 62 (4): 745–65. https://doi.org/10.1111/1467-9248.12048.

CBC News. 2015. "Conservatives Recruiting High-Profile Candidates in Push to Regain Lost Quebec Seats." Canadian Press, 26 April 2015. http://www.cbc.ca/news/canada/montreal/conservatives-recruiting-high-profile-candidates-in-push-to-regain-lost-quebec-seats-1.3049332.

CTV News. 2007. "Garneau Pledges to Fight for 'Liberal Values.'" 19 October 2007. http://www.ctvnews.ca/garneau-pledges-to-fight-for-liberal-values-1.260933.

Daoust, Jean-François, and André Blais. 2018. "How Much Do Voters Care about the Electoral Outcome in Their District?" *Representation* 53 (3–4): 233–46. https://doi.org/10.1080/00344893.2018.1424028.

Gallagher, Michael, and Paul Mitchell. 2005. *The Politics of Electoral Systems*. Oxford: Oxford University Press.

Glasgow, Garrett, and R. Michael Alvarez. 2000. "Uncertainty and Candidate Personality Traits." *American Politics Research* 28 (1): 26–49. https://doi.org/10.1177/1532673X00028001002.

Górecki, Maciej A. 2013. "Electoral Context, Habit-Formation and Voter Turnout: A New Analysis." *Electoral Studies* 32 (1): 140–52. https://doi.org/10.1016/j.electstud.2012.09.005.

Górecki, Maciej A., and Michael Marsh. 2012. "Not Just 'Friends and Neighbours': Canvassing, Geographic Proximity and Voter Choice." *European Journal of Political Research* 51 (5): 563–82. https://doi.org/10.1111/j.1475-6765.2011.02008.x.

Heixweg, Susan. 1979. "An Examination of Voter Conceptualizations of the Ideal Political Candidate." *Southern Speech Communication Journal* 44 (4): 373–85. https://doi.org/10.1080/10417947909372427.

Irvine, William. 1982. "Does the Candidate Make a Difference? The Macro-politics and Micro-politics of Getting Elected." *Canadian Journal of Political Science* 15 (4): 755–82. https://doi.org/10.1017/S0008423900052045.

Johnston, Richard. 1992. "Party Identification Measures in the Anglo-American Democracies: A National Survey Experiment." *American Journal of Political Science* 36 (2): 542–59. https://doi.org/10.2307/2111490.

Keeter, Scott. 1987. "The Illusion of Intimacy: Television and the Role of Candidate Personal Qualities in Voter Choice." *Public Opinion Quarterly* 51 (3): 344–58. https://doi.org/10.1086/269040.

Krashinsky, Michael, and William J. Milne. 1986. "The Effect of Incumbency in the 1984 Federal and 1985 Ontario Elections." *Canadian Journal of Political Science* 19 (2): 337–43. https://doi.org/10.1017/S0008423900054056.

Krebs, Timothy. 2001. "Political Experience and Fundraising in City Council Elections." *Social Science Quarterly* 82 (3): 536–51. https://doi.org/10.1111/0038-4941.00041.

Loewen, Peter. 2015. "Loewen: Do Local Candidates Even Matter to Voters?" *Ottawa Citizen*, 18 September 2015. http://ottawacitizen.com/news/politics/loewen-do-local-candidates-even-matter-to-voters.

Marsh, Michael. 1987. "Electoral Evaluations of Candidates in Irish General Elections 1948–82." *Irish Political Studies* 2 (1): 65–76. https://doi.org/10.1080/07907188708406437.

– 2007. "Candidates or Parties? Objects of Electoral Choice in Ireland." *Party Politics* 13 (4): 500–27. https://doi.org/10.1177/1354068807075944.

McAllister, Ian. 2013. "The Personalization of Politics in Australia." *Party Politics* 21 (3): 337–45. https://doi.org/10.1177/1354068813487111.

Moser, Robert G., and Ethan Scheiner. 2005. "Strategic Ticket Splitting and the Personal Vote in Mixed-Member Electoral Systems." *Legislative Studies Quarterly* 30 (2): 259–76. https://doi.org/10.3162/036298005X201545.

National Post. 2014. "Liberal Convention Will Showcase Justin Trudeau's Star Candidates as Leader Seeks to Add Heft to Image." Canadian Press, 19 February 2014. http://nationalpost.com/news/politics/liberal-convention-will-showcase-justin-trudeaus-star-candidates-as-leader-seeks-to-add-heft-to-image.

Roy, Jason, and Christopher Alcantara. 2015. "The Candidate Effect: Does the Local Candidate Matter?" *Journal of Elections, Public Opinion & Parties*. 25 (2): 195–214. https://doi.org/10.1080/17457289.2014.925461.

Schoen, Harald, and Siegfried Schumann. 2007. "Personality Traits, Partisan Attitudes, and Voting Behavior: Evidence from Germany." *Political Psychology* 28 (4): 471–98. https://doi.org/10.1111/j.1467-9221.2007.00582.x.

Shugart, Matthew Søberg, Melody Ellis Valdini, and Kati Suominen. 2005. "Looking for Locals: Voter Information Demands and Personal Vote-Earning Attributes of Legislators under Proportional Representation."

American Journal of Political Science 49 (2): 437–49. https://doi.org/10.1111/j.0092-5853.2005.00133.x.

Squire, Peverill. 1991. "Preemptive Fund-Raising and Challenger Profile in Senate Elections." *Journal of Politics* 53 (4): 1150–64. https://doi.org/10.2307/2131872.

Tavits, Margit. 2010. "Effect of Local Ties on Electoral Success and Parliamentary Behaviour: The Case of Estonia." *Party Politics* 16 (2): 215–35. https://doi.org/10.1177/1354068809341053.

Zaller, John. 1992. *The Nature and Origins of Mass Opinion*. Cambridge: Cambridge University Press.

Appendix 5.1. Candidate profiles available to participants

Strong Candidate Professional Biography:

Awards and Achievements:
- Founder of Free Breakfast for Students Program
- Friend of the Arts recognition
- 2011 Local business development man of the year
- 2010 Community leader award
- Established after-school youth activities program

Committee Work:
- Metcalf environmental association
- Library Board of Directors
- Local Chamber of Commerce (committee chair)

Volunteer Work:
- Reading to the elderly
- Cooking for the local soup kitchen program
- Member of local parks and trails maintenance team
- Local youth soccer team coach

Personal:
- Married
- Two children

Qualifications and Occupation before Entering Government Service:
- Master's degree
- Community development coordinator
- Humanitarian affairs officer

Weak Candidate 1 Professional Biography:

Awards and Achievements:
- Local newspaper People to Watch in 2008 list
- Founder of Metcalf entrepreneurship association

Committee Work:
- Town and Gown Finance Chair
- Citizens' Budget Task Force

Volunteer Work:
- Track and field club assistant
- Annual Relay for Life participant

Personal:
- Married
- Two children

Qualifications and Occupation before Entering Government Service:
- Master's degree
- Plant manager

Weak Candidate 2 Professional Biography:

Awards and Achievements:
- Community Spirit Award (2007)
- Co-creator of high school science competition

Committee Work:
- Library Board of Directors
- 2010 High School Reunion Planning Committee

Volunteer Work:
- Meals on Wheels volunteer
- Christmas food hamper distributor
- Metcalf annual community clean-up volunteer

Personal:
- Married
- Two children

Qualifications and Occupation before Entering Government Service:
- Master's degree
- Journalist
- Sales executive

Weak Candidate 3 Professional Biography:

Awards and Achievements:
- Metcalf Award of Merit
- Nominee for Citizenship in Action Award

Committee Work:
- Municipal Heritage Advisory Board
- Oktoberfest Fundraising Committee
- Metcalf annual community clean-up volunteer

Volunteer Work:
- Collecting donations for Halloween for Hunger
- Arts in the Park festival volunteer

Personal:
- Married
- Two children

Qualifications and Occupation before Entering Government Service:
- Master's degree
- Lawyer

Appendix 5.2: Newspaper story available to participants

Newspaper Story: Joseph Adams Praised for Role in Job Creation

The city of Metcalf, whose citizens suffered the loss of over 3,000 jobs as a result of the economic downturn of 2007–8, received a much-needed boost with the announcement of the reopening of two factories at a town hall meeting.

Mayor Anica Rosthow opened the event, saying, "I'm overjoyed to be able to share this news with you. Job loss has taken its toll on our community, and while this isn't the end, we now have something to celebrate. I ask that you all join me in thanking Joseph Adams for his tireless efforts in bringing this work back to our community!"

Joseph Adams, a candidate running in the upcoming election and who has been praised for his job-creation efforts, also spoke to the crowd. "My own family was hit hard by the economic crisis, losing their jobs when the factories closed, and for a time they struggled to make ends meet," Adams admitted. "I know how hard the economic downturn has been for you and how important it is to know that there's a brighter future ahead." He concluded, "I not only understand the issues, I've lived them myself, which has given me the strength to work towards rebuilding our economic base through job creation!"

Other candidates in the upcoming election were also on hand for the announcement. George Stevens congratulated Adams, acknowledging that "Joseph has done a great job bringing this work back to Metcalf, but we must remain vigilant in our efforts to create even more opportunities for this area." Stevens concluded that he was the person to do just that: "While Joseph has brought us back to where we were four years ago, my promise to the citizens is to work towards securing even more jobs in the future to see our community strive!"

Paul Smith also praised Adams for his role in bringing these jobs back to Metcalf, but pointed out that he was only one of many people involved in the process. "There is no doubt Joseph played an important role in bringing this work back to our community," said Smith, "but let's not forget that he was part of a much larger team that worked equally as hard to recover these jobs."

Robert Johnson was quick to agree with Smith, adding that "Joseph is undoubtedly a talented individual, but as my platform points out, I have a number of ideas that will lead us into a future of economic prosperity. I'm not saying Joseph doesn't deserve this recognition," said Johnson, "but to suggest that he is the only person capable of bringing jobs back to our community is going too far."

Appendix 5.3. Summary statistics

Variable	Election 1	Election 2	Election 3	Election 4
Age	21 (4.18)	21.60 (5.06)	22.03 (5.75)	22.48 (7.63)
Female	0.60 (0.49)	0.62 (0.49)	0.63 (0.48)	0.69 (0.46)
Satisfaction	2.17 (0.58)	2.29 (0.63)	2.19 (0.65)	2.08 (0.54)
Political interest	5.93 (2.34)	6.00 (2.31)	6.01 (2.51)	5.72 (2.45)
Political knowledge	0.66 (0.29)	0.67 (0.28)	0.66 (0.28)	0.68 (0.28)
Political ideology	4.82 (2.15)	5.19 (2.26)	4.71 (2.16)	4.81 (2.09)
CPC PID	0.13 (0.34)	0.15 (0.36)	0.17 (0.37)	0.09 (0.29)

(Continued)

Appendix 5.3. Summary statistics (Continued)

Variable	Election 1	Election 2	Election 3	Election 4
GRN PID	0.02 (0.15)	0.03 (0.17)	0.01 (0.08)	0.05 (0.21)
LIB PID	0.13 (0.34)	0.16 (0.37)	0.15 (0.36)	0.17 (0.37)
NDP PID	0.09 (0.29)	0.12 (0.32)	0.13 (0.34)	0.08 (0.27)
N	123	152	138	139

Note: The cells contain averages, with standard deviations in parentheses. Age is the respondents' age in years. Female is dichotomous, coded "1" for female. Political interest and ideology are the average responses reported based on a scale of 0 (no interest) to 10 (extremely interested). Political knowledge is an index (alpha = 0.59) based on five factual questions: the name of the British prime minister, the name of the most recent Republican candidate for US president, the name of the federal finance minister, the name of the governor general, and the number of seats in the House of Commons. The respondents were assigned a point for each correct question. This variable was rescaled to fit between 0 and 1. PID is a dichotomous measure of strong or very strong party identifiers. N = number of usable cases in each treatment.

Appendix 5.4. Multinomial logistic regression results for test of random assignment to treatments

Variable	CPC Strong	LIB Strong	NDP Strong
Age	0.00 (0.03)	0.03 (0.02)	0.05 (0.02)*
Female	0.05 (0.27)	0.05 (0.26)	0.41 (0.27)
Satisfaction	−0.48 (0.22)*	−0.44 (0.21)*	−0.81 (0.22)***
Political interest	0.02 (0.06)	−0.01 (0.06)	0.02 (0.06)
Political knowledge	0.06 (0.48)	−0.29 (0.46)	0.11 (0.48)
Political ideology	−0.11 (0.07)[a]	−0.13 (0.06)*	−0.09 (0.07)
LIB PID	−0.69 (0.39)[a]	−0.30 (0.36)	−0.32 (0.36)
CPC PID	−0.18 (0.40)	0.18 (0.38)	−0.57 (0.42)
NDP PID	−0.63 (0.45)	−0.13 (0.41)	−0.70 (0.46)
GRN PID	−0.57 (0.89)	−1.24 (1.14)	0.38 (0.73)
Constant	1.41 (0.85)	1.28 (0.79)	0.83 (0.82)

N = 543
χ^2 (df = 30) = 37.43
Pseudo R^2 = 0.02

Note: The cells report multinomial logistic regression coefficients, with standard errors in parentheses. The GRN strong candidate treatment is set as the base outcome (largest N). Age is the respondents' age in years. Female is dichotomous, coded "1" for female. Political interest and political ideology are self-reported positions on an eleven-point scale running from "No interest" to "Great deal of interest" and "Left–Right," respectively. Political knowledge is an index (alpha = 0.59) based on five factual questions: the name of the British prime minister, the name of the most recent Republican candidate for US president, the name of the federal finance minister, the name of the governor general, and the number of seats in the House of Commons. The respondents received one point for each correct response. The variable was then rescaled to fit between 0 and 1. PID is a dichotomous measure of strong or very strong party identifiers. N = number of cases with full response set.
*** $p < 0.001$; ** $p < 0.01$; * $p < 0.05$; [a] $p < 0.10$.

Appendix 5.5. Full results for figure 5.2
Results for figure 5.2: Treatment effects on vote choice by partisanship

	CPC	GRN	LIB	NDP
Strong candidate	0.57 (0.27)* [0.07]	1.03 (0.28)*** [0.10]	0.69 (0.23)** [0.12]	0.73 (0.25)** [0.10]
Strong candidate PID	3.39 (0.40)***	2.86 (0.62)***	1.74 (0.28)***	2.16 (0.33)***
Other PID	−1.90 (0.41)***	−0.82 (0.31)**	−1.94 (0.32)***	−1.50 (0.33)***
Constant	−1.32 (0.16)***	−2.14 (0.20)***	−0.65 (0.13)***	−1.38 (0.16)***
Pseudo R^2	0.31	0.12	0.18	0.17
N	552	552	552	552

Note: The cells report logistic regression coefficients, with standard errors in parentheses and marginal effects/discrete changes reported in square brackets. PID is included in the model as a control, with no or weak PID set as the reference category.
***$p < 0.001$; **$p < 0.01$; *$p < 0.05$; ᵃ$p < 0.10$.

PART TWO

Keeping Power – Public Opinion and Incumbency

Chapter Six

Parliamentary Configurations and Assigning Political Responsibility

We will always be open to working with others. ... But the fact is Canadians aren't interested in formal coalitions. Canadians want a clear government, with a strong plan and come Oct. 19, that's exactly what they're going to get if they vote for the Liberal Party. (Justin Trudeau, federal Liberal leader, quoted in Hayward 2015)

"[A minority government] would force the parties to work co-operatively, it would be more representative, because different party platforms would have to be reconciled, so a wider spectrum of voters [sic] interests would be represented in the platforms that would eventually be made into policy," University of Toronto constitutional law professor Yasmin Dawood told CBC News Network's *Power & Politics*. (Harris 2015)

Canada's main political parties have long preferred winning majority governments to other configurations, such as minority and coalition governments, for fairly obvious reasons. Majority governments allow the winning party to pass whatever legislation it wishes since, by definition, it controls enough seats to always win every vote in the House. If politics is fundamentally about capturing and exercising power, then having a monopoly over it is generally preferable to sharing it with your political opponents.

Fortunately for Canada's two dominant parties, the Liberals (LIB) and the Conservatives (CPC), Canada's electoral system has tended to favour majority governments over other configurations, even when the winning party has failed to capture a majority of the popular vote (Massicotte 2005; Russell 2008). This is because our single-member plurality (SMP) system requires the winning candidate to capture only a plurality of the votes (more than any other candidate but not an absolute majority) to win a riding (Cairns 1968). If the electorate is unevenly dispersed across constituencies (e.g., some ridings have much larger electorates than others), then disproportionate results are more likely to occur. In 1993 and 2000, for instance, the LIB won majority governments despite receiving only 38.5% and 41% of the national vote, respectively (Massicotte 2005, 68).

As a result of these dynamics, critics have been advocating for electoral reform for some time, suggesting that Canada needs to adopt a fairer and more democratic system, which produces fewer majority governments and more minority and coalition ones (Massicotte 2005; Milner 1999; Russell 2008). However, defenders of the current system and of majority governments in general point to a chief strength of the status quo, which is that voters are routinely presented with clear lines of accountability (Blais 1991, 242; Loewen 2015). When the government acts, voters know exactly who is to be blamed or credited for a particular decision or outcome: the government, the official Opposition, or the other parties in the House. In minority and coalition situations, this task is more difficult because the opposition parties may sometimes cooperate with the government, either formally or informally, on an issue-by-issue basis.

A key part of winning and keeping power is ensuring that one's party receives proper credit for producing publicly popular decisions and avoiding the blame for the unpopular ones. What are the implications of different parliamentary configurations for how voters assign blame and credit for government actions? Is it preferable for governing parties to have clear lines of accountability to maximize their re-election chances, or is it better to blur the lines of accountability by cooperating with other parties in trying to pass legislation?

In this chapter, we use data gathered from an online voting experiment to answer these questions. Specifically, we consider how vote shares differ according to whether legislation passes under different parliamentary configurations. The chapter begins by summarizing the literature on accountability and vote choice. It then draws upon this literature to formulate expectations before explaining the experimental design and analysing the data collected from the experiment. It concludes with a discussion of the implications of our findings for winning and keeping power in Canada.

Background, Theory, and Expectations

Accountability is a core feature of democracy, and political scientists have spent considerable time and effort mapping the relationship

Parliamentary Configurations 131

between these concepts and practices across time and jurisdictions. A major feature of this relationship is the idea that citizens hold politicians accountable for their actions primarily through the vote. Governments that perform well are thought to be rewarded with strong voter support, while governments that perform poorly are thought to be punished with weak voter support. Thus, political parties face strong incentives to maximize their performance while in government (Tilley and Hobolt 2011, 316–17; Marsh and Tilley 2009; Hellwig and Samuels 2007).

To what extent do voters actually assign blame and credit to the various political actors involved in guiding, supporting, and opposing government action? Generally speaking, the literature suggests that this behaviour, labelled the *responsibility hypothesis*, does, in fact, occur (Anderson 1995, 352; Kramer 1971; Nannestad and Paldam 1993). The strongest evidence for this hypothesis comes from the economic voting literature, which investigates the effects of different economic conditions on vote choice. These scholars assume and have found evidence that a strong economy, measured by GDP, unemployment, and inflation rates (Hellwig and Samuels 2007, 72), tends to increase voter support for the incumbent governing party, while a weak economy tends to reduce it as voters blame the government for the poor economic conditions.

These initial assumptions have been challenged by a variety of scholars, who contend that, among other things, economic voting and the responsibility hypothesis are very much affected by different political and institutional contexts. At the core of this argument is the notion that different institutional and political configurations create different levels of complexity and clarity for voters, making it easier or more difficult for them to assign blame and credit for policy decisions and behaviour to political actors (Anderson 1995, 350–1). Lewis-Beck (1988), for instance, found that variations in coalition government structures created different levels of clarity with respect to the ability of voters to correctly assign responsibility for policymaking to the different political parties involved in these governments. When coalition governments were less complex and had clear lines of responsibility, economic voting was more likely to have a significant effect on vote choice. When coalition governments were more complex and had unclear lines of responsibility, the effects of economic voting were greatly reduced (see also Schram 1989). Anderson's (1995, 380) comparison of Dutch and Danish coalition governments found something similar:

> Complex institutional arrangements such as coalition governments either may inhibit the assignment of credit and blame, or the economic effects

may wash out because voters shift support among political parties within governments. The analysis presented above strongly suggests that investigations of government support must take into account the role played by political institutions.

Others have moved beyond coalition governments to look more broadly at other institutional configurations. De Vries, Edwards, and Tillman (2011), for instance, analysed European Union issue voting in nineteen European countries and found that higher-clarity systems, defined as systems "where a single, unified party has primary control over policy making" (341), such as majority governments, tend to reward or punish voting behaviour, while lower-clarity systems, defined as systems where "power is dispersed among multiple parties or in which policy-making coalitions are continuously shifting" (344), such as minority governments, tend to suppress such behaviour. Powell and Whitten (1993) examined a variety of institutional contexts, such as one-party versus multi-party rule, bicameral opposition, opposition influence over decision making, and party cohesion, finding that economic voting had a stronger effect in countries where there were clear lines of responsibility in the legislatures (see also Lewis-Beck 1988, 108–10; Powell 1989).

Anderson (2000), building on the work of Powell and Whitten (1993), moved beyond coalition governments to examine the effects of economic voting in three types of political and institutional context. Using data from the Eurobarometer 42.0, he examined the effect of economic conditions against three measures relating to clarity of responsibility (conceptualized as a relatively stable "structure of formal and informal power relationships and policymaking authority" (Anderson 2000, 156), the governing party's target size (conceptualized as the share of the number of seats and Cabinet posts that the main governing party holds), and the clarity of available party alternatives (conceptualized as the number of opposition parties and their share of seats in the legislature). He found that the ability of voters "to express discontent with economic performance is enhanced when accountability is simple. Voters' economic assessments have stronger effects on government support when it is clear who the target is, when the target is sizable, and when voters have only a limited number of viable alternatives" (168).

Overall, the existing research suggests that institutional and political arrangements exert a significant effect on voting behaviour by structuring the lines of responsibility among voters, parties, and policymaking in particular ways. Specifically, those configurations that create complex and blurry lines of responsibility as they relate to policy decisions tend to suppress the effects of policymaking on vote choice, while configurations that reduce complexity and clarify responsibility tend to enhance the effects of policymaking on vote choice.

In this chapter, we contribute to the literature by examining how variation in one particular type of institutional context, Westminster parliamentary configurations, can affect vote choice. Drawing upon data gathered from an online voting experiment, we first consider how voters assign credit or blame to incumbent governments according to whether a piece of legislation passes. We then examine the clarity of responsibility in two ways – whether the legislation passes with the support of all parties and the type of parliamentary configuration involved – and measure the extent to which voters assign blame and credit by examining how they vote across the scenarios.

Surprisingly, very little empirical attention has been directed towards the effects of majority, minority, and coalition configurations on accountability, responsibility, and vote choice. Yet discussions about majority, minority, and coalition structures have been front and centre in countries that have SMP systems, such as Canada and the United Kingdom, mainly because debate about electoral reform has concentrated on the desirability of these different configurations (Massicotte 2005). Supporters of SMP systems, for instance, argue that they are preferable because they tend to produce majority governments more often, thus allowing voters to easily and clearly assign blame and credit to the political parties in the legislature for their political and policy decisions. Minority and coalition governments, on the other hand, occur less frequently, and, when they do occur, voters are thought to find it more difficult to correctly assign blame and credit to the political parties for the decisions they make in the legislature. Our experimental design allows us to test these assumptions directly and assess how each government configuration affects vote choice.

We begin by assessing incumbent-party vote (as a proxy for blame or credit) according to whether legislation passes or not. All things being equal, we assume that voters will reward (punish) government with their vote when "positive" legislation passes (fails). By *positive legislation*, we are referring to policy that is widely agreed upon as being beneficial to society. In our study, we use health care as a valence issue based on the empirical work of others (see Nadeau et al. 2015, 50; Pattie and Johnston 2008, 107), offering the participants information that indicates that the policy will have a positive yet unspecified effect on health care (see below). Accordingly, our first hypothesis expects incumbent governments to receive a boost in their overall vote share under conditions where legislation passes (e.g., government is credited for successful legislation) relative to the vote they receive when legislation fails to pass (e.g., government is blamed for the failure).

> H1: The incumbent vote share will be higher when legislation passes relative to incumbent vote share when legislation fails to pass.

Our second hypothesis considers the clarity of responsibility. We expect that the increase in the incumbent vote share should be greatest under conditions where the government is clearly responsible for the successful legislation. In the case of a minority government, assigning credit or blame is expected to be more difficult relative to a majority configuration because support from parties other than the governing party is necessary for the legislation to pass. A coalition government may also increase the difficulty of assigning blame or credit for successful legislation, although less so than under a minority government configuration given that the coalition partner is clearly identified and expected to support its governing partner. This reasoning is consistent with the broader theoretical arguments made by de Vries, Edwards, and Tillman (2011, 344–5), who argue that higher-clarity systems, which they define as regimes in which "a single, unified party has primary control over policy making," tend to reward or punish voting behaviour compared with lower-clarity systems, defined as regimes where "power is dispersed among multiple parties or in which policymaking coalitions are continuously shifting." Given that our design maintains a single coalition partner under the two coalition treatments, we contend that voters should be better able to assign responsibility under coalition conditions relative to minority configurations. Following from this logic, when legislation passes, we expect incumbent vote share to be higher in majority situations relative to incumbent vote share in minority and coalition situations.[1]

> H2: When legislation passes, incumbent vote share will be higher in majority situations relative to incumbent vote share in minority and coalition situations.

In regard to our expectations for differences between minority and coalition configurations, we expect incumbent vote share to be higher when there is a minority government in place based on the assumption

---

1 Here we focus exclusively on successful legislation since it is extremely unlikely for legislation to be defeated in a vote in a majority situation.

that minority situations diffuse support across multiple parties compared with a formal government coalition, when the coalition partner(s) is (are) easily identified. The logic for this assumption is based on the idea that, under a coalition configuration, votes for the government will be split among the coalition partners, which will result in a lower vote share for the incumbent party relative to the vote share it would receive in a minority situation. Following this logic, we should also see an increase in the vote share of the coalition partner, when it supports legislation, based on the same assumptions that led to our expectation that incumbent vote share will increase as a reward for successful legislation. Formally, we expect:

> H3: When legislation passes, the incumbent's vote share will be higher in minority situations compared with coalition governments.
>
> H4: When legislation passes under a coalition configuration, the vote share that the minor coalition partner receives will be higher compared with the vote share it receives under majority or minority governments.

What about blame? To this point, our arguments have focused on increased support following successful legislation. But do governments pay a price at the ballot box for failed legislation? Our final set of hypotheses examines whether governments are blamed as much as they are rewarded for legislative outcomes. We put forth the following set of hypotheses based on the logic outlined above, that clarity of responsibility will affect public support at the ballot box. Our underlying assumption is that governments will pay the price when they fail to pass legislation, with the extent of the loss of support a function of clarity of responsibility. Similarly, in the case of a single coalition partner, we expect the partner's vote support to be lowest when it votes against its coalition partner, leading to failed legislation. Following from this logic, we expect:

> H5: When legislation fails, the incumbent's vote share will be higher in coalition situations compared with minority governments.
>
> H6: When legislation fails under a coalition configuration, the vote share that the minor coalition partner receives will be lower compared with the vote share it receives under majority or minority governments.

In sum, we expect that parties will be rewarded (punished) with increased (decreased) vote support under conditions in which voters can clearly assign responsibility for the success (failure) of legislation. We contend that clarity of responsibility will vary according to the type of government configuration, with majority governments offering voters the most direct means of assigning responsibility and minority configurations the most blurred lines of responsibility. We turn now to our data and methods section, where we explain the experimental design used to test these hypotheses.

Methodology

As with the other studies in this book, we employed an online experimental platform that first had the participants complete a brief survey and then randomly assigned them to one of six treatments, in which they were asked to take part in a mock election contested by four fictitious parties (see table 6.1 for treatments and number of participants in each group; see chapter 1 for additional sample information and study dates). In all treatments, the parties were represented by fictional candidates, all men with Anglo-Saxon names, in their early fifties, and married with children (see chapter 1 for further discussion of our choice of candidates). All candidates were similar in regard to education and work experience. Voters could access all this information through a static Election campaign information screen, which allowed the participants to consider information on each candidate and party before voting (see appendix 6.1). Additional information on the candidates included a non-cueing quote by each candidate from a television broadcast, a human-interest story covering an event that the candidate had recently attended, and an excerpt from the party's environmental-policy position paper; these positions were indistinguishable across candidates (e.g., neutral position balancing environmental protection and job growth). In all treatments, candidate and party information were held constant, with the order of candidates and information links randomized for each participant.

The experimental manipulation involved altering the outcome of a vote on a piece of legislation (which parties supported or opposed) and the government configuration (majority, minority, or coalition). In all treatments, the participants were informed of the outcome (pass or fail) of a recent vote on "a piece of legislation that reports say will greatly improve health care service in Canada" before starting the mock campaign. They were also told of the type of government configuration: Party D was identified as the governing party and Party B the official Opposition in all cases. Party A was presented as the minor coalition partner in the two treatments with coalition configurations. The title "Governing Party," "Official Opposition," and "Coalition Partner" was listed next to each of the parties on the instruction screen, the Election

Table 6.1. Government configuration treatments

Treatment number	Government configuration	Legislation supported by	Legislation outcome	N
1	Majority	All parties	Pass	155
2	Majority	Governing party only	Pass	119
3	Minority	All parties	Pass	153
4	Minority	Governing party only	Fail	159
5	Coalition	All parties	Pass	173
6	Coalition	Governing party only	Fail	148
Total				907

Note: The cells indicate the configuration and vote outcome for each treatment. The number of participants in each group is listed in the last column.

campaign information screen, and the vote screen to ensure that the participants were clear as to which party was the governing party, the Opposition, and the coalition partner.

In the elections that were held after the legislation had passed (e.g., both majority configurations and the minority and coalition treatments in which all parties supported the legislation), the participants were told, "As the final piece of business to be voted upon before the upcoming election, it is likely that this vote will serve as a central part of the election campaign." In the treatments in which none of the opposition parties supported the legislation, they were told, "With all three opposition parties [the opposition parties and the coalition partner] opposing the bill, the government fell, triggering an early election. It is likely that this vote will serve as a central part of the election campaign." After reading the background information on the introduction screen, the participants advanced to the Election campaign information screen, where information on the vote outcome was repeated in the form of two information links for each candidate: one was a newspaper story that repeated the information outlining the outcome of the recent vote, which had appeared on the instruction screen, and the second offered the voting record of the parties on the legislation referred to in the newspaper story (see appendix 6.2). The participants were free to access as much of the information on the Election campaign information screen as they wished before voting.

We tested the participants for random assignment to each of our treatments according to socio-demographic characteristics, ideology, political knowledge (a scale based on their responses to five factual, political-knowledge questions), political interest, PID (strong or very strong attachments to a federal political party), and level of satisfaction with the way democracy works in Canada as well as whether a respondent correctly answered a careless-response question administered during the survey (see appendix 6.3 for summary statistics). The results of our multinomial logistic regression estimate confirmed that the groups did not include any systematic differences ($\chi^2 = 89.06; p = 0.36$).[2] Given these results, we are satisfied that our randomization process worked, creating groups similar to each other in make-up. As such, we proceeded with our assessment without any of these factors included in our models as controls.

We had a total of 982 individuals complete our study. Unlike some of our other experiments, this study provided the treatment cue on the instruction screen for all participants. However, the time spent reviewing this information varied considerably across the sample: the average time spent was fifty-three seconds, with a sizeable standard deviation of eighty-two seconds. Further assessment of the time spent on the instruction screen revealed that just over 10% of the sample spent less than eight seconds reviewing the entire instruction screen, well below the estimated time of twenty-four seconds to read the treatment information.[3] Of course, it is possible that while individuals may not have been exposed to the treatment in their haste to move past the instruction screen, they may have been exposed to the information using one of the cueing links presented on the Election campaign information screen. In an effort to remove respondents who were not exposed to the treatment cue, we excluded all individuals who had not viewed any of the cueing links and spent less than eight seconds on the instruction screen (the fastest 10% of respondents). The removal of these individuals left us with a final sample of 907 respondents, 92% of the total sample.

Results

We begin our assessment by examining whether legislation success affects vote choice. Recall that we expect the incumbent governing party to increase its vote share when it is successful at achieving its legislative goal (elections 1, 2, 3, and 5). To test this relationship, we use a logistic

---

2 See appendix 6.4 for full multinomial logistic regression results.
3 Time estimated based on average adult reading speed of approximately 3.33 words per second. The treatment cue text consisted of eighty-two words, estimated to take twenty-four seconds to read (see http://niram.org/read/). This estimate does not include the additional instruction text presented to the respondents. The estimate for the full text (200 words) on the instruction screen is sixty seconds, consistent with the average time spent on the instruction screen.

Figure 6.1. Impact of legislation passing on incumbent vote

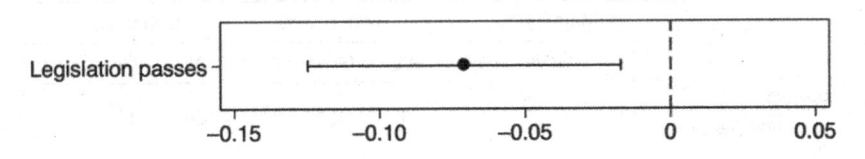

regression model with a vote for the governing party (= 1) as our dependent variable. We include a dichotomous variable for whether or not the legislation passed (passed = 1) to assess our hypothesis. The results from this model are presented graphically in figure 6.1 and included in full in appendix 6.5.[4]

As we can see from the results, our hypothesis is not supported: the governing party does *not* receive an increase in vote share when legislation passes. In fact, the coefficient for whether or not legislation passed is negative, with the probability of voting for the governing party found to decrease by 7 percentage points ($p < 0.05$) when legislation passes relative to the likelihood of voting for the governing party when legislation does not pass (see appendix 6.5). Contrary to expectations, it is the non-governing parties that appear to benefit in terms of vote support when legislation passes.

While our first hypothesis finds no support, we expect that this reflects the fact that our initial model fails to account for the conditions under which assigning responsibility (blame or credit) for successful legislation is linked directly to the governing party – in other words, clarity of responsibility. To fully explore this possibility and test our remaining hypotheses, we employ a multinomial logistic regression model to estimate the vote probability for each party by treatment. We report the results of the full model in appendix 6.6, with the incumbent governing party omitted as the reference category. In the results that follow, we use Stata's post-estimation margins commands to estimate the vote share, and the significance of any changes in vote share, across parties and treatments. Table 6.2 provides a summary of the vote share for each party according to treatment.

Our second hypothesis contends that the incumbent vote share will be higher in majority situations (elections 1 and 2) relative to

---

[4] See chap. 1 for an overview of how to read the results reported in the tables and graphs.

Table 6.2. Estimated vote share by party and treatment

	Majority, %		Minority, %		Coalition, %	
	All	Government	All	Government	All	Government
Party A (coalition partner)	13	11	21	18	26	14
Party B (opposition)	22	20	23	21	20	18
Party C	16	19	17	13	15	17
Party D (governing party)	49	50	39	48	39	51

Note: The cells report estimated vote share (percentage). Coalition party identified only for coalition treatments.

incumbent vote share in minority and coalition situations in which legislation passes (elections 3 and 5). Our argument is that voters will be more apt to assign responsibility to a governing party when they can clearly attribute responsibility to a single party. As such, majority governments should provide the clearest line of responsibility, followed by minority configurations and then coalitions. Our reasoning for assuming that coalition configurations will provide voters with the least clarity of responsibility follows from the work of Anderson (1995), which contends that, in coalition situations, voters are more apt to divide responsibility across coalition partners. While a minority configuration still requires support from at least one of the opposition parties for legislation to succeed, the informal nature of the alliances is expected to make it less clear which parties should be credited for successful legislation relative to the conditions observed under coalition configurations.

Based on the results reported in table 6.2, we find evidence supportive of our expectations. In both elections where legislation passes under a majority government, the incumbent party receives nearly identical levels of support: 49% of the vote share in election 1 and 50% of the vote share in election 2. In contrast, the incumbent's vote share drops to 39% in both the minority government treatment and the coalition government treatment when legislation passes. This drop of more than 10 percentage points is found to be statistically significant ($p < 0.10$) regardless of the majority government treatment.

In response to our first set of results reported for hypothesis 1, it appears that voters do reward the incumbent party with votes for successful legislation, but only when it is clearly the incumbent that is responsible for passing the legislation (majority configurations). In both the minority and the coalition configurations, other parties benefit when they cooperate with the governing party to pass legislation.

Contrary to our third hypothesis, which expected a higher level of incumbent support under minority governments compared with coalition conditions, the level of support for the incumbent party when legislation passes is identical under both minority and coalition configurations (39%). Ironically, the results suggest that opposition parties stand the best chance of gaining vote support under conditions where their support for the governing party means that the incumbent succeeds at passing legislation.

Is increased support split equally across opposition parties under minority and coalition configurations when legislation passes? Our fourth hypothesis states that a minor coalition partner will reap a greater reward for successful legislation under a coalition configuration relative to the other conditions. Referring to table 6.2, we find evidence of this phenomenon: The vote share of Party A (identified as coalition partner only in coalition treatments) increases from 13% under a majority government, when all parties support legislation, to 21% under the minority configuration and 26% when the party is identified as the coalition partner. However, while the difference in the vote share across configurations fits with expectations, the difference in Party A's vote share under the coalition treatment is found to be statistically significant ($p < 0.05$) only when compared with the vote share it receives under a majority configuration.

Our final two hypotheses consider how clarity of responsibility affects the vote when legislation is unsuccessful. Hypothesis 5 assumes that the incumbent will do better when legislation fails in a coalition configuration relative to a minority situation due to the fact that voters can clearly assign blame for the failed legislation to the minor coalition partner, the party that had agreed to support the larger coalition partner. Our results are somewhat supportive of this hypothesis: the governing party receives 51% of the vote when legislation fails under a coalition government compared with 48% of the vote when legislation fails under a minority configuration. However, this 3-percentage-point difference is not statistically significant.

In the case of the assignment of blame to the coalition partner for failed legislation, we once again find limited differences across treatments where the legislation fails. However, the difference in the vote share for the minor coalition partner when the party is identified under the coalition configurations is substantial across these two treatments. When the minor coalition partner supports its governing partner, it receives 26% of the vote. In contrast, when it votes against legislation, its vote share drops 12 points ($p < 0.05$) (see table 6.2). Taken together, these results suggest that the minor partner in a coalition government benefits, vis-à-vis successful legislation, when it supports the larger governing party. When the minor partner votes against legislation, all bets are off.

Discussion and Conclusion

Using an online experimental platform to assess the extent to which voters assign credit or blame to incumbent parties for successful or unsuccessful legislation, we have shown a somewhat counterintuitive relationship: incumbent parties are penalized for successful legislation, at least when the legislation receives the support of opposition parties to pass. However, the reverse is not true: incumbent governments do not receive increased support when opposition parties vote against government legislation.

Our analyses of how clarity of responsibility affects voters' ability to assign credit and blame offer more insight into this relationship. Our results show that the minor-coalition partner has the most to gain by propping up the government, netting a 13-percentage-point increase in vote share in a coalition setting compared with when legislation passes under a majority configuration. It also has the most to lose when it votes against its larger coalition partner, netting a 12-percentage-point decrease when the legislation fails.

So what are the implications of our findings for winning and keeping power in Canadian politics? When it comes to maximizing public credit for successful legislation, incumbent parties benefit the most in majority government situations. Our data show that an incumbent's vote share decreases by approximately 10 percentage points under minority and coalition configurations, relative to majority ones. If winning power is a key consideration, party leaders and elites should oppose any form of electoral reform that promotes the more frequent election of minority and coalition configurations.

For those who are perpetually on the other side of the House, however, minority and coalition configurations are likely preferable, and so electoral reform is clearly an important and worthwhile avenue for achieving democratic alternation and the sharing of power (Milner 1999; Russell 2008). Perhaps ironically, opposition parties may benefit the most from cooperating with the government in coalition situations, with coalition support at 26 percentage points when it supports the government as a formal partner compared with 14 percentage points when it votes against government legislation. In that sense, these parties may be "damned if they do and damned if they don't."

Of course, our study examines fictional configurations involving legislation addressing a single valence issue. Many issues in Canadian politics are not valence issues, and so, in those cases, the effects of parliamentary configuration may be overcome by other factors, such as partisanship or ideology. Nonetheless, our study suggests that governing parties are best served by the status quo and therefore face strong incentives to oppose any form of electoral reform that might undermine the frequency of majority governments in Canada. This latter observation does not bode well for supporters of electoral reform.

REFERENCES

Anderson, Christopher J. 1995. "The Dynamics of Public Support for Coalition Governments." *Comparative Political Studies* 28 (3): 350–83. https://doi.org/10.1177/0010414095028003002.

– 2000. "Economic Voting and Political Context: A Comparative Perspective." *Electoral Studies* 19 (2–3): 151–70. https://doi.org/10.1016/S0261-3794(99)00045-1.

Blais, André. 1991. "The Debate over Electoral Systems." *International Political Science Review* 12 (3): 239–60. https://doi.org/10.1177/019251219101200304.

Cairns, Alan. 1968. "The Electoral System and the Party System in Canada, 1921–1965." *Canadian Journal of Political Science* 1 (1): 55–80. https://doi.org/10.1017/S0008423900035228.

de Vries, Catherine E., Erica E. Edwards, and Erik R. Tillman. 2011. "Clarity of Responsibility beyond the Pocketbook: How Political Institutions Condition EU Issue Voting." *Comparative Political Studies* 44 (3): 339–63. https://doi.org/10.1177/0010414010384373.

Harris, Katelyn. 2015. "Minority Outcome Could Produce Political and Constitutional Squabbling for Months." *CBC News*, 17 October 2015. http://www.cbc.ca/news/politics/canada-election-2015-minority-government-power-1.3271483.

Hayward, Jonathan. 2015. "Canadians Don't Want a Coalition Government, Trudeau Says." *Globe and Mail*, 8 September 2015. https://www.theglobeandmail.com/news/politics/canadians-dont-want-a-coalition-government-trudeau-says/article26247346/.

Hellwig, Timothy, and David Samuels. 2007. "Electoral Accountability and the Variety of Democratic Regimes." *British Journal of Political Science* 38 (1): 65–90. https://doi.org/10.1017/S0007123408000045.

Kramer, Gerald. 1971. "Short-Term Fluctuations in U.S. Voting Behavior, 1896–1964." *American Political Science Review* 65 (1): 131–43. https://doi.org/10.2307/1955049.

Lewis-Beck, Michael. 1988. *Economics and Elections: The Major European Democracies*. Ann Arbor: University of Michigan Press.

Loewen, Peter. 2015. "First-Past-the-Post Electoral Systems May Still Be the Best." *Province* (Vancouver), 2 July 2015. https://theprovince.com/opinion/peter-loewen-first-past-the-post-electoral-systems-may-still-be-best.

Marsh, Michael, and James Tilley. 2009. "The Attribution of Credit and Blame to Governments and Its Impact on Vote Choice." *British Journal of Political Science* 40 (1): 115–34. https://doi.org/10.1017/S0007123409990275.

Massicotte, Louis. 2005. "Changing the Canadian Electoral System." In *Strengthening Canadian Democracy*, edited by Paul Howe, Richard Johnston, and André Blais, 65–98. Montreal: IRPP.

Milner, Henry. 1999. "The Case for Proportional Representation in Canada." In *Steps toward Making Every Vote Count: Electoral System Reform in Canada and Its Provinces*, 2nd ed., edited by Henry Milner, 37–50. Toronto: University of Toronto Press. www.jstor.org/stable/10.3138/j.ctt2tv1bb.8.

Nadeau, Richard, Éric Bélanger, François Pétry, Stuart N. Soroka, and Antonia Maioni. 2015. *Health Care Policy and Opinion in the United States and Canada*. London: Routledge.

Nannestad, Peter, and Martin Paldam. 1993. *The VP-Function: A Survey of the Literature on Vote and Popularity Functions*. Arhus, Denmark: Arhus University.

Pattie, Charles, and Ron Johnston. 2008. "Positional Issues, Valence Issues and the Economic Geography of Voting in British Elections." *Journal of Economic Geography* 8 (1): 105–26. https://doi.org/10.1093/jeg/lbm032.

Powell, G. Bingham, Jr. 1989. "Constitutional Design and Citizen Electoral Control." *Journal of Theoretical Politics* 1 (2): 107–30. https://doi.org/10.1177/0951692889001002001.

Powell, G. Bingham, Jr., and Guy D. Whitten. 1993. "A Cross-National Analysis of Economic Voting: Taking Account of the Political Context." *American Journal of Political Science* 37 (2): 391–414. https://doi.org/10.2307/2111378.

Russell, Peter. 2008. *Two Cheers for Minority Government: The Evolution of Canadian Parliamentary Democracy*. Toronto: Edmond Publishing.

Schram, A.J.H.C. 1989. *Voter Behaviour in Economic Perspective*. Alblasserdam, The Netherlands: Offsetdrukkerij Kauters.

Tilley, James, and Sara B. Hobolt. 2011. "Is the Government to Blame? An Experimental Test of How Partisanship Shapes Perceptions of Performance and Responsibility." *Journal of Politics* 73 (2): 316–30. https://doi.org/10.1017/S0022381611000168.

Parliamentary Configurations   145

Appendix 6.1. Election campaign information screen

Election Campaign

Click on a link below to view more information.

George Stevens - Party B (Official Opposition)	Robert Johnson - Party D (Governing Party)	Joseph Adams - Party C	Paul Smith - Party A
Campaign Information	Campaign Information	Campaign Information	Campaign Information
Quote from TV Debate	Quote from TV Debate	Quote from TV Debate	Quote from TV Debate
Voting Record	Voting Record	Voting Record	Voting Record
Professional Biography	Professional Biography	Professional Biography	Professional Biography
Newspaper Story	Newspaper Story	Newspaper Story	Newspaper Story

Appendix 6.2. Sample newspaper story and voting record cues

George Stevens
Party B

NEWSPAPER STORY

Health Care Bill Passes

In a recent vote, the governing party, Party D, gained the full support of the house in passing a piece of legislation that reports say will "greatly improve health care service in Canada". Given Party D's minority government status, the support of the opposition parties was necessary for the bill to pass. As the final piece of business to be voted upon before the upcoming election, it is likely that this vote will serve as a central part of the election campaign.

George Stevens
Party B

VOTING RECORD

A recent bill in the legislature contained the following text:

"...this legislation will ensure the long-term stability of our health care system, guaranteeing its sustainability for future generations."

The party voted as follows:

Party B: Support

Given Party D's minority government status, the support of the opposition parties was necessary for the bill to pass.

Appendix 6.3. Summary statistics

	Treatment 1	Treatment 2	Treatment 3	Treatment 4	Treatment 5	Treatment 6
Age	48.24 (15.98)	47.14 (17.28)	47.55 (17.21)	47.43 (16.41)	45.40 (16.66)	46.34 (17.58)
Female	0.51 (0.50)	0.47 (0.50)	0.51 (0.50)	0.50 (0.50)	0.54 (0.50)	0.48 (0.50)
No high school	0.06 (0.24)	0.07 (0.26)	0.07 (0.26)	0.06 (0.25)	0.06 (0.23)	0.06 (0.24)
University graduate	0.37 (0.48)	0.33 (0.47)	0.31 (0.46)	0.33 (0.47)	0.42 (0.50)	0.38 (0.49)
Income	3.57 (1.80)	3.55 (1.76)	3.81 (1.86)	3.53 (1.76)	3.73 (1.82)	3.97 (1.78)
Prairies	0.26 (0.44)	0.31 (0.46)	0.26 (0.44)	0.28 (0.45)	0.25 (0.43)	0.30 (0.46)
Ontario	0.45 (0.50)	0.46 (0.50)	0.54 (0.50)	0.45 (0.50)	0.52 (0.50)	0.52 (0.50)
Atlantic	0.14 (0.35)	0.15 (0.36)	0.08 (0.27)	0.11 (0.31)	0.12 (0.32)	0.08 (0.27)
Satisfaction	0.81 (0.39)	0.80 (0.40)	0.74 (0.44)	0.75 (0.43)	0.80 (0.40)	0.75 (0.44)
Political interest	6.10 (2.61)	6.22 (2.27)	6.27 (2.59)	5.60 (2.71)	5.99 (2.70)	6.04 (2.69)
Political knowledge	0.53 (0.34)	0.55 (0.29)	0.53 (0.31)	0.50 (0.31)	0.55 (0.29)	0.57 (0.31)
Political ideology	5.31 (2.08)	4.97 (2.16)	5.00 (2.42)	4.92 (1.83)	5.24 (2.22)	4.91 (2.30)
CPC PID	0.22 (0.42)	0.20 (0.40)	0.25 (0.44)	0.18 (0.39)	0.23 (0.42)	0.15 (0.36)
GRN PID	0.03 (0.18)	0.03 (0.17)	0.03 (0.16)	0.02 (0.13)	0.03 (0.16)	0.06 (0.25)
LIB PID	0.22 (0.41)	0.27 (0.44)	0.20 (0.40)	0.19 (0.39)	0.23 (0.42)	0.21 (0.41)
NDP PID	0.10 (0.30)	0.13 (0.34)	0.16 (0.37)	0.06 (0.24)	0.08 (0.27)	0.08 (0.28)
Response check	0.91 (0.29)	0.93 (0.26)	0.90 (0.31)	0.92 (0.27)	0.91 (0.29)	0.92 (0.27)
N	182	141	172	177	201	161

Note: The cells report averages, with standard deviations in parentheses. Age is the respondents' age in years. Female, no high school, university graduate, regional variables, PID, and response check are dichotomous measures, coded "1" in correspondence with the variable name. Political interest and political ideology are self-reported positions on an eleven-point scale running from "No interest" to "Great deal of interest" and "Left–Right," respectively. Political knowledge is an index (alpha = 0.60) based on five factual questions: the name of the British prime minister, the level of government that has primary responsibility for education and health care in Canada, the name of the federal finance minister, the name of the governor general, and the number of seats in the House of Commons. The respondents received one point for each correct response. The variable was then rescaled to fit between 0 and 1. N = number of usable cases in each treatment.

Appendix 6.4. Multinomial logistic regression results for test of random assignment to treatments

	Treatment 2	Treatment 3	Treatment 4	Treatment 5	Treatment 6
Age	−0.01 (0.01)	−0.01 (0.01)	−0.00 (0.01)	−0.01 (0.01)	−0.01 (0.01)
Female	−0.20 (0.27)	0.02 (0.26)	−0.10 (0.25)	0.09 (0.24)	−0.21 (0.26)
No high school	0.24 (0.65)	0.57 (0.57)	−0.05 (0.58)	0.25 (0.58)	0.53 (0.59)
University graduate	−0.19 (0.30)	−0.38 (0.28)	−0.33 (0.28)	0.06 (0.26)	−0.23 (0.28)
Income	0.01 (0.08)	0.12 (0.08)	−0.04 (0.08)	0.04 (0.07)	0.13 (0.08)[a]
Prairies	0.77 (0.50)	0.38 (0.43)	−0.12 (0.40)	0.50 (0.41)	0.94 (0.46)*
Ontario	0.81 (0.46)[a]	0.58 (0.39)	−0.15 (0.36)	0.67 (0.37)[a]	0.89 (0.42)*
Atlantic	1.02 (0.55)[a]	−0.01 (0.53)	−0.70 (0.49)	0.42 (0.48)	0.24 (0.55)
Satisfaction	−0.28 (0.36)	−0.36 (0.33)	−0.33 (0.32)	−0.30 (0.32)	−0.40 (0.33)
Political interest	0.02 (0.06)	0.02 (0.06)	−0.05 (0.05)	0.00 (0.05)	0.02 (0.06)
Political knowledge	0.34 (0.49)	0.07 (0.45)	−0.04 (0.44)	0.23 (0.42)	0.55 (0.45)
Political ideology	−0.07 (0.07)	−0.07 (0.06)	−0.09 (0.06)	−0.00 (0.06)	−0.08 (0.07)
CPC PID	0.40 (0.40)	0.49 (0.36)	−0.22 (0.37)	0.17 (0.34)	−0.55 (0.39)
GRN PID	0.15 (0.81)	0.20 (0.75)	−0.65 (0.80)	0.01 (0.71)	0.60 (0.65)
LIB PID	0.35 (0.36)	0.13 (0.35)	−0.11 (0.33)	−0.01 (0.32)	−0.17 (0.34)
NDP PID	0.82 (0.46)[a]	0.97 (0.44)*	−0.31 (0.49)	−0.04 (0.47)	−0.40 (0.50)
Response check	0.63 (0.56)	−0.35 (0.42)	−0.11 (0.43)	−0.01 (0.41)	0.09 (0.45)
Constant	−1.13 (1.03)	0.01 (0.89)	1.90 (0.85)*	0.03 (0.85)	−0.37 (0.91)

$N = 795$
χ^2 (df = 85) = 89.06
Pseudo R^2 = 0.03

Note: The cells report multinomial logistic regression coefficients, with standard errors in parentheses. Treatment 1 is set as the base outcome. Age is the respondents' age in years. Female, no high school, university graduate, regional variables, PID, and response check are dichotomous measures, coded "1" in correspondence with the variable name. Political interest and political ideology are self-reported positions on an eleven-point scale running from "No interest" to "Great deal of interest" and "Left–Right," respectively. Political knowledge is an index (alpha = 0.60) based on five factual questions: the name of the British prime minister, the level of government that has primary responsibility for education and health care in Canada, the name of the federal finance minister, the name of the governor general, and the number of seats in the House of Commons. The respondents received one point for each correct response. The variable was then rescaled to fit between 0 and 1. N = number of cases with full response set.
***$p < 0.001$; **$p < 0.01$; *$p < 0.05$; [a]$p < 0.10$.

Appendix 6.5. Full results for figure 6.1

Legislation passes	−0.29 (0.13)*
	[−0.07]
Constant	−0.02 (0.10)
Pseudo R²	0.00
N	907

Note: Cells report logistic regression coefficients, with standard errors in parentheses and marginal effects/discrete changes reported in square brackets.
***$p < 0.001$; **$p < 0.01$; *$p < 0.05$; ᵃ$p < 0.10$.

Appendix 6.6. Full multinomial logistic regression results for table 6.2

	Party A (coalition partner)	Party B (opposition)	Party C
Treatment 2	−0.18 (0.40)	−0.10 (0.32)	0.17 (0.34)
Treatment 3	0.71 (0.33)*	0.27 (0.30)	0.28 (0.33)
Treatment 4	0.36 (0.33)	−0.04 (0.29)	−0.24 (0.34)
Treatment 5	0.92 (0.32)**	0.11 (0.29)	0.15 (0.33)
Treatment 6	0.06 (0.35)	−0.22 (0.30)	0.01 (0.33)
Constant	−1.34 (0.25)***	−0.80 (0.21)***	−1.11 (0.23)***

$N = 907$
χ^2 (df = 15) = 21.86
Pseudo R² = 0.01

Note: The cells report multinomial logistic regression coefficients, with standard errors in parentheses. Party D, the incumbent governing party in all treatments, is set as the base outcome. Treatment 1 is the reference category. Coalition party identified only for coalition treatments. N = number of cases with full response set.
***$p < 0.001$; **$p < 0.01$; *$p < 0.05$; ᵃ$p < 0.10$.

Chapter Seven

Election Timing[1]

The significance of this [fixed-election-date legislation] is that politicians, the Premier, will no longer be able to play games with the election date. As we've seen over a number of years, Premiers do in fact play games with the public and with the political process in trying to choose an election date to their best advantage. We're fixing this election date so that the election will be at the convenience of the public, not at the convenience of the Premier, whoever that Premier might happen to be. (Ontario MPP Liz Sandals, Sandals 2004, 3215)

"Fixed election dates will improve the fairness of Canada's electoral system by eliminating the ability of governing parties to manipulate the timing of elections for partisan advantage." (Rob Nicholson, federal minister of democratic reform, quoted in *CBC News* 2007)

In the 2006 federal election, the Conservative Party of Canada (CPC) ended thirteen years of Liberal Party (LIB) rule by winning a minority government. Shortly after his party's victory, CPC leader Stephen Harper announced that his government planned to introduce fixed-election-date legislation because "fixed election dates prevent governments from calling snap elections for short-term political advantage. Fixed election dates stop leaders from trying to manipulate the calendar. They level the playing field for all parties. The rules are clear for everybody" (Stephen Harper, quoted in Aucoin, Jarvis, and Turnbull 2011, 131). With this legislation, Harper's plan was to prevent future incumbent leaders from using the election-timing power in the

---

1 This chapter has been adapted and updated from work originally published in *Electoral Studies* (Roy and Alcantara 2012).

way that his predecessor, LIB Prime Minister Jean Chrétien, had to "unfairly" win consecutive majority governments.

One year after this announcement, the federal government amended the *Canada Elections Act* by setting the date for all future federal elections to the third Monday in October every four years (Pepall 2010, 11). The law also permitted elections to occur outside this date, but only if the government had lost the confidence of the House or if the Crown had exercised its royal prerogative of dissolution. In practical terms, the amendment "partially fixed" the federal election date by acknowledging the governor general's discretion to dissolve Parliament and call an election (White and Alcantara 2018).[2]

Harper's decision to introduce this legislation at the federal level was part of a broader trend. According to Henry Milner (2005), many democratic countries – Austria, Belgium, Chile, Costa Rica, Czech Republic, Finland, France, Germany, Greece, Hungary, Israel, Italy, Latvia, Luxembourg, and Mexico – have adopted this kind of law. In Canada, nine provinces have passed this legislation, with BC the first to do so in 2001 and Quebec the last in 2013. These trends are likely the result of a growing public awareness that the power of first ministers and their advisers to opportunistically time elections is unfair and undemocratic (Alcantara and Roy 2014; Docherty 2010).

To what extent does having control over the timing of elections provide first ministers and their parties with an electoral advantage?[3] Surprisingly, only a handful of empirical studies have been published on this question, with most relying on cross-national (Schleiter and Tavits

---

2 Generally speaking, even with fixed-election-date legislation, it is still possible for an election to occur outside the dates specified in the legislation. This possibility is more likely to occur in minority, coalition, and minority-coalition government situations as well as when a first minister in a majority single-party-government situation is faced with wholesale defections or a major scandal. Bonga (2010, 9) defines coalition governments as follows: "Formal coalitions can be categorized into two main types: legislative coalitions 'which sustain the government in office' and executive coalitions which are 'the collection of parties which between them make up the cabinet' according to the relative proportion of their seats in parliament." We make no distinction between the two types in our experimental design given Canada's inexperience with both.

3 Of course, commentators are also aware that election timing is an inexact science and can sometimes produce disastrous results for the incumbent party. One example of this scenario is the 1990 Ontario provincial election, when then LIB premier David Peterson called an election three years into his mandate, only to be defeated by Bob Rae and the NDP. Similarly, federal LIB Prime Minister Pierre Trudeau used the election-timing power to stretch out the length of his government's mandate beyond the typical four-year term, resulting in a significant electoral defeat to Joe

2016) or British observational data (Schleiter and Belu 2018); only one uses Canadian provincial data (White and Alcantara 2018). In this chapter, we employ an online voting experiment to test whether the power to time an opportunistic election matters for incumbent vote support at the federal level in Canada. We do so by comparing incumbent support in a context of positive (negative) government (opposition) coverage in opportunistic and delayed election-timing scenarios. Our results support the argument that incumbents do gain a significant electoral advantage when they control the timing of an election. This advantage, however, is limited to conditions in which a government receives favourable coverage immediately before the vote.

Background, Theory, and Expectations

The literature on election timing suggests that there are four main reasons why first ministers in parliamentary democracies might opportunistically time elections. First, they call elections when public support for them and their parties is strong and therefore likely to improve their re-election chances (Aucoin, Jarvis, and Turnbull 2011, 131; Bakvis 2001; Docherty 2010; Wearing 1971). Frequently, leaders and strategists rely on polling numbers to assess their party's popularity (Aucoin, Jarvis, and Turnbull 2011, 130; Smith 1971, 317). In the Canadian context, Prime Minister Jean Chrétien asked the governor general in 1997 to dissolve Parliament and call an election only three and a half years into his mandate due to an upswing in polling numbers for his party (Clarkson 2005, 183). Similarly, John Turner called an election in 1984 on the basis of a 10-point lead in the polls (Clarkson 2005, 117–19), as did Brian Mulroney in 1988 and Kim Campbell in 1993, albeit with different polling numbers (Frizzell, Pammett, and Westell 1989, 1994, 15–17). Some commentators blame Pierre Trudeau's defeat in the 1979 election on the fact that the prime minister did not listen to the advice of campaign adviser Keith Davey and party pollster Allan Goldfarb to call an election a year or two earlier, when Trudeau's popularity was much higher (Clarkson, 2005, 60–1).

A second reason why first ministers opportunistically call elections is to capitalize electorally on a strong economy. The logic here is that

---

Clark and his Progressive Conservative Party in 1979. Thus, it is commonly assumed that incumbent first ministers should strategically time elections to occur only sometime between fifteen months and four years into their mandates. Calling an election outside this strategic window invites charges of illegitimacy, thus potentially cancelling out any positive effects that may accrue from the election-timing advantage (see Blais et al. 2004; Pepall 2010; White and Alcantara 2018).

the state of the economy is likely to impact voter assessments of the government's overall performance and ability to govern, which may, in turn, affect its re-election chances. Ito and Park (1988, 234–7) and Ito (1990), for instance, found that incumbent Japanese governments tended to call elections when economic growth was high and inflation was low. Other scholars have focused on the extent to which incumbent governments are able to manipulate the economy to create the ideal economic conditions for an opportunistic election call or whether incumbent governments simply try to predict and ride the economic waves. Using the same data as Ito and Park (1988), Cargill and Hutchinson (1991) found only moderate support for the ability of Japanese governments to opportunistically time elections with strong economic conditions. Chowdhury (1993) applied these arguments about manipulation and "surfing" to India, finding some evidence in support of surfing but none for manipulation. Alesina and Roubini (1992) attempted to replicate Ito and Park's findings by looking at Japan and eleven other democratic countries in the Organisation for Economic Co-operation and Development between 1960 and 1987. Although they did successfully replicate Ito's findings for Japan, their evidence for the other eleven countries was inconclusive.

On the other hand, Palmer and Whitten (2000) examined twelve parliamentary democracies using a different data set and found stronger evidence of opportunistic election timing. Alastair Smith's (2004) book on opportunistic election timing in British parliamentary elections found that incumbent prime ministers did attempt to synchronize elections with healthy economic conditions and that British governments frequently tried to call elections before the onset of economic decline. More recently, White and Alcantara (2018) found that as short-term economic conditions (measured in terms of six- and three-month unemployment and inflation trends) worsened at the provincial level, and before the passage of partially fixed election-date legislation, premiers were more likely to call an election, a move that usually resulted in increased electoral support for their parties.

In addition to timing elections to coincide with strong polling numbers or economic conditions, first ministers call elections to maintain discipline within their caucus and Cabinet (Bakvis 2001, 75; Schindler 1971, 30; Smith 1971, 315–16; White 2005, 176). Janice MacKinnon (2003, 123–4), for instance, recalls the circumstances surrounding the 1993 Saskatchewan provincial budget in which New Democratic Party (NDP) Premier Roy Romanow visited the lieutenant governor, Sylvia Fedoruk, before meeting with his divided Cabinet about the budget. At that meeting, he threatened to call an election unless the members united behind his budget, which they eventually did, unanimously. Similarly, in 2002, the federal Speech from the Throne contained a single sentence that promised "legislative changes to the financing of political parties and candidates for office" (Docherty 2004, 142). Many LIB members of Parliament were surprised later to find that the details of these legislative changes severely restricted their ability, and significantly increased the opposition parties' ability, to wage effective election campaigns. Faced with significant opposition from his caucus, the outgoing prime minister, Jean Chrétien, told his party that the legislative changes were a matter of confidence and that they had to support him or face an election (Docherty 2004, 143).

Finally, first ministers may time elections to take advantage of opposition parties that are in disarray and/or unprepared for an election (Aucoin, Jarvis, and Turnbull 2011, 130–1; Docherty 2010, 77). The classic example is the 2000 Canadian federal election, in which Prime Minister Chrétien called an election three years into his mandate to take advantage of the Canadian Alliance's new leader and lack of nominated candidates, fundraising structures, and campaign staffers (Pammett and Dornan 2001, 8; Wolinetz 2005, 212). Similarly, in the 1997 election, Prime Minister Chrétien called an election three and a half years into his mandate, partly to take advantage of "the Bloc Québécois's self-destructive leadership campaign to replace Lucien Bouchard (who had moved on to become the premier of Quebec)." Indeed, LIB elites believed that "the BQ's disarray also promised Liberal gains in Chrétien's home province" (Clarkson 2005, 183).

In sum, there are two broad scenarios in which first ministers tend to opportunistically call elections. The first occurs when they want to maintain party discipline and Cabinet solidarity. The second occurs when the incumbent government calls "an election at a time most conducive to its re-election prospects" (White 2005, 176). In particular, this latter scenario involves incumbent governments trying to time elections to correspond with periods in which they enjoy high levels of public support, the economy is strong, or the opposition is in disarray.

Existing studies suggest that the election-timing power does produce an advantage for first ministers who wield it. Schleiter and Tavits (2016, 847) found that the ability to time elections correlated "with an 8 percentage point vote share bonus and a 10 percentage point seat share bonus for PMs [prime ministers]. Such elections are also associated with 26%–30% greater odds of survival for the PMs." In a similar vein, White and Alcantara (2018) found that first ministers who had control over election timing benefited significantly when they could call early elections. In this chapter, we contribute to the debate by focusing on situations in which the government is receiving positive news coverage, and when the opposition is in disarray, to assess the impact of election timing on electoral success.[4]

Methodology

To test electoral timing, we employed an online voting platform that drew upon the student population at Wilfrid Laurier University, using an email to invite participants (see chapter 1 for additional sample information and study dates). This design allowed us to create an electoral environment where all factors were held constant, with the exception of our election-timing and context stimuli.[5] Students who opted to participate – approximately 20% of the student population – were first directed to a consent form that required their acceptance before entering the experiment. Upon giving their consent, they completed a survey that gathered a number of individual-level measures, including level of political interest, questions pertaining to issue priorities, measures of political knowledge, and a host of socio-demographic characteristics. Once the survey was completed, the participants were randomly assigned to one of five elections.

We designed our experiment to isolate the effects of election timing based on both positive public support for the fictitious incumbent party and negative public opinion towards the Opposition party. Two other parties were included as "neutral" actors, to simulate a multi-party system in a Westminster parliamentary democracy like Canada. In all elections, the incumbent and official Opposition candidates were clearly indicated by having these titles next to their names (see figure 7.1). These labels were also placed next to their names on the Election campaign information screen. No distinctions were offered for the two neutral parties.

To convey levels of support, we relied upon newspaper stories that presented the incumbent (Opposition) in a positive (negative) frame. While we note that this strategy may be capturing media effects as much as it offers a test of election-timing effects, we contend that this approach approximates the real-world context, where voters receive

---

4 We do so mainly because there is little evidence to suggest that first ministers in Canada have frequently called an election to maintain party discipline and Cabinet solidarity.
5 Given that we manipulate the amount of information participants can review as part of our experimental treatments, we do not consider the information search that the individuals undertake before casting a ballot, as we do in other chapters.

Figure 7.1. Election campaign information screen

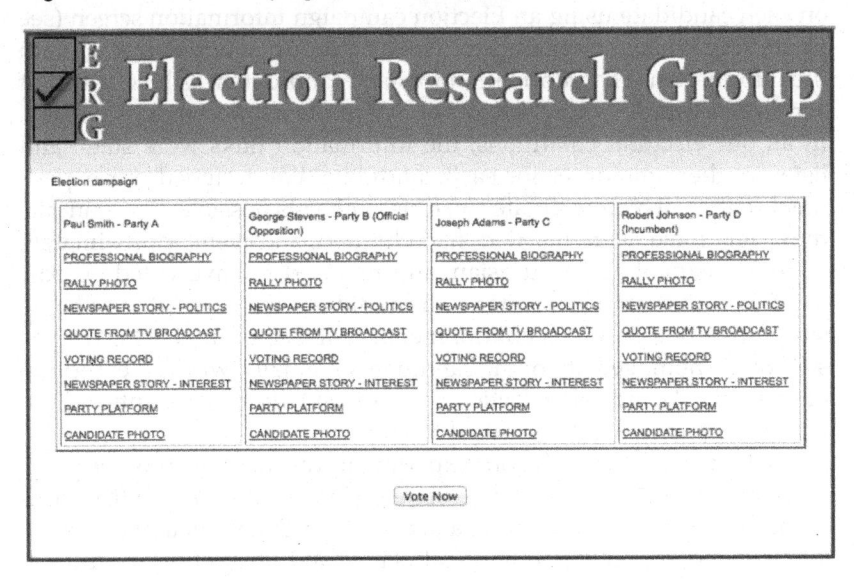

Paul Smith - Party A	George Stevens - Party B (Official Opposition)	Joseph Adams - Party C	Robert Johnson - Party D (Incumbent)
PROFESSIONAL BIOGRAPHY	PROFESSIONAL BIOGRAPHY	PROFESSIONAL BIOGRAPHY	PROFESSIONAL BIOGRAPHY
RALLY PHOTO	RALLY PHOTO	RALLY PHOTO	RALLY PHOTO
NEWSPAPER STORY - POLITICS	NEWSPAPER STORY - POLITICS	NEWSPAPER STORY - POLITICS	NEWSPAPER STORY - POLITICS
QUOTE FROM TV BROADCAST	QUOTE FROM TV BROADCAST	QUOTE FROM TV BROADCAST	QUOTE FROM TV BROADCAST
VOTING RECORD	VOTING RECORD	VOTING RECORD	VOTING RECORD
NEWSPAPER STORY - INTEREST	NEWSPAPER STORY - INTEREST	NEWSPAPER STORY - INTEREST	NEWSPAPER STORY - INTEREST
PARTY PLATFORM	PARTY PLATFORM	PARTY PLATFORM	PARTY PLATFORM
CANDIDATE PHOTO	CANDIDATE PHOTO	CANDIDATE PHOTO	CANDIDATE PHOTO

information regarding the performance of political actors, and political information in general, mainly through media sources (Nye, Zelikow, and King 1997; Savoie 2010). Ideally, we would be able to capture unmediated contextual effects, such as positive economic conditions or job growth, to further examine the potential that incumbents are taking advantage of the political business cycle.[6] However, our experimental design employs a fictional context, making such an assessment impossible.

In future work, we would recommend employing a detailed analysis of real-world examples, contrasting the objective national economic conditions with media coverage using content analysis to disentangle the impact of national conditions with what the media reports. In part, such an analysis would build upon the work of Palmer and Whitten (2000), Smith (2004), and White and Alcantara (2018). While we expect the correlation between objective national conditions and media coverage to be strong, we acknowledge the potential for the media to engage in priming some issues over others and framing this coverage in either a negative or a positive light (Cohen 1963; Soroka 2002, 2003).

---

6 We are grateful to an anonymous reviewer of our previously published article (Roy and Alcantara 2012), from which this chapter is adapted, for highlighting this point.

In all elections, the participants were presented with information on each candidate using an Election campaign information screen (see figure 7.1). When they clicked on a link, a pop-up window opened with the information. The information for each candidate was held constant across all elections, with the exception of the newspaper story – politics. In all our electoral conditions, the information links were static and listed in the same order for each candidate. We designed our experiment so that all our candidates were as similar as possible. For example, they were male, were married, had children, and were approximately 51 to 53 years of age, Caucasian, and reported to have voted on past legislation in a similar manner. (All candidates were reported as being supportive of a fictitious environmental bill. See chapter 1 for discussion of the homogeneity of the candidates.)[7] Finally, with the exception of our control condition (election 5, see below), the participants did not know when they would be asked to vote.

The first manipulation in our experiment was the content of the political news story. In the case of positive government coverage (elections 1 and 3), the participants read a story in which the incumbent party was praised by both international actors and competing candidates for recent government policies that balanced environmental protection with job growth. In the negative Opposition elections (elections 2 and 4), participants received a story that reported the Opposition party in complete disarray following a messy internal leadership battle. The political news was the same for each candidate by treatment (e.g., it conveyed either the positive incumbent story or the negative Opposition story, depending on the treatment).

Our second manipulation reflects election timing directly. In one scenario (election 1), the participants were forced to vote immediately after reading the positive-government newspaper story. This scenario was designed to simulate a situation in which a sitting government calls an election when the conditions are most favourable to re-election. Our expectation was that this election would yield the highest level of incumbent vote support relative to all other electoral treatments. Election timing was similar for a second election (election 2), except that an

---

[7] Of course, in an SMP electoral system, such as that used in Canada, it would not be possible to have all four candidates contesting the same riding vote on a previous bill since that would mean that all four had served at the same time. This was an oversight on our part. Instead of the reported "candidate vote," the text should have read "party vote." However, there is no indication that this oversight was identified by the participants and, given that the error was consistent across the treatments, we do not believe that it had any impact on the results presented below.

immediate vote followed after the participants had accessed a negative Opposition story.

In a second set of elections (election 3 and election 4), we tested whether the positive (negative) coverage of the government (Opposition) had an effect after a short period of time between accessing the information and casting the vote. This condition tested limits on election timing by delaying the vote, even though the conditions were advantageous for the incumbent. To simulate this scenario, we created a delay between the time the participants accessed the news story conveying the positive (negative) message and the time they voted. To do this, we launched the vote screen only after they had accessed three additional information links following the newspaper story. Our expectation for these cases was based on our assumptions regarding electoral timing. We expected that the immediate-vote conditions would yield greater incumbent support, all else being equal, than the delayed effect.

Some might question whether our experimental design captures what occurs when a first minister exercises the election-timing power in the real-world context. We agree that our design does not perfectly reflect this situation, especially given that federal election campaigns can vary anywhere between twenty days (in 1874) and seventy-eight days (in 2015). Indeed, the average campaign length from 1872 to 2015 was fifty days (Deachman 2015). What our experimental design does accomplish is to simulate, on a much shorter time scale, whether a positive cue about the incumbent governing party or a negative cue about the official Opposition has an effect on vote choice immediately before voting versus voting after a delay. To test this, we need to isolate the effect of election timing from the other individual and contextual factors likely to influence vote choice. Our research design allows us to do just that. What we are left with, in our controlled environment, is an observable measure of the change in the probability of voting for the incumbent as a result of timing an election when it is to the government's advantage (or the Opposition's disadvantage). While we accept that external factors may exaggerate or diminish the results produced in this experimental design, our contribution is to assess whether such an effect exists in the first place. Insomuch as one adheres to the belief that no party should gain an advantage at the ballot box as a result of institutional rules, our experimental design offers a means by which we can directly test the effect of the governing party controlling election dates. We are also encouraged by the similarity between the results reported here and those from observational studies (e.g., Schleiter and Tavits 2016; White and Alcantara 2018).

Table 7.1. Election-timing treatments

Treatment	News coverage	Timing	N
1	Positive incumbent story	Immediate vote	141
2	Negative Opposition story	Immediate vote	158
3	Positive incumbent story	Delayed vote	113
4	Negative Opposition story	Delayed vote	103
5 (control)	Neutral	User determined vote timing	233
Total			748

Note: The elections are listed in descending order according to expected highest to expected lowest incumbent vote support. The number of participants in each group is listed in the last column.

In sum, we assume that positive coverage will yield greater support for the incumbent than negative coverage of the Opposition. We believe that it is reasonable to expect positive coverage to accrue directly to the incumbent, whereas negative coverage of the Opposition should lead voters to throw their support to any other party except the official Opposition, which may or may not be the incumbent. As such, we expect support for the incumbent to be highest in election 1 (positive-immediate), followed by election 2 (negative-immediate), election 3 (positive-delayed), and finally election 4 (negative-delayed). As a control, we added a fifth election (control group), in which the participants could choose to vote at any time. In this election, all information was identical to that of the others, with the exception of the news story. In the control group, the newspaper story was neutral. Table 7.1 summarizes the five elections based on our expectations of highest to lowest incumbent vote support, along with the number of participants in each group.

Results

In total, we have a sample of 748 participants.[8] As might be expected from a university student sample, our respondents are relatively young

---

[8] The total number of participants was 2,480. However, nearly half were randomly assigned to a different study twinned with this research. Of the 1,265 individuals assigned to our five elections, we have full data on only 748 due to participants dropping out of the study before casting a ballot. We note that this number differs from that reported in Roy and Alcantara (2012), where the sample included only 709 respondents. The reason for this difference reflects the testing used for random assignment to the treatment groups. Given the results from the test applied within the current work, we do not include controls within the vote model, as we did in our earlier work. Substantively, the results are unaffected by the difference in sample size and model

(approximately 22.6 years of age, on average), fall just left of centre on our measure of ideology (4.7 on a 0–10 scale), and tend to be fairly or very satisfied with the way democracy works in Canada (74% of the sample). Few were strong or very strong partisans (approximately 22% of the sample) – again, unsurprising given the nature of the population from which we drew our sample. Women were also more likely to complete the study relative to men (63% of the sample was female).[9]

It is reassuring that while the raw number of participants in each treatment varies, there are limited differences across groups. To confirm, we modelled assignment to treatment groups as a function of socio-demographic characteristics, satisfaction with the way democracy works in Canada, political interest, political knowledge (a scale based on the participants' responses to five factual, political-knowledge questions), political ideology, and PID (strong or very strong partisans) to test whether random assignment to our groups produced similar samples. Our likelihood ratio statistic (χ^2 statistic, 45.97) indicates that assignment to group is independent of the respondents' characteristics, suggesting balance on observables between conditions ($p = 0.39$; see appendix 7.2). As such, we can be confident that random assignment was successful, all groups are similar, and, therefore, we exclude any controls in the models that follow.

To test the relationship between electoral timing and incumbent vote share, we use logistic regression. In all models, our dependent variable is coded "1" if a participant voted for the incumbent candidate and "0" otherwise. We test the impact of electoral timing by first regressing the incumbent vote on each of the election treatments (coded "1" for stated treatment and "0" otherwise) independently (models 1, 2, 3, and 4). This strategy allows us to test the impact of each of the treatments against all other elections. If our assumptions are correct, then we should find the strongest boost to incumbent support in the positive-immediate election (election 1), decreasing in strength through negative-immediate, positive-delayed, and negative-delayed treatments (elections 2, 3, and 4, respectively). To simplify interpretation, we display the results graphically.[10]

---

specification. It is also worth noting that the highest rate of attrition was observed in elections with delayed timing effects (approximately 54% dropped out compared with approximately 45% in the immediate-election conditions and only 11% in the control group). Attrition was not random: younger individuals, males, and less politically interested and politically informed participants were more apt to quit the study before completion than their older, female, more politically interested and informed counterparts.

9 See appendix 7.1 for summary statistics by treatment.
10 See chap. 1 for an overview of how to read the results reported in the tables and graphs. See appendix 7.3 for full results.

Figure 7.2. Electoral timing and incumbent vote share

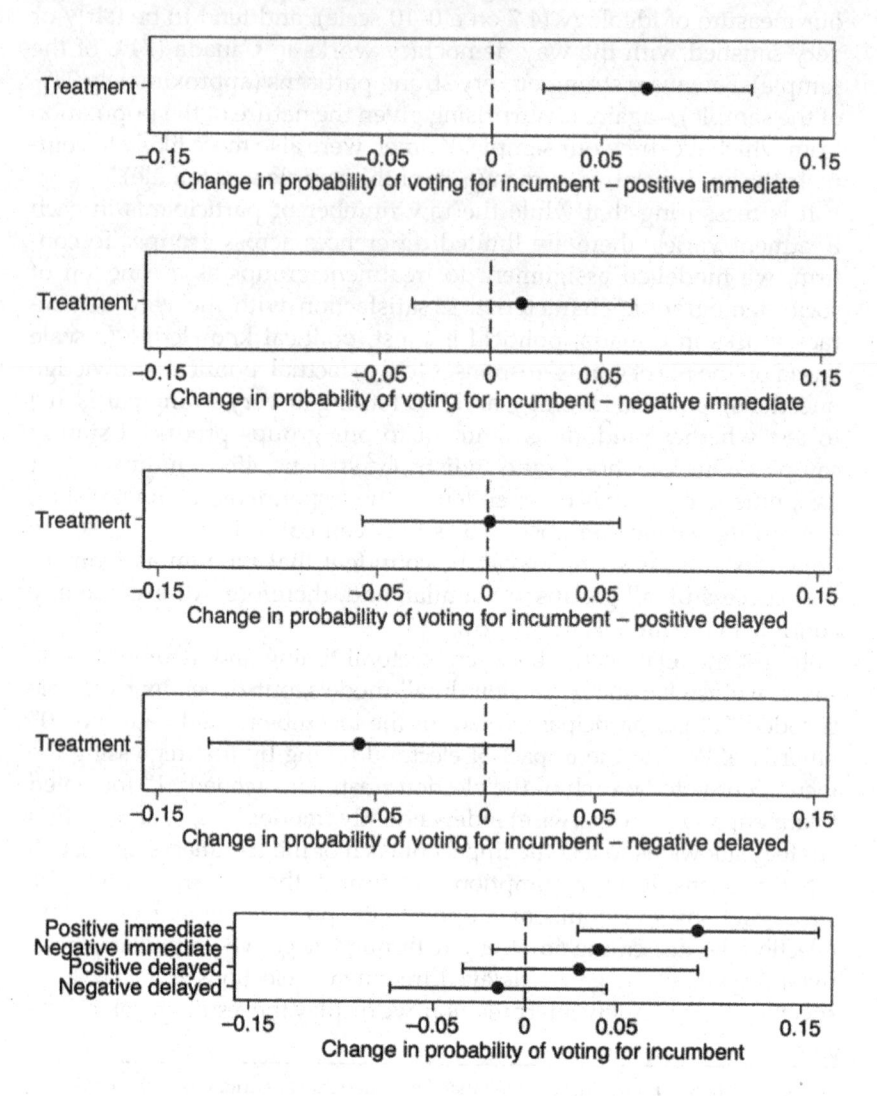

Change in probability of voting for incumbent – positive immediate

Change in probability of voting for incumbent – negative immediate

Change in probability of voting for incumbent – positive delayed

Change in probability of voting for incumbent – negative delayed

Change in probability of voting for incumbent

The point estimates report the change in the probability of voting for the incumbent according to treatment. We also include 90% confidence intervals for each estimate. The results are statistically significant ($p < 0.10$) when both tails of the confidence interval fall on the same side of the "0." Figure 7.2 presents the results from these models, by treatment, as well as a final model, with all treatments included in a single model and with the control group (treatment 5) set as the reference category. This full model serves as a check on the results we report when we estimate the effects of each treatment independently.

Based on the results, it is clear that only one of our treatments had a significant impact: the probability of voting for the incumbent increased significantly when the participants were exposed to a positive incumbent story followed by an immediate vote. In the first model, where we compare the impact of an immediate election following exposure to a positive incumbent message, the probability of voting for the incumbent increases by 7 percentage points ($p < 0.05$) relative to all the other elections. Similarly, when we run the full model, in which all four treatments are included, we find that the only treatment that yields a significant change is once again election 1: in this case, we observe a 9-percentage-point increase in incumbent vote probability relative to the control category. Put simply, our results concur with the assumption that an incumbent gains a significant electoral advantage when given the opportunity to call an election when support is most favourable. However, this effect appears to be observed only when the government is experiencing positive coverage and the election takes place immediately. In the case of negative opposition coverage or a delayed vote, no significant effects are found.

Although the incumbent vote share is improved significantly when voters are exposed to a positive incumbent story followed by an immediate election, it is important to note that in none of the five elections did the incumbent actually "win." In fact, in all five scenarios, the incumbent candidate finished last. Tests of the factors relevant to explaining this outcome revealed that younger voters were more apt to vote against the incumbent, regardless of treatment (results not shown). It may be that our incumbent was disadvantaged from the start given the population from which our sample was drawn. However, this observation does not change the conclusions inferred from this study. Our interest is the performance of the incumbent candidate across different election scenarios. Our results clearly show that controlling election timing can increase incumbent support, at least under certain conditions; all else being equal, the incumbent party does gain an advantage by calling elections when the "timing is right."

Discussion and Conclusion

Up until 2007, Canadian prime ministers had full discretion over the timing of federal elections, and they used that power, as much as they could, to take advantage of situations in which they enjoyed strong public support or economic conditions to increase their re-election chances. Things changed, however, after the LIB won a string of three majority victories dating back to 1993, which coincided with an emerging climate of democratic malaise to produce legislative changes that constrained, at least somewhat, the discretionary use of this power (Alcantara and Roy 2014). Amendments to the *Canada Elections Act* have been only partially constraining due to that crucial feature of Westminster systems that requires governments to maintain the confidence of the House. Technically, a prime minister can still manufacture a scenario for strategically triggering an election. This is especially true in minority situations, where it is generally expected that minority governments never govern for the full four or five years (see chapter 6 for more on government configurations).

As recently as fall 2018, there were rumours and rumblings that LIB strategists were pressuring the prime minister to call a snap spring election based on the fact that the main opposition parties seemed unprepared and vulnerable (Sears 2018; *CBC News* 2018). The legitimacy of such action, especially in majority situations, would be quite low and likely cause significant public backlash. Such an action would require not only introducing legislation and a confidence motion that none of the opposition parties could support but also encouraging government MPs to skip the vote to produce the desired outcome. Most observers would likely agree that such an action would be viewed quite negatively by the general public and result in the kind of punishment that some incumbent parties have received when they have called elections "too early" (Blais et al. 2004; White and Alcantara 2018).

To what extent does the election-timing power matter for incumbent vote share? The results in this chapter suggest that the critics were right to be concerned. Incumbents do seem to gain an electoral advantage when they dictate the timing of an election. However, this advantage seems to exist only when a government receives positive attention immediately before voting. Indeed, it is only in this single election (election 1) that we observe a significant advantage for the government. These findings are consistent with others that rely on observational data to show that incumbent parties generally benefit at the ballot box when the election-timing power is used opportunistically (Schleiter and Belu 2018; Schleiter and Tavits 2016; White and Alcantara 2018).

Thus, the implications for winning and keeping power are clear. Opportunistically timing elections can provide incumbent parties with a powerful tool for improving their re-election chances. The key to using this power today is to find (or create) the right mix of conditions to exercise it without suffering electoral and public backlash. The window for using this power in Canada, however, is likely closing given election-timing legislation. We suspect that such efforts will become even less likely as time passes and fixed election dates become more entrenched within the Canadian population.

REFERENCES

Alcantara, Christopher, and Jason Roy. 2014. "Reforming Election Dates in Canada: Towards an Explanatory Framework." *Canadian Public Administration* 57 (2): 256–74. https://doi.org/10.1111/capa.12067.

Alesina, Alberto, and Nouriel Roubini. 1992. "Political Cycles in OECD Economies." *Review of Economic Studies* 59 (4): 663–88. https://doi.org/10.2307/2297992.

Aucoin, Peter, Mark Jarvis, and Lori Turnbull. 2011. *Democratizing the Constitution: Reforming Responsible Government*. Toronto: Edmond Publishing.

Bakvis, Herman. 2001. "Prime Minister and Cabinet in Canada: An Autocracy in Need of Reform?" *Journal of Canadian Studies* 35 (4): 60–79. https://doi.org/10.3138/jcs.35.4.60.

Bakvis, Herman, and Steven B. Wolinetz. 2005. "Canada: A Case of Hyper-presidentialism?" In *The Presidentialization of Politics: A Study in Comparative Politics*, edited by Paul Webb and Thomas Poguntke, 199–220. Oxford: Oxford University Press.

Blais, André, Elizabeth Gidengil, Neil Nevitte, and Richard Nadeau. 2004. "Do (Some) Canadian Voters Punish a Prime Minister for Calling a Snap Election?" *Political Studies* 52 (2): 307–23. https://doi.org/10.1111/j.1467-9248.2004.00481.x.

Bonga, Melissa. 2010. "The Coalition Crisis and Competing Visions of Canadian Democracy." *Canadian Parliamentary Review* 33 (2). https://www.canlii.org/en/commentary/journals/18/924/.

Cargill, Thomas F., and Michael M. Hutchinson. 1991. "Political Business Cycles with Endogenous Election Timing: Evidence from Japan." *Review of Economics and Statistics* 73 (4): 733–9. https://doi.org/10.2307/2109416.

CBC News. 2007. "Bill Setting Federal Elections Every 4 Years about to Become Law." *CBC News*, 2 May 2007. http://www.cbc.ca/news/canada/bill-setting-federal-elections-every-4-years-about-to-become-law-1.669836.

– 2018. "Trudeau Rules Out Snap Election, So Vote Will Fall Oct. 21." Canadian Press, 16 December 2018. https://www.cbc.ca/news/politics/trudeau-rules-out-snap-election-1.4948404.

Chowdhury, Abdur R. 1993. "Political Surfing over Economic Waves: Parliamentary Election Timing in India." *American Journal of Political Science* 37 (4): 1100–18. https://doi.org/10.2307/2111545.

Clarkson, Stephen. 2005. *The Big Red Machine: How the Liberal Party Dominates Canadian Politics*. Vancouver: UBC Press.

Cohen, Bernard C. 1963. *The Press and Foreign Policy*. Princeton, NJ: Princeton University Press.

Deachman, Bruce. 2015. "78 Days? The Long and the Short of Canadian Campaigns." *Ottawa Citizen*, 3 August 2015. https://ottawacitizen.com/news/politics/two-down-76-to-go-the-longest-election-campaign-since-we-first-re-elected-john-a.

Docherty, David C. 2004. *Legislatures*. Vancouver: UBC Press.

– 2010. "Legislatures." In *Auditing Canadian Democracy*, edited by William P. Cross, 65–92. Vancouver: UBC Press.

Frizzell, Alan, Jon H. Pammett, and Anthony Westell. 1989. *The Canadian General Election of 1988*. Ottawa: Carleton University Press.

– 1994. *The Canadian General Election of 1993*. Ottawa: Carleton University Press.

Ito, Takatoshi. 1990. "The Timing of Elections and Political Business Cycles in Japan." *Journal of Asian Economics* 1 (1): 135–56. https://doi.org/10.1016/1049-0078(90)90011-O.

Ito, Takatoshi, and Jin Hyuk Park. 1988. "Political Business Cycles in the Parliamentary System." *Economic Letters* 27 (3): 233–8. https://doi.org/10.1016/0165-1765(88)90176-0.

King, Gary, Robert Keohane, and Sidney Verba. 1994. *Designing Social Inquiry: Scientific Inference in Qualitative Research*. Princeton, NJ: Princeton University Press.

MacKinnon, Janice. 2003. *Minding the Public Purse: The Fiscal Crisis, Political Trade-Offs and Canada's Future*. Montreal and Kingston: McGill-Queen's University Press.

Milner, Henry. 2005. "Fixing Canada's Unfixed Election Dates: A Political Season to Reduce the Democratic Deficit." *IRPP Policy Matters* 6 (6): 1–44. https://irpp.org/research-studies/policy-matters-vol6-no6/.

Nye, Joseph S., Jr., Philip D. Zelikow, and David C. King. 1997. *Why People Don't Trust Government*. Cambridge, MA: Harvard University Press.

Palmer, Harvey D., and Guy D. Whitten. 2000. "Government Competence, Economic Performance and Endogenous Election Dates." *Electoral Studies* 19 (2–3): 413–26. https://doi.org/10.1016/S0261-3794(99)00059-1.

Pammett, Jon H., and Christopher Dornan, eds. 2001. *The Canadian General Election of 2000*. Toronto: Dundurn Press.

Pepall, John. 2010. *Against Reform*. Toronto: University of Toronto Press.
Roy, Jason, and Christopher Alcantara. 2012. "The Election Timing Advantage: Empirical Fact or Fiction?" *Electoral Studies* 31 (4): 774–81. https://doi.org/10.1016/j.electstud.2012.06.005.
Sandals, Liz. 2004. Ontario. Legislative Assembly. *Hansard*, 38th Parliament, 1st Session, 23 June.
Savoie, Donald J. 2010. *Power: Where Is It?* Montreal and Kingston: McGill-Queen's University Press.
Schindler, Fred, 1971. "The Prime Minister and Cabinet: History and Development." In *Apex of Power: The Prime Minister and Political Leadership in Canada*, edited by Thomas A. Hockin, 22–47. Scarborough, ON: Prentice-Hall.
Schleiter, Petra, and Valerie Belu. 2018. "Electoral Incumbency Advantages and the Introduction of Fixed Parliamentary Terms in the United Kingdom." *British Journal of Politics and International Relations* 20 (2): 303–22. https://doi.org/10.1177/1369148117739858.
Schleiter, Petra, and Margit Tavits. 2016. "The Electoral Benefits of Opportunistic Election Timing." *Journal of Politics* 78 (3): 836–50. https://doi.org/10.1086/685447.
Sears, Robin. 2018. "Early Federal Election Rumours Build." *Toronto Star*, 9 September 2018. https://www.thestar.com/opinion/star-columnists/2018/09/09/early-federal-election-rumours-build.html.
Smith, Alastair. 2004. *Election Timing*. Cambridge: University of Cambridge Press.
Smith, Denis. 1971. "President and Parliament: The Transformation of Parliamentary Government in Canada." In *Apex of Power: The Prime Minister and Political Leadership in Canada*, edited by Thomas A. Hockin, 308–25. Scarborough, ON: Prentice-Hall.
Soroka, Stuart N. 2002. *Agenda-Setting Dynamics in Canada*. Vancouver: UBC Press.
– 2003. "Media, Public Opinion, and Foreign Policy." *Press/Politics* 8 (1): 27–48. https://doi.org/10.1177/1081180X02238783.
Wearing, Joseph. 1971. "President or Prime Minister." In *Apex of Power: The Prime Minister and Political Leadership in Canada*, edited by Thomas A. Hockin, 326–43. Scarborough, ON: Prentice-Hall.
White, Graham. 2005. *Cabinets and First Ministers*. Vancouver: UBC Press.
White, Steve, and Christopher Alcantara. 2018. "Do Constraints Limit Opportunism? Incumbent Electoral Performance before and after (Partially) Fixed-Term Laws." *Political Behavior* 41 (3): 657–75. https://doi.org/10.1007/s11109-018-9467-3.

Appendix 7.1. Summary statistics

Variable	Election 1	Election 2	Election 3	Election 4	Control
Age	22.74 (6.74)	22.29 (5.62)	23.03 (5.61)	23.49 (8.27)	22.27 (6.11)
Female	0.64 (0.48)	0.67 (0.47)	0.56 (0.50)	0.67 (0.47)	0.62 (0.49)
Satisfaction	2.24 (0.69)	2.23 (0.61)	2.33 (0.68)	2.24 (0.59)	2.25 (0.57)
Political interest	6.35 (2.23)	5.81 (2.42)	6.19 (2.34)	5.64 (2.40)	6.10 (2.33)
Political knowledge	0.71 (0.24)	0.68 (0.24)	0.70 (0.25)	0.67 (0.24)	0.65 (0.24)
Political ideology	4.68 (2.10)	4.71 (2.10)	4.55 (2.10)	4.71 (2.02)	4.92 (2.25)
CPC PID	0.06 (0.23)	0.04 (0.19)	0.06 (0.24)	0.06 (0.24)	0.06 (0.24)
GRN PID	0.01 (0.08)	0.01 (0.11)	0.01 (0.09)	0.03 (0.17)	0.01 (0.11)
LIB PID	0.09 (0.28)	0.07 (0.26)	0.12 (0.32)	0.03 (0.17)	0.05 (0.22)
NDP PID	0.08 (0.27)	0.08 (0.27)	0.10 (0.30)	0.05 (0.22)	0.09 (0.28)
N	141	158	113	103	233

Note: The cells contain averages, with standard deviations in parentheses. Age is the respondents' age in years. Female is dichotomous, coded "1" for female. Political interest and ideology are the average responses reported based on a 0 (no interest) to 10 (extremely interested) scale. Political knowledge is an index (alpha = 0.68) based on five factual questions: the name of each of the four federal party leaders (CPC, GRN, LIB, and NDP), the name of the most recent Republican candidate for US president, the name of the federal finance minister, the name of the governor general, and the number of seats in the House of Commons. The respondents were assigned a point for each correct question. This variable was rescaled to fit between 0 and 1. PID is a dichotomous measure of strong or very strong party identifiers. N = number of usable cases in each treatment.

Appendix 7.2. Multinomial logistic regression results for test of random assignment to treatments

Variable	Election 1	Election 2	Election 3	Election 4
Age	0.01 (0.02)	0.00 (0.02)	0.01 (0.02)	0.03 (0.02)[a]
Female	0.25 (0.24)	0.27 (0.24)	−0.21 (0.26)	0.21 (0.27)
Satisfaction	−0.12 (0.19)	−0.14 (0.19)	0.21 (0.20)	−0.19 (0.21)
Political interest	−0.01 (0.06)	−0.10 (0.06)[a]	−0.08 (0.06)	−0.12 (0.06)[a]
Political knowledge	1.11 (0.57)[a]	1.02 (0.55)[a]	0.98 (0.62)	1.05 (0.62)[a]
Political ideology	−0.04 (0.06)	−0.04 (0.05)	−0.06 (0.06)	−0.07 (0.06)
CPC PID	−0.48 (0.56)	−0.31 (0.52)	0.31 (0.53)	−0.12 (0.56)
GRN PID	−0.56 (1.17)	0.11 (0.93)	−14.37 (1,167.70)	0.76 (0.86)
LIB PID	0.51 (0.46)	0.48 (0.46)	1.13 (0.45)*	−0.53 (0.68)

Appendix 7.2. Multinomial logistic regression results for test of random assignment to treatments (Continued)

Variable	Election 1	Election 2	Election 3	Election 4
NDP PID	−0.30 (0.43)	−0.18 (0.41)	−0.01 (0.45)	−0.77 (0.55)
Constant	−1.05 (0.75)	−0.17 (0.74)	−1.30 (0.81)	−0.86 (0.81)
$N = 679$				
χ^2 (df = 40) = 42.53				
Pseudo R^2 = 0.02				

Note: The cells report multinomial logistic regression coefficients, with standard errors in parentheses. The control is set as the base outcome. Age is the respondents' age in years. Female is dichotomous, coded "1" for female. Political interest and political ideology are self-reported positions on an eleven-point scale running from "No interest" to "Great deal of interest" and "Left–Right," respectively. Political knowledge is an index (alpha = 0.68) based on five factual questions: the name of each of the four federal party leaders (CPC, GRN, LIB, and NDP), the name of the most recent Republican candidate for US president, the name of the federal finance minister, the name of the governor general, and the number of seats in the House of Commons. The respondents received one point for each correct response. The variable was then rescaled to fit between 0 and 1. PID is a dichotomous measure of strong or very strong party identifiers. N = number of cases with full response set.
*** $p < 0.001$; ** $p < 0.01$; * $p < 0.05$; ᵃ $p < 0.10$.

Appendix 7.3. Full results for figure 7.2

	Model 1	Model 2	Model 3	Model 4	Model 5
Positive-Immediate	0.59 (0.24)* [0.07]				0.72 (0.29)* [0.09]
Negative-Immediate		0.12 (0.25) [0.01]			0.35 (0.30) [0.04]
Positive-Delayed			0.01 (0.29) [0.00]		0.27 (0.34) [0.03]
Negative-Delayed				−0.47 (0.35) [−0.06]	−0.16 (0.39) [−0.01]
Constant	−1.94 (0.12)***	−1.84 (0.12)***	−1.81 (0.11)***	−1.76 (0.11)***	−2.07 (0.21)***
Pseudo R^2	0.01	0.00	0.00	0.00	0.01
N	748	748	748	748	748

Note: The cells report logistic regression coefficients, with standard errors in parentheses and marginal effects/discrete changes reported in square brackets.
*** $p < 0.001$; ** $p < 0.01$; * $p < 0.05$; ᵃ $p < 0.10$.

Chapter Eight

The Supreme Court of Canada, Parliament, and the Role of Experts

Faced with loud provincial objections to his plan to change the Senate via a simple federal law without a constitutional change approved by the provinces – as well as the ire of some of his own appointed senators – Harper is throwing his contentious plan into the lap of the country's top judges. (MacCharles 2013)

Prime Minister Justin Trudeau may not like it, but experts agree that he and his government have limited options when it comes to challenging a new law in Quebec that forbids people from giving or receiving government services with their faces covered. (Scotti 2017)

Over the last thirty-five years, Canadian judges have "abandoned the deference and self-restraint that characterized their pre-Charter jurisprudence and become more active players in the political process" (Morton and Knopff 2000, 13). This transformation from parliamentary to constitutional, or judicial, supremacy was the result of three factors. The first was the emergence of a support structure for legal mobilization, which encouraged and empowered judicial actors to move beyond constitutional interpretation and venture into policymaking and the political process (Epp 1998, 3). Second, Canada adopted the Canadian Charter of Rights and Freedoms, providing the courts with a new set of constitutional rights and freedoms from which they could justify their new interventionist role (Howe and Russell 2001). Finally, Canadian political elites voluntarily facilitated this transfer of power "in response to perceived threats by peripheral groups." They assumed that Canada's judicial elites not only shared the same set of policy preferences that they possessed but would also be better positioned to protect those preferences because of their long-standing reputation for "political impartiality and rectitude" (Hirschl 2000, 91).

In many ways, the rise of judicial and constitutional supremacy has been a double-edged sword for Canadian politicians. On the one hand, they have seen their power diminish collectively relative to the judiciary as the latter has taken a more activist role, not only in adjudicating the constitutionality of a wider range of laws but in directly amending many of them as well (Morton and Knopff 2000). On the other hand, the Supreme Court has given politicians a useful and convenient mechanism for shielding themselves occasionally from highly contentious policy and political issues. When faced with the decision of whether to legalize same-sex marriage, for instance, then prime minister Jean Chrétien turned to the Supreme Court, using the reference power, to determine the government's constitutional obligations before it introduced legislation (Puddister 2019, 574). Similarly, in confronting the issue of Quebec secession, the government of Canada turned to the court for guidance before introducing the Clarity Act rather than setting the rules of secession unilaterally. In both instances, Canadian political leaders and their operatives believed that the court would deliver their preferred outcome, while at the same time insulating them from any public-opinion fallout that might result (Radmilovic 2010, 852; Russell 2004).

Of course, these kinds of decisions and situations do not occur in a political vacuum. Instead, experts frequently comment on them in the public sphere in hopes of influencing not only the outcomes themselves but also how the public perceives those outcomes. Between 1982 and 1985, for instance, the government of Quebec included the notwithstanding clause in every bill that it introduced in the Quebec National Assembly as a means of insulating its legislation against any future interference and intrusion by the Supreme Court (Johansen and Rosen 2008). According to Peter Russell, one of Canada's pre-eminent constitutional scholars, "The Supreme Court of Canada upheld this blanket use of the legislative override in the same decision in which it struck down Quebec's sign law. But it was wrong to do so" (2007). Similarly, in the debate leading up to the Supreme Court's ruling on same-sex marriage, political scientist Christopher Manfredi (2003) argued that "if courts declare that the definition of marriage should change, but Parliament determines that a plausible alternative interpretation of the Charter leads to a different conclusion, then the notwithstanding clause is the constitutionally authorized mechanism for asserting that alternative interpretation." In both instances, high-profile experts in Canadian politics and law waded into the public sphere to influence the judicial outcome in some way. To what extent, however, do these interventions affect public opinion?

In this chapter, we present two experiments that investigate the effects of institutional choice and expert opinion on public attitudes towards the Parliament of Canada and the Supreme Court of Canada. Our main goals are to sort out the level of public support that these institutions enjoy, the extent to which it makes strategic sense for politicians to push political issues to the court for adjudication, and whether expert opinion matters for how citizens view these situations. We test these arguments using a survey wording experiment that allows us to assess the extent to which citizens view each body as having not only the authority to pass legislation but also the authority to block the other's efforts to do so. In addition, we consider how stable these opinions are by introducing an expert cue in support of, or in opposition to, each institution blocking the decision of the other.

Background, Theory, and Expectations

The adoption of the Constitution Act, 1982 and the Canadian Charter of Rights and Freedoms were major instances of institutional change in Canada. In one fell swoop, Canadian leaders had nudged our political system away from its long-standing tradition of parliamentary supremacy (Ajzenstat 2007; Smith 2007) towards constitutional and judicial supremacy. Whereas before 1982, Parliament was the key political and legal actor in Canada, this was no longer to be the case. Instead, judges were to either share that distinction with elected officials (Baker 2010; Hogg and Bushell 1997) or supersede them by engaging in what some scholars negatively describe as judicial activism and the erosion of Canadian democracy (Morton and Knopff 2000). While the drafters of the 1982 constitutional documents did envision the possibility of legislative checks on judicial power in the form of sections 1 (the reasonable limits clause, which allows limits to be placed on Charter rights as long as such limits can be justified) and 33 (the notwithstanding clause, which allows a legislature to insulate a law from sections 2 and 7 to 15 of the Charter for a period of up to five years), these sections proved to be relatively ineffective, with the latter falling into disuse after its highly unpopular application (at least among residents outside Quebec) by the Quebec government (Leeson 2001; Russell 2004).

Generally speaking, there has been only a handful of studies published on Canadian public opinion as it relates to the judicial system. Yet these studies generally agree that Canadians tend to have strong, positive feelings about the courts and that they prefer the courts to every other political and legal body in Canada (Hausegger and Riddell 2004; Sniderman et al. 1996). Fletcher and Howe (2001), for instance, asked the respondents in 1987 and 1999 whether the legislature or the courts should have the final say over the constitutionality of a piece of legislation. They found that 62% and 62% of the respondents, respectively, preferred the courts, whereas only 28% and 30% preferred the legislature (with the remaining 10% and 8% stating that they did not know) (Fletcher and Howe 2001, 261). When they examined regional and partisan differences, they found no statistically significant differences among regions, but they did find that the "supporters of most federal parties [with the exception of the Reform Party] also strongly favour the courts over the legislature" (262).

Using data from the 2006 Canadian Election Study, Goodyear-Grant, Matthews, and Hiebert (2013, 385) found almost identical results, with 61% of the respondents choosing the courts versus 26% choosing the elected representatives when asked whether the courts or elected representatives should have the final say on issues related to same-sex marriage and the death penalty (383). These results, they suggest, were driven by citizens fixated on outcome-oriented evaluations rather than process-oriented ones. "It is significant that nearly all of the significant effects in the regression analysis can be interpreted as reflecting, at least in part, [citizens'] evaluations of the incoming Conservative minority government, rather than [citizens'] views of the policy output of the courts" (394). In other words, partisan dynamics seemed to be driving public considerations with respect to Parliament and the Supreme Court rather than particular court decisions or organizational features of the institutions.

The popularity of the Supreme Court of Canada in comparison to Parliament seems to be consistent and durable over time. A 2015 Angus Reid study, for instance, found that 74% of the respondents had a favourable opinion of the Supreme Court of Canada (compared with 26% who had an unfavourable opinion) and that 61% expressed "a great deal" or "quite a lot" of confidence in the Supreme Court, followed by 51% for the courts, 31% for the media, 28% for the House of Commons, 13% for political parties, 12% for politicians, and 10% for the Senate. In short, Canadians hold the Supreme Court in high esteem. Given these consistent findings in the literature, our first hypothesis is as follows:

H1: Individuals will be more supportive of the Supreme Court of Canada determining the laws of Canada relative to the Parliament of Canada.

While most of the time, Parliament has tended to be deferential to the judgments of the Supreme Court, it has at its disposal a variety of mechanisms, such as the notwithstanding clause, and others that it has used, such as the tools of coordinate interpretation (e.g., minority retort, in which the legislature implements the minority opinion in a judicial decision, or textual retort, in which the legislature inserts Charter language directly into the legislation), to disagree with it (Baker 2010; Leeson 2001). What impact might these disagreements have on public opinion towards both institutions? Public opinion data suggest that it should have no effect on support for the court. According to the authors of the Angus Reid report, "In nearly every case, the court prevailed" when the respondents were "asked a variety of questions about the interaction between the court and the elected branch of government." When Parliament and the Supreme Court come into conflict with each other, "Canadians' affection for the court leads them to side with it more often than not" (Angus Reid Institute 2015).

To what extent this argument is true likely depends on the basis on which individual public opinion on these institutions was formed. If support for the Supreme Court is a normative commitment, a belief that it *should* determine what legislation passes, then public support for it will remain stable regardless of other considerations. Alternatively, if public support for the court assumes that the court is the final arbiter in Canada, then we should see public support for it decrease when this assumption is challenged in light of new (factual) information (Bullock 2009). Our second hypothesis assesses the validity of each possibility. Given earlier findings that support for the court tends to prevail, we base our hypothesis on the former assumption:

> H2: Individuals will be more supportive of the Supreme Court of Canada determining the laws of Canada relative to the Parliament of Canada, even when primed to consider the two institutions in conflict with each other.

While studies of Canadian public opinion have uncovered what seem to be relatively stable patterns of public support for the Supreme Court relative to Parliament, there do not appear to be any published results that report the effects of expert opinion on those evaluations.[1] Should we expect experts to have any influence on them? The comparative-public-opinion literature suggests that they should, arguing that "people will believe the opinions of someone who is assumed to have a lot of relevant knowledge" (Klucharev, Smidts, and Fernández 2008, 353; see also Page, Shapiro, and Dempsey 1987). In one study, the authors "found that experts made the attitude toward objects more favorable by 12% and increased the probability of object recognition by 10%. In everyday life, the apparent expertise of the

---

[1] We note that experts weigh in on a variety of issues of the day, including court decisions, the focus of this study.

communicator has a striking impact on persuasion" (Klucharev, Smidts, and Fernández 2008, 361). Similarly, Coppock, Ekins, and Kirby (2018, 82) found that op-eds, which are normally written by experts on particular topics, generate "statistically significant average treatment effects ... between 0.30 and 0.50 standard deviations on policy attitudes."

Based on these observations, we included a second experiment in this study, in which we assess the impact of expert opinion. If it does influence public preferences, we should find that support for the Supreme Court increases when a decision is supported by expert opinion. Accordingly, we expect the following:

H3: Support for the Supreme Court of Canada determining the laws of Canada will increase when citizens are informed that an expert has praised a decision by the court.

Perhaps unsurprisingly, the effects of experts on public opinion are not always uniform (Nadeau et al. 1999). Jennifer Jerit (2009, 454) found that political knowledge varies "across people with varying socioeconomic status. Expert commentary reinforces these differences and makes the distribution of knowledge more unequal." As well, the effectiveness of expert influence depends on the extent to which experts agree or disagree on a particular issue. In their study of public support for Europe, Gabel and Scheve (2007, 1023) found that citizens were more supportive of Europe only "when the informational environment is characterized by consistent elite messages favoring the process of integration." Similarly, Darmofal (2005, 381) found that citizens are more likely to disagree with expert opinion when "political elites they favor challenge this opinion." These effects, which are similar to the effects of confirmation bias, are magnified especially among individuals with low levels of political knowledge and certain life experiences and political beliefs (391–2). Given these findings, our final hypothesis tests for a potential conditional effect of political sophistication (a combined measure of political knowledge and interest):

H4: Support for the Supreme Court of Canada determining the laws of Canada will increase more for citizens with lower levels of political sophistication, relative to their more sophisticated counterparts, when they are informed that an expert has praised a decision by the court.

Methodology

To assess public support for Parliament and the Supreme Court, we used a web-based study that randomly assigned the participants to

Table 8.1. Public support for the PoC and SCC treatments

Treatment	Outcome	N
1	PoC control	737
2	SCC control	803
3	SCC overturns Parliament – Support for SCC	770
4	PoC overturns SCC – Support for PoC	726
5	SCC overturns Parliament and expert disagrees with decision – Support for SCC	727
6	PoC overturns SCC and expert disagrees with decision – Support for PoC	727
7	SCC overturns PoC and expert agrees with decision – Support for SCC	744
8	PoC overturns SCC and expert agrees with decision – Support for PoC	697
Total		5,931

one of six experimental treatments or one of two control groups (see table 8.1; see chapter 1 for additional sample information and study dates). The two controls asked the respondents, "Please indicate the extent to which you agree or disagree that the [Parliament or Supreme Court of Canada] should determine the laws of Canada." From these controls, we established a base measure of support for each institution and compared it against that reported following six possible manipulations, which asked the same question, preceded by one of the following statements: "In a recent decision, the [Parliament or Supreme Court of Canada] overruled legislation passed by the [Supreme Court of Canada or Parliament]" or "In a recent decision, the [Supreme Court of Canada or Parliament] overruled legislation passed by the [Parliament or Supreme Court of Canada]. According to a distinguished expert in the field of Canadian law and politics, this decision is [excellent or terrible] and should be [supported or opposed] by everyone in Canada." In sum, the manipulations allowed us to assess how the level of support for each institution changed when we primed the respondents to consider one overturning a decision of the other (hypothesis 2) as well as the influence that public commentators had on public opinion (hypothesis 3 and hypothesis 4).[2]

---

[2] See chap. 1 for further discussion of the strength of experimental designs to isolate causal relationships. For brevity, the Results section uses the abbreviations PoC and SCC.

Results

Our sample for this experiment consisted of 5,931 respondents, with the number in each condition reported in table 8.1.[3] To test for random assignment to groups, we use a multinomial logistic regression in which treatment is set as the dependent variable. We assess this as a function of socio-demographic characteristics, satisfaction with the way democracy works in Canada, political interest, political knowledge (a scale based on the participants' responses to five factual, political-knowledge questions), political ideology, and PID (strong or very strong partisans) as well as a careless-response question embedded in the survey. Our likelihood ratio statistic (χ^2 statistic, 104.43; $p = 0.83$) indicates that assignment to group is independent of the respondents' characteristics (see appendix 8.2). As such, we are confident that the groups do not vary systematically.

Our first hypothesis states that Canadians will be more supportive of the SCC determining the laws of Canada relative to the PoC. To test this hypothesis, we generate a dichotomous measure of support (agree or strongly agree = 1) for all conditions. We then use a logistic regression specification to model support as a function of treatment. For the first hypothesis, we are interested in comparing the two control groups to assess the difference in support for the SCC determining the laws of Canada relative to the PoC. If our assumption is correct, we should find a stronger level of support for the SCC. The results are reported in figure 8.1.[4]

While the difference is not overly large (4 percentage points), it is statistically significant ($p < 0.10$); it appears that the public is more likely to agree that the SCC should determine Canadian laws relative to the PoC.[5] Thus, we find support for our first hypothesis.

Do the results hold after we prime consideration of the two institutions in conflict? To answer this question, we compare the difference

---

3 See appendix 8.1 for summary statistics for each condition.
4 Full results for figures 8.1 to 8.4 are reported in appendix 8.3. See chap. 1 for an overview of how to read the results reported in the tables and graphs.
5 We also used a nearest-neighbour matching technique, which allowed us to isolate treatment effects by comparing the level of agreement between matched individuals in the two control treatments. We matched on socio-demographic characteristics including age, sex, education, region, and income. The results hold, indicating a 5-percentage-point difference ($p < 0.10$) after accounting for socio-demographic factors. Results not reported.

176   Winning and Keeping Power in Canadian Politics

Figure 8.1. Support for the SCC determining Canadian laws relative to the PoC

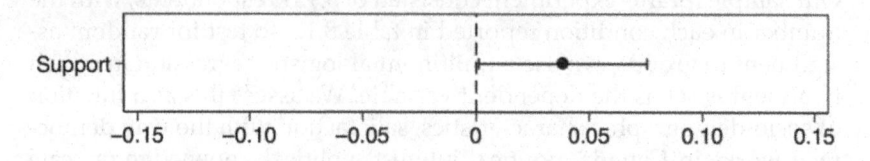

Figure 8.2. Support for the SCC determining Canadian laws relative to the PoC when one institution overrules a decision by the other

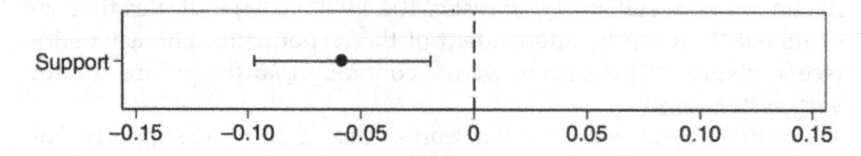

in level of agreement for each institution's responsibility for determining Canadian laws after one institution overrules a decision of the other. We once again model support as a dichotomous measure (agree or strongly agree that the SCC or PoC should determine Canadian laws = 1), comparing the level of support for each institution when the other challenges its authority to determine Canadian laws. The results are reported in figure 8.2.

While Canadians may generally feel more supportive of the SCC than the PoC when it comes to determining legislation (see figure 8.1), it appears that this support waivers when the SCC challenges the authority of the PoC to set laws relative to the support the PoC receives when it challenges the SCC's legislative authority (see figure 8.2). The results indicate that the PoC receives relatively higher levels of support (6 percentage points; $p < 0.05$) when it overrules the SCC compared with the SCC overruling the PoC. Contrary to our second hypothesis, citizens are *not* more supportive of the SCC determining the laws of Canada relative to the PoC when primed to consider the two institutions in conflict with each other. This finding suggests that the basis of public support for the SCC may be rooted less in normative commitment and more in perceptions of legal fact. We can further dissect this finding by comparing the level of agreement that each institution should determine legislation by comparing the change in support for each institution separately, with and without the stimulus. The results are reported in figures 8.3 and 8.4.

Figure 8.3. Change in PoC support when it overrules the SCC

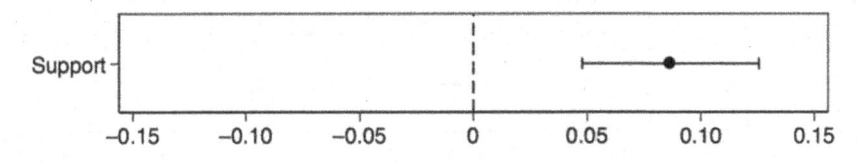

Figure 8.4. Change in SCC support when it overrules the PoC

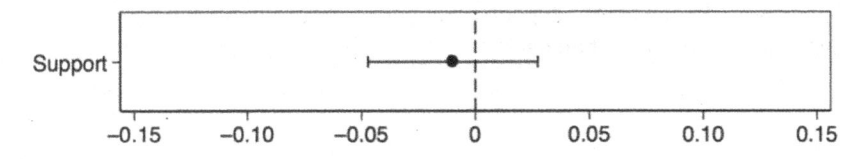

Figure 8.5. Change in SCC support after an expert says that the SCC overruling the PoC is a bad decision

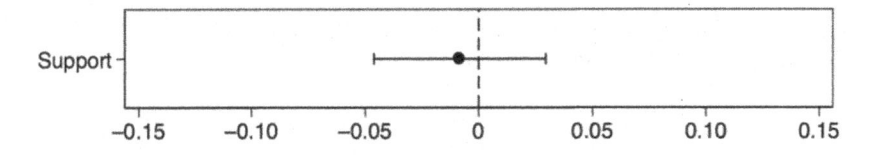

The results from these additional tests are revealing. While the PoC overruling the SCC yields a 9-percentage-point ($p < 0.001$) increase in agreement that the PoC should determine the laws of Canada relative to the level of PoC support in the control (see figure 8.3), the SCC treatment shows no effect (see figure 8.4). Based on these results, it would appear that while the overall level of support for the SCC determining Canadian laws is higher than that of the PoC in general (figure 8.1), this relationship is reversed when the SCC attempts to assert authority over the PoC's right to set legislation (figure 8.2). Furthermore, unlike the PoC, the SCC does not receive any boost in support when it challenges the other institution's legislative authority (figure 8.4). These results run contrary to our second hypothesis.

Are these findings robust to expert cues? Our final set of hypotheses (and the second experiment reported in this chapter) considers how public support changes when presented with expert opinion. To test the impact of expert cues, we compare the level of agreement with the statement that the SCC should determine Canadian laws after the SCC overrules PoC legislation against an identical scenario in which an expert indicates that this outcome was a bad decision (figure 8.5) or a

Figure 8.6. Change in SCC support after an expert says that the SCC overruling the PoC is a good decision

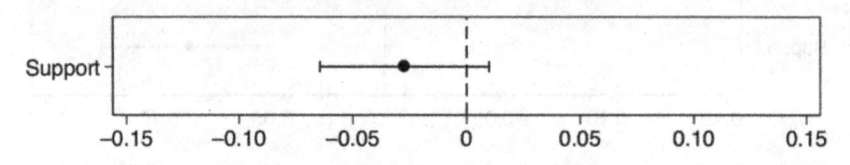

Figure 8.7. Change in PoC support after an expert says that the PoC overruling the SCC is a bad decision

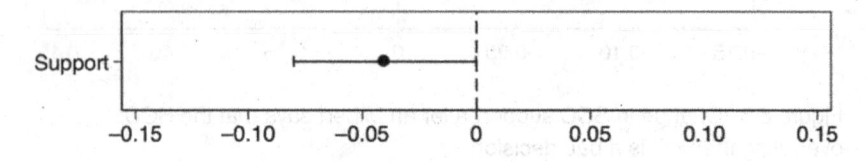

Figure 8.8. Change in PoC support after an expert says that the PoC overruling the SCC is a good decision

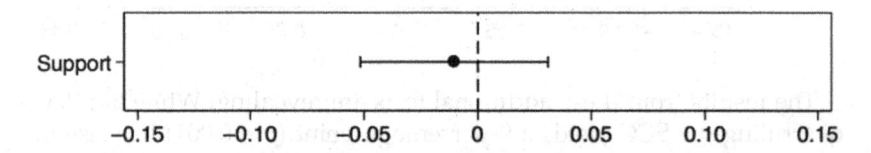

good decision (figure 8.6). We then compare the same treatments for the PoC (figure 8.7 and figure 8.8, respectively).[6]

What impact does expert opinion have on public opinion? Not much. In only one instance (when the expert states that the PoC overruling the SCC was a bad decision) do we find a significant change in opinion given an expert cue (see figure 8.7). In the other three treatments, the impact is negligible. Contrary to our expectations, expert cues, regardless of their tone, have only limited influence on public opinion, at least when it comes to support for the PoC or SCC determining Canadian legislation.

As a final consideration, we reassess the expert-cueing models to test the potential conditional effect of political sophistication (a combination of political interest and political knowledge). As noted above

---

6 Full results for figures 8.5 to 8.8 are reported in appendix 8.4.

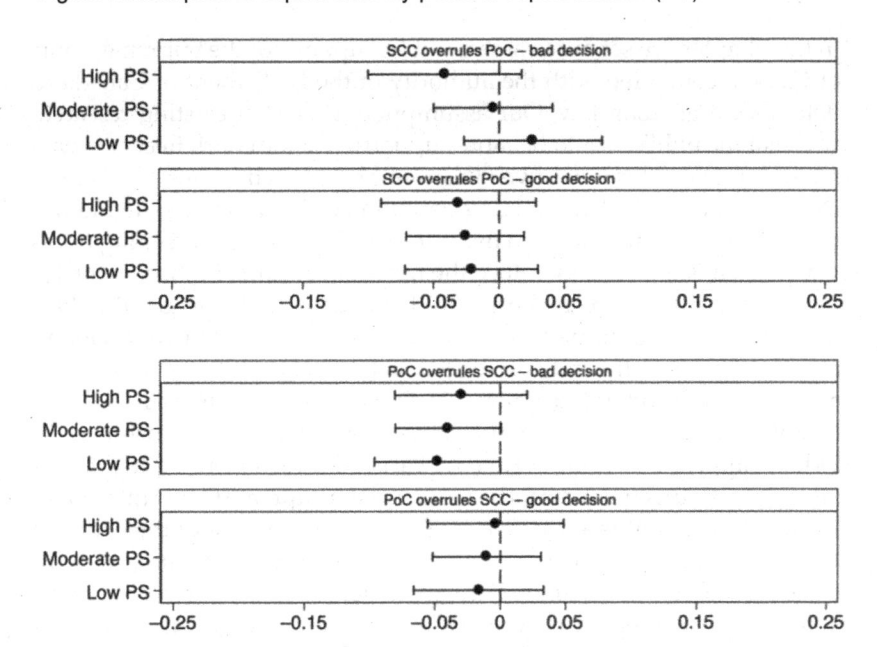

Figure 8.9. Impact of expert cues by political sophistication (PS)

(hypothesis 4), it may be that those with lower levels of political sophistication are more susceptible to expert opinions compared with their more politically sophisticated counterparts. We present the results graphically (see figure 8.9), with political sophistication estimated at the 25th, 50th, and 75th percentiles (low, moderate, and high sophistication).[7]

It appears that level of political sophistication has a very limited impact on susceptibility to expert cues. The single exception is the case of an expert disagreeing with the SCC's decision to overrule the PoC. In this case, we find that low sophisticates are significantly different ($p < 0.05$) from their high-sophisticate counterparts. However, neither group differs significantly from the treatment absent the expert cues. Overall, the conclusion drawn before testing for conditional effects holds: expert cues appear to have little impact on public support for the SCC or the PoC determining Canadian laws, with the possible exception of when an expert states that the PoC overruling the SCC was a bad decision.

---

7 Full results for figure 8.9 are reported in appendix 8.5.

Discussion and Conclusion

In this chapter, we set out to assess public support for the Supreme Court of Canada compared with the authority of the Parliament of Canada to determine Canadian law. Our assumption, based on existing research, was that the public would be more supportive of the court. Recent events seem to support this idea, given the public backlash that Ontario Premier Doug Ford provoked when he declared in 2018 that he intended to use the notwithstanding clause to overturn a judicial decision relating to his government's decision to reduce the number of wards in the City of Toronto during the municipal election (De Luca 2018; Weinrib 2018). Our research results confirmed this assumption, at least when we excluded any cues to prime the individuals to consider one institution overruling a decision of the other (see figure 8.1). Based on the results from the latter conditions, however, we found a somewhat different relationship: individuals appear more supportive of Parliament determining legislation after learning that it has recently overruled the Supreme Court than when the prime is absent (see figure 8.3). The same is not true of the court. In fact, the negative coefficient, albeit non-significant (see figure 8.4), indicates that the court overruling Parliament decreases support for the court.

In regard to keeping power in Canadian politics, governments that wish to protect themselves against politically difficult policy decisions (e.g., same-sex marriage) may find it useful to shift such responsibility to the Supreme Court. On the other hand, support for Parliament's right to determine legislation is highest when the court overrules laws enacted by Parliament. Taken together, these findings suggest that governments may be able to use the court strategically to "have their cake and eat it too."

Our findings also suggest that expert opinion has little effect on public support for the Supreme Court and Parliament even when we consider the level of political sophistication among the respondents. However, we must be cautious not to overstate these findings. It may be that the issue, which is the right to determine (or more specifically, overrule) Canadian laws, is not as susceptible to expert cues as other issues. It may also be that our "distinguished expert in the field of Canadian law and politics" does not resonate with the general public. Future research might consider varying the "expert" credentials, along with the issue, to test for such differences. Additional studies that consider experts versus other types of public figures (e.g., celebrities) may also help advance our understanding of the influence that such cues may have on public opinion.

In short, the implications in this chapter for winning and keeping power are clear. Our findings suggest that political elites can use the Supreme Court to strategically implement their policy preferences and insulate themselves, at least somewhat, from any public fallout. Indeed, this strategy is exactly what then prime minister Jean Chrétien did when he used reference power on the issue of same-sex marriage (Puddister 2019, 574). Should the court not implement its desired outcome, Parliament can then overrule the judicial decision by making use of the various tools that are available to it. Section 33, for instance, allows the government to circumvent certain judicial decisions for a renewable five-year period. Alternatively, Parliament might respond to judicial decisions using what Dennis Baker (2010, 19) refers to as "minority retort," which involves implementing the decision of the minority opinion of the court, or "textual retort," which involves passing new legislation or amending existing ones that simply restate "the constitutional provision to defeat the judicial addition" (24).

Historically speaking, at least since 1982, Canadian governments have been reluctant to use any of these remedies, perhaps due to fears about the political fallout that might occur given the popularity of the Supreme Court. Our study, however, suggests that such fears may be unwarranted. Government officials and political strategists might draw upon our findings to convince policymakers and politicians to make greater use of these mechanisms to implement their policy preferences, especially when the normal parliamentary process may seem uncertain or dangerous from a public relations perspective.

REFERENCES

Ajzenstat, Janet. 2007. *The Canadian Founding: John Locke and Parliament.* Montreal and Kingston: McGill-Queen's University Press.

Angus Reid Institute. 2015. "Canadians Have a More Favourable View of Their Supreme Court Than Americans Have of Their Own." 17 August 2015. http://angusreid.org/supreme-court/.

Baker, Dennis. 2010. *Not Quite Supreme: The Courts and Coordinate Constitutional Interpretation.* Montreal and Kingston: McGill-Queen's University Press.

Bullock, John G. 2009. "Partisan Bias and the Bayesian Ideal in the Study of Public Opinion." *Journal of Politics* 71 (3): 1109–24. https://doi.org/10.1017/S0022381609090914.

Coppock, Alexander, Emily Ekins, and David Kirby. 2018. "The Long-Lasting Effects of Newspaper Op-eds on Public Opinion." *Quarterly Journal of Political Science* 13 (1): 59–87. https://doi.org/10.1561/100.00016112.

Darmofal, David. 2005. "Elite Cues and Citizen Disagreement with Expert Opinion." *Political Research Quarterly* 58 (3): 381–95. https://doi.org/10.1177/106591290505800302.

De Luca, Rob. 2018. "The Notwithstanding Clause: A Dangerous Precedent Has Been Set." *Toronto Star*, 19 September 2018. https://www.thestar

.com/opinion/contributors/2018/09/19/the-notwithstanding-clause-a
-dangerous-precedent-has-been-set.html.
Epp, Charles. 1998. *The Rights Revolution: Lawyers, Activists, and Supreme Courts in Comparative Perspective.* Chicago: University of Chicago Press.
Fletcher, Joseph, and Paul Howe. 2001. "Public Opinion and Canada's Courts." In *Judicial Power and Canadian Democracy*, edited by Paul Howe and Peter Russell, 255–96. Montreal and Kingston: McGill-Queen's University Press.
Gabel, Matthew, and Kenneth Scheve. 2007. "Estimating the Effect of Elite Communications on Public Opinion Using Instrumental Variables." *American Journal of Political Science* 51 (4): 1013–28. https://doi.org/10.1111/j.1540-5907.2007.00294.x.
Goodyear-Grant, Elizabeth, J. Scott Matthews, and Janet Hiebert. 2013. "The Courts/Parliament Trade-Off: Canadian Attitudes on Judicial Influence in Public Policy." *Commonwealth & Comparative Politics* 51 (3): 377–97. https://doi.org/10.1080/14662043.2013.805540.
Hausegger, Lori, and Troy Riddell. 2004. "The Changing Nature of Public Support for the Supreme Court of Canada." *Canadian Journal of Political Science* 37 (1): 23–50. https://doi.org/10.1017/S000842390404003X.
Hirschl, Ran. 2000. "The Political Origins of Judicial Empowerment through Constitutionalization: Lessons from Four Constitutional Revolutions." *Law & Social Inquiry* 25 (1): 91–149. https://doi.org/10.1111/j.1747-4469.2000.tb00152.x.
Hogg, Peter W., and Allison A. Bushell. 1997. "The Charter Dialogue between Courts and Legislatures (or Perhaps the Charter of Rights Isn't Such a Bad Thing after All." *Osgoode Hall Law Journal* 35 (1): 75–124. https://digitalcommons.osgoode.yorku.ca/ohlj/vol35/iss1/2/.
Howe, Paul, and Peter Russell, eds. 2001. *Judicial Power and Canadian Democracy.* Montreal and Kingston: McGill-Queen's University Press.
Jerit, Jennifer. 2009. "Understanding the Knowledge Gap: The Role of Experts and Journalists." *Journal of Politics* 71 (2): 442–56. https://doi.org/10.1017/S0022381609090380.
Johansen, David, and Philip Rosen. 2008. "The Notwithstanding Clause of the Charter." Publication no. BP-194-E. Ottawa: Parliamentary Information and Research Service, Library of Parliament, 16 October. https://firstamendmentlawyers.org/wp-content/uploads/2019/07/2014_2_0304materials.pdf.
Klucharev, Vasily, Ale Smidts, and Guillén Fernández. 2008. "Brain Mechanisms of Persuasion: How 'Expert Power' Modulates Memory and Attitudes." *Social Cognitive and Affective Neuroscience* 3 (4): 353–66. https://doi.org/10.1093/scan/nsn022.
Leeson, Howard. 2001. "Section 33, the Notwithstanding Clause: A Paper Tiger?" In *Judicial Power and Canadian Democracy*, edited by Paul Howe and Peter Russell, 297–327. Montreal and Kingston: McGill-Queen's University Press.

MacCharles, Tonda. 2013. "Stephen Harper Wants Supreme Court's Opinion on Senate Reform." *Toronto Star*, 1 February 2013. https://www.thestar.com/news/canada/2013/02/01/stephen_harper_wants_supreme_courts_opinion_on_senate_reform.html.

Manfredi, Christopher P. 2003. "Same-Sex Marriage and the Notwithstanding Clause." *Policy Options*. 1 October. http://policyoptions.irpp.org/magazines/who-decides-the-courts-or-parliament/same-sex-marriage-and-the-notwithstanding-clause/.

Morton, F.L., and Rainer Knopff. 2000. *The Charter Revolution and the Court Party*. Peterborough: Broadview Press.

Nadeau, Richard, Richard G. Niemi, David P. Fan, and Timothy Amato. 1999. "Elite Economic Forecasts, Economic News, Mass Economic Judgments, and Presidential Approval." *Journal of Politics* 61 (1): 109–35. https://doi.org/10.2307/2647777.

Page, Benjamin, Robert Shapiro, and Glenn Dempsey. 1987. "What Moves Public Opinion?" *American Political Science Review* 81 (1): 23–43. https://doi.org/10.2307/1960777.

Puddister, Kate. 2019. "The Canadian Reference Power: Delegation to the Courts and the Navigation of Federalism." *Publius: Journal of Federalism* 49 (4): 561–86. https://doi.org/10.1093/publius/pjy034.

Radmilovic, Vuk. 2010. "Strategic Legitimacy Cultivation at the Supreme Court of Canada: Quebec *Secession Reference* and Beyond." *Canadian Journal of Political Science* 43 (4): 843–69. https://doi.org/10.1017/S0008423910000764.

Russell, Peter. 2004. *Constitutional Odyssey*. Toronto: University of Toronto Press.

– 2007. "The Notwithstanding Clause: The Charter's Homage to Parliamentary Democracy." *Policy Options*. 1 February. http://policyoptions.irpp.org/fr/magazines/the-charter-25/the-notwithstanding-clause-the-charters-homage-to-parliamentary-democracy/.

Scotti, Monique. 2017. "Bill 62: Could Ottawa Really Do Anything about Quebec's Face-Veil Ban?" *Global News*, 19 October 2017. https://globalnews.ca/news/3813986/bill-62-quebec-trudeau-intervene/.

Smith, David E. 2007. *The People's House of Commons: Theories of Democracy in Contention*. Toronto: University of Toronto Press.

Sniderman, Paul, Joseph Fletcher, Peter Russell, and Phillip Tetlock. 1996. *The Clash of Rights: Liberty, Equality and Legitimacy in a Pluralist Democracy*. New Haven, CT: Yale University Press.

Weinrib, Lorraine. 2018. "Doug Ford Can't Apply the Notwithstanding Clause Retroactively to Impede Democracy." *Globe and Mail*, 18 September 2018. https://www.theglobeandmail.com/opinion/article-doug-ford-cant-apply-the-notwithstanding-clause-retroactively-to/.

Appendix 8.1. Summary statistics

	Treatment 1	Treatment 2	Treatment 3	Treatment 4	Treatment 5	Treatment 6	Treatment 7	Treatment 8
Age	45.90 (16.84)	46.16 (16.73)	44.85 (16.78)	45.77 (17.35)	45.71 (16.32)	45.32 (16.74)	45.93 (16.25)	45.82 (16.46)
Female	0.49 (0.50)	0.50 (0.50)	0.52 (0.50)	0.50 (0.50)	0.53 (0.50)	0.53 (0.50)	0.51 (0.50)	0.50 (0.50)
No high school	0.05 (0.21)	0.05 (0.21)	0.04 (0.19)	0.05 (0.22)	0.04 (0.21)	0.05 (0.22)	0.04 (0.20)	0.06 (0.24)
University graduate	0.35 (0.48)	0.34 (0.47)	0.37 (0.48)	0.32 (0.47)	0.33 (0.47)	0.36 (0.48)	0.36 (0.48)	0.33 (0.47)
Income	3.72 (1.77)	3.69 (1.88)	3.71 (1.81)	3.74 (1.80)	3.65 (1.81)	3.75 (1.86)	3.71 (1.81)	3.58 (1.79)
Prairies	0.26 (0.44)	0.26 (0.44)	0.25 (0.43)	0.28 (0.45)	0.24 (0.43)	0.24 (0.43)	0.23 (0.42)	0.26 (0.44)
Ontario	0.50 (0.50)	0.51 (0.50)	0.48 (0.50)	0.51 (0.50)	0.54 (0.50)	0.52 (0.50)	0.51 (0.50)	0.52 (0.50)
Atlantic	0.09 (0.29)	0.12 (0.32)	0.12 (0.32)	0.10 (0.30)	0.09 (0.29)	0.12 (0.33)	0.11 (0.31)	0.10 (0.30)
Satisfaction	0.77 (0.42)	0.80 (0.40)	0.77 (0.42)	0.81 (0.39)	0.76 (0.42)	0.81 (0.39)	0.80 (0.40)	0.78 (0.42)
Political interest	6.20 (2.46)	6.05 (2.63)	6.04 (2.61)	6.17 (2.54)	6.14 (2.63)	6.04 (2.61)	6.06 (2.66)	6.02 (2.65)
Political knowledge	0.53 (0.31)	0.53 (0.31)	0.53 (0.31)	0.55 (0.30)	0.53 (0.32)	0.54 (0.32)	0.51 (0.30)	0.53 (0.30)
Political ideology	5.07 (2.15)	5.12 (2.24)	4.92 (2.25)	5.00 (2.26)	5.01 (2.18)	5.02 (2.16)	5.07 (2.11)	5.09 (2.12)
CPC PID	0.23 (0.42)	0.19 (0.39)	0.20 (0.40)	0.19 (0.39)	0.20 (0.40)	0.20 (0.40)	0.19 (0.39)	0.20 (0.40)
GRN PID	0.04 (0.19)	0.04 (0.20)	0.03 (0.17)	0.04 (0.20)	0.02 (0.15)	0.04 (0.18)	0.04 (0.19)	0.03 (0.17)
LIB PID	0.23 (0.42)	0.24 (0.43)	0.23 (0.42)	0.22 (0.42)	0.24 (0.42)	0.23 (0.42)	0.24 (0.43)	0.21 (0.41)
NDP PID	0.09 (0.29)	0.09 (0.29)	0.10 (0.29)	0.09 (0.29)	0.09 (0.29)	0.08 (0.27)	0.08 (0.26)	0.10 (0.31)
Response check	0.91 (0.29)	0.91 (0.28)	0.90 (0.30)	0.90 (0.30)	0.93 (0.26)	0.90 (0.30)	0.90 (0.30)	0.90 (0.30)
N	737	803	770	726	727	727	744	697

Note: The cells report averages, with standard deviations in parentheses. Age is the respondents' age in years. Female, no high school, university graduate, regional variables, PID, and response check are dichotomous measures, coded "1" in correspondence with the variable name. Political interest and political ideology are self-reported positions on an eleven-point scale running from "No interest" to "Great deal of interest" and "Left–Right," respectively. Political knowledge is an index (alpha = 0.61) based on five factual questions: the name of the British prime minister, the level of government that has primary responsibility for education and health care in Canada, the name of the federal finance minister, the name of the governor general, and the number of seats in the House of Commons. The respondents received one point for each correct response. The variable was then rescaled to fit between 0 and 1. N = number of usable cases in each treatment.

Appendix 8.2. Multinomial logistic regression results for test of random assignment to treatments

	Treatment 2	Treatment 3	Treatment 4	Treatment 5	Treatment 6	Treatment 7	Treatment 8
Age	0.00 (0.00)	−0.00 (0.00)	0.00 (0.00)	0.00 (0.00)	0.00 (0.00)	0.00 (0.00)	−0.00 (0.00)
Female	0.02 (0.12)	0.16 (0.12)	0.07 (0.12)	0.14 (0.12)	0.14 (0.12)	0.03 (0.12)	0.08 (0.12)
No high school	0.11 (0.31)	−0.04 (0.32)	0.29 (0.31)	0.12 (0.32)	0.35 (0.31)	0.09 (0.32)	0.43 (0.30)
University graduate	−0.02 (0.13)	0.12 (0.13)	−0.21 (0.13)	−0.07 (0.13)	0.07 (0.13)	0.13 (0.13)	−0.03 (0.14)
Income	−0.01 (0.03)	−0.01 (0.03)	0.00 (0.03)	−0.02 (0.03)	0.02 (0.03)	−0.01 (0.03)	−0.05 (0.04)
Prairies	0.20 (0.20)	−0.16 (0.19)	0.24 (0.21)	−0.06 (0.20)	−0.09 (0.20)	−0.20 (0.20)	0.05 (0.21)
Ontario	0.27 (0.19)	−0.15 (0.18)	0.28 (0.19)	0.14 (0.18)	0.13 (0.18)	−0.01 (0.18)	0.14 (0.19)
Atlantic	0.52 (0.25)*	0.17 (0.24)	0.30 (0.26)	0.07 (0.26)	0.30 (0.25)	0.12 (0.25)	0.15 (0.26)
Satisfaction	0.09 (0.15)	−0.04 (0.15)	0.23 (0.16)	−0.08 (0.15)	0.17 (0.16)	0.09 (0.15)	0.05 (0.15)
Political interest	−0.03 (0.03)	−0.04 (0.03)	−0.00 (0.03)	0.01 (0.03)	−0.03 (0.03)	−0.02 (0.03)	−0.04 (0.03)
Political knowledge	0.05 (0.20)	0.10 (0.20)	0.23 (0.21)	−0.05 (0.21)	0.11 (0.21)	−0.26 (0.20)	0.21 (0.21)
Political ideology	0.05 (0.03)	−0.01 (0.03)	0.03 (0.03)	0.00 (0.03)	0.01 (0.03)	0.02 (0.03)	0.03 (0.03)
CPC PID	−0.25 (0.17)	−0.01 (0.17)	−0.37 (0.18)*	−0.26 (0.17)	−0.20 (0.17)	−0.27 (0.17)	−0.09 (0.17)
GRN PID	0.59 (0.32)[a]	0.10 (0.35)	0.23 (0.34)	−0.41 (0.40)	0.20 (0.35)	0.20 (0.34)	−0.04 (0.37)
LIB PID	0.04 (0.16)	−0.06 (0.16)	−0.22 (0.16)	−0.05 (0.16)	−0.08 (0.16)	−0.07 (0.16)	−0.09 (0.16)
NDP PID	0.12 (0.22)	0.09 (0.22)	−0.05 (0.22)	−0.03 (0.22)	−0.16 (0.23)	−0.20 (0.23)	0.21 (0.22)
Response check	0.05 (0.21)	−0.04 (0.21)	−0.20 (0.20)	0.25 (0.22)	−0.17 (0.20)	−0.07 (0.20)	−0.14 (0.21)
Constant	−0.47 (0.40)	0.50 (0.40)	−0.36 (0.41)	−0.12 (0.41)	−0.11 (0.41)	0.21 (0.40)	0.12 (0.41)

N = 4,709
χ^2 (df = 119) = 104.43
Pseudo R^2 = 0.01

Note: The cells report multinomial logistic regression coefficients, with standard errors in parentheses. Treatment 1 is set as the base outcome. Age is the respondents' age in years. Female, no high school, university graduate, regional variables, PID, and response check are dichotomous measures, coded "1" in correspondence with the variable name. Political interest and political ideology are self-reported positions on an eleven-point scale running from "No interest" to "Great deal of interest" and "Left–Right," respectively. Political knowledge is an index (alpha = 0.61) based on five factual questions: the name of the British prime minister, the level of government that has primary responsibility for education and health care in Canada, the name of the federal finance minister, the name of the governor general, and the number of seats in the House of Commons. The respondents received one point for each correct response. The variable was then rescaled to fit between 0 and 1. N = number of cases with full response set.
*** $p < 0.001$; ** $p < 0.01$; * $p < 0.05$; [a] $p < 0.10$.

Appendix 8.3. Full results for figures 8.1 to 8.4

	Figure 8.1	Figure 8.2	Figure 8.3	Figure 8.4
SCC support	0.21 (0.12)[a] [0.04]			
SCC support when SCC overrules PoC		−1.29 (0.12)* [−0.06]		
PoC support vs. PoC support when PoC overrules SCC			0.45 (0.12)*** [0.09]	
SCC support vs. SCC support when SCC overrules PoC				−0.05 (0.12) [−0.01]
Constant	−1.25 (0.09)***	−0.80 (0.08)***	−1.25 (0.09)***	−1.04 (0.08)***
Pseudo R^2	0.00	0.00	0.01	0.00
N	1,442	1,141	1,372	1,484

Note: The cells report logistic regression coefficients, with standard errors in parentheses and marginal effects/discrete changes reported in square brackets.
***$p < 0.001$; **$p < 0.01$; *$p < 0.05$; [a]$p < 0.10$.

Appendix 8.4. Full results for figures 8.5 to 8.8

	Figure 8.5	Figure 8.6	Figure 8.7	Figure 8.8
SCC support – expert says SCC overruling PoC a bad decision	−0.05 (0.12) [−0.01]			
SCC support – expert says SCC overruling PoC a good decision		−0.15 (0.12) [−0.03]		
PoC support – expert says PoC overruling SCC a bad decision			−0.20 (0.12)[a] [−0.04]	
PoC support – expert says PoC overruling SCC a good decision				−0.05 (0.12) [−0.01]
Constant	−1.09 (0.09)***	−1.09 (0.09)***	−0.80 (0.08)***	−0.80 (0.08)***
Pseudo R^2	0.00	0.00	0.00	0.00
N	1,409	1,422	1,376	1,347

Note: The cells report logistic regression coefficients, with standard errors in parentheses and marginal effects/discrete changes reported in square brackets.
***$p < 0.001$; **$p < 0.01$; *$p < 0.05$; [a]$p < 0.10$.

Appendix 8.5. Full results for figure 8.9

	Support SCC	Support PoC
SCC support – expert says SCC overruling PoC a bad decision	−0.01 (0.13)	-
SCC support – expert says SCC overruling PoC a good decision	−0.14 (0.13)	-
PoC support – expert says PoC overruling SCC a bad decision	-	−0.20 (0.12)
PoC support – expert says PoC overruling SCC a good decision	-	−0.05 (0.12)
Political sophistication	0.49 (0.11)***	0.18 (0.10)[a]
Political sophistication × SCC support – expert says SCC overruling PoC a bad decision	−0.31 (0.16)*	-
Political sophistication × SCC support – expert says SCC overruling PoC a good decision	−0.01 (0.16)	-
Political sophistication × PoC support – expert says PoC overruling SCC a bad decision	-	0.10 (0.16)
Political sophistication × PoC support – expert says PoC overruling SCC a good decision	-	0.06 (0.15)
Constant	−1.13 (0.09)***	−0.81 (0.08)***
Pseudo R^2	0.02	0.01
N	2,100	2,036

Note: The cells report logistic regression coefficients, with standard errors in parentheses.
***$p < 0.001$; **$p < 0.01$; *$p < 0.05$; [a]$p < 0.10$.

Chapter Nine

Framing Public Budgeting

Infrastructure spending [promised in 2015] is shaping up to be the Liberals' biggest single policy response to the dramatic changes in the Canadian economy. (*Globe and Mail* 2016)

Tuesday's [2018 federal] budget nonetheless amounts to a swap – dollars for roads and transit [infrastructure] delayed in favor of new departmental spending. (Wingrove 2018)

Creating a [health care] premium, as opposed to hiking PST or income tax, is all about the packaging, he said. ... "This is about a spoonful of sugar making the pill go down. That's really what this is. It's selling it to the electorate in a way that makes it as easy as possible." (Colin Busby of the C.D. Howe Institute, quoted in Geary 2017)

Modern democratic governments cannot govern without revenue. Building and maintaining infrastructure, delivering programs and services, and enforcing the rule of law require money. The government's main method for raising that money is to impose one or more revenue-collection tools on society, such as an income tax, a sales tax, a premium or special tax, a user fee, and a property tax, among others. While revenue collection is the primary objective for most taxes, sometimes they are used as a public policy tool to nudge or incentivize citizens to behave in certain ways. In 2017, for instance, a Health Canada report surfaced, urging the federal government to massively hike tobacco-tax rates because research had shown that doing so was an effective way to reduce long-term-smoking rates (Beeby 2017).

Generally speaking, most Canadians realize that modern governments cannot function or deliver programs and services without the revenues collected through the taxes they impose. At the same time, however, Canadians do not like taxes, and they especially do not like tax increases or the imposition of new taxes. This situation puts policymakers and political leaders in a tough situation. To win elections, politicians must promise new or increased spending on various salient issues, but they must do so without raising or imposing new taxes; sometimes they are expected to lower or even eliminate them. Once in office, whether it be as a result of changing economic conditions, inaccurate forecasting of costs and revenues, or some other reason, governments must sometimes impose new taxes, raise existing ones, or impose spending cuts and reallocations, much like what occurred with respect to Justin Trudeau's promise to invest in infrastructure. The trick for governments in these situations is to find a way to deliver on their commitments, using existing or new public-budgeting tools, but in a way that does not drastically erode public support.

When it comes to citizens' preferences about public budgeting, the relationship between them is not well understood. A variety of studies have found that voters are generally uninformed (Bartels 2005) and ignorant about tax and spending policies or have unrealistic expectations about what governments can accomplish (Edlund 2003, 148; Hansen 1998, 513; Winter and Mouritzen 2001, 110). Others have found confirmatory or contradictory evidence about why citizens pay or evade taxes or why they support or oppose varying tax and funding increases and reductions (Edlund and Seva 2013; MacManus 1995; Steel and Lovrich 1998). Surprisingly, the literature on the relationship between mass opinion and the selection of different public budgeting tools and mechanisms (e.g., funding and spending decisions) is relatively modest. Although some scholars have looked at this topic by examining public opinion against a limited selection of taxes imposed by different levels of governments (e.g., state versus federal income taxes or property taxes versus state sales taxes), few have investigated citizens' preferences as they relate to a broad and *concurrent* range of tax and funding options at *one* government level (Beck and Dye 1982; Bowler and Donovan 1995). This is especially true in Canada, where our search of the literature found no studies of Canadian public opinion on these issues.

In this chapter, we investigate public support for different public budgeting mechanisms by examining the extent to which public opinion varies as it relates to the use of the following five public-budgeting tools to invest in public infrastructure: an increased sales tax, a new user fee, a new infrastructure premium or special infrastructure tax attached to income taxes, a general increase in income taxes, and the reallocation of existing funds earmarked for existing programs and services. We present these tools in two ways: one with actual amounts (e.g., a 1% increase or transfer) and one without them. To investigate their effects on Canadian public opinion, we draw on data collected from an online experiment, which we embedded in a national survey that was distributed to a representative sample of Canadians. In the pages that follow, we describe the theoretical assumptions underpinning our expectations, our research design and data, and our main findings before discussing their implications for winning and keeping power in Canada.

Background, Theory, and Expectations

The general assumption in the literature is that most citizens in advanced democratic countries are self-interested in their outlook and behaviour towards public budgeting (Beck and Dye 1982, 175; Beck, Rainey, and Traut 1990, 74–5). Most citizens prefer governments that deliver robust and effective programs and services, while at the same time minimizing the taxes that they have to pay to fund these programs and services. In short, they "believe in the free lunch; they want something for nothing" (Hansen 1998, 513; see also Edlund 2003; Steel and Lovrich 1998; Winter and Mouritzen 2001).

There is disagreement in the literature over why citizens hold these views. Some researchers believe that they are the result of political ignorance or information about how public budgeting works and how much programs and services actually cost to deliver. Others argue the opposite, that citizens are more or less fully informed and adopt these preferences because they are fundamentally self-interested. A more useful way of theorizing about these views is to assume that all citizens operate under conditions of *bounded rationality*, which manifests itself in three ways. According to Winter and Mouritzen (2001, 111–12),

> First, the capacity, opportunities, and incentives of individuals to calculate consequences is limited (limited knowledge). Second, the capacity of individuals to process various sorts of information and to calculate consequences is limited (limited cognitive abilities). Third, the value functions of individuals are not entirely clear and consistent in the sense that they rank neatly all their different goals.

Based on these assumptions, it is possible that citizens may make paradoxical demands, such as lower taxes and higher spending on government services. Indeed, this perspective is exactly what Winter and Mouritzen (2011, 119–20) found in their study of citizens living in the municipality of Odense, Denmark. These assumptions form the basis of our first hypothesis:

> H1: Citizens will be more supportive of government infrastructure spending when a funding mechanism is not outlined relative to when a funding mechanism is provided.

If citizens do operate in accordance with the characteristics of bounded rationality, then they are likely to base their choice of funding instruments on some sort of heuristic. One highly plausible heuristic, which seems to have strong empirical support in the literature, is a particular cognitive bias called *loss aversion*. According to Tversky and Kahneman (1992), people are much more sensitive to potential and actual losses than they are to gains across a variety of phenomena, so much so that individuals are likely to pursue gains only when they are at least double the amount of the losses. Otherwise, individuals will make choices that avoid losses. If we apply these insights to the question of individual opinions towards different funding instruments, we expect similar dynamics when funding mechanisms for spending are noted; citizens will assume the worst when actual costs (losses) are not provided. In formal terms, we hypothesize the following:

> H2: Citizens will prefer funding mechanisms that state the actual costs compared with those that omit the costs.

In practice, we expect individuals to prefer the redistribution of existing funds to all other options because redistribution involves no new taxes or fees to be paid to the government; in this way, there are no new losses to individual incomes or savings. Although redistribution could impact an individual's preferred government program or service and, hence, cause a significant loss to be incurred, it is equally likely, absent any specific information provided to the individual, that the transfer of funds could involve other, less preferable or relevant public goods, thus minimizing individual losses.

Following the redistribution of funds, an increase in sales tax would be the next preferable option, followed by new user fees and new special taxes. According to Bowler and Donovan (1995), individuals react negatively and strongly to the introduction of new taxes in places where such taxes never existed. They note, "In places where a tax is absent (e.g., the state individual income tax in Texas, Florida or Washington), political discussion about implementing the tax often generates conflict and information. Proposals for new taxes, moreover, cannot be disguised as easily as marginal changes in established taxes due to the political controversy involved" (84). Indeed, these dynamics were on full display when then Liberal (LIB) leader Stéphane Dion floated the idea of a national carbon tax plan in 2008 (*CBC News* 2008) and when former Alberta premier Rachel Notley implemented a carbon tax in 2017 (Graney 2017).

Given these assumptions and findings, we expect citizens to prefer an increase in sales tax because they are likely to view it as a marginal loss; new user fees and new special taxes, in comparison, are likely to be viewed as new, more significant losses. We also anticipate that citizens will prefer new user fees over new special taxes attached to a specific policy objective or field because they can exercise some control over how often they use the service and therefore have to pay the user fee. In sum, we expect citizens to prefer the redistribution of existing funds over user fees, an increased sales tax, a new special tax, and increased income taxes, in that order. More generally, this forms the basis of our third and final hypothesis:

H3: Citizens will prefer funding mechanisms that minimize personal costs.

Methodology

To test our assumptions, we randomly assigned the participants to one of ten treatment groups or a control group and asked them to indicate their level of support for infrastructure spending along a five-point scale ("strongly agree" to "strongly disagree"; see chapter 1 for additional sample information and study dates). The control provided no information on how the government would pay for the infrastructure and simply asked the participants, "Please indicate the extent to which you agree or disagree that the federal government should invest in infrastructure across Canada (e.g., roads, highways, power lines, etc.)." The treatment groups included the same question except that the participants were provided with information on how the infrastructure would be paid for. For example, "Please indicate the extent to which you agree or disagree that the federal government should *raise income taxes* to invest in infrastructure across Canada (e.g., roads, highways, power lines, etc.)."[1]

The ten treatments allow us to assess a range of funding mechanisms: five of the treatments offer the participants no indication of the

---

1 Italics added for emphasis; not included in actual experiment.

Table 9.1. Support for infrastructure spending treatments

	N
Control	411
Treatment 1: Transfer	435
Treatment 2: Transfer 1%	425
Treatment 3: User fees	437
Treatment 4: User fees approx. $500/yr.	413
Treatment 5: HST/GST	416
Treatment 6: HST/GST 1%	400
Treatment 7: New tax	468
Treatment 8: New tax 1%	469
Treatment 9: Income tax	423
Treatment 10: Income tax 1%	439
Total	4,736

amount of tax, tax increase, or user fee, while the other five provide this information. They also enable us to test our loss-adverse assumptions (hypothesis 2 and hypothesis 3). If we are correct, we should see an increase in support for all treatments when we provide an actual amount relative to the same treatment when the increase is not specified. The reasoning for this assumption is based on the belief that the less detailed treatment will lead the respondents to assume a greater loss. Finally, given the five types of funding tools included in the various treatments, we can test the validity of our third hypothesis, which considers individual-ordered preference for funding mechanisms that minimize personal costs. We list each of the treatments in table 9.1, along with the number of respondents in each group. The full wording for each treatment is included in appendix 9.1.

In total, our sample includes 4,736 respondents.[2] As with earlier chapters, we test random assignment to each group by regressing socio-demographic characteristics, political ideology, political interest, political knowledge (a scale based on the participants' responses to five factual, political-knowledge questions), partisanship (PID), and satisfaction with the way democracy works in Canada as well as response to an attention-check question included in the pre-survey onto the treatments. The results show no systematic bias ($\chi^2 = 203.24$; $p = 0.50$).[3] Thus, we proceed without any additional controls in our statistical models.

---

2 See appendix 9.2 for summary statistics for each group.
3 See appendix 9.3 for full results.

Figure 9.1. Impact of cueing a funding mechanism

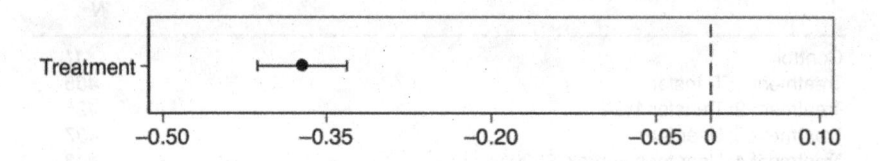

```
Treatment  ├───●───┤
       -0.50   -0.35   -0.20   -0.05  0   0.10
```

Results

Our first hypothesis states that citizens will be more supportive of government infrastructure spending when a funding mechanism is not outlined relative to when a funding mechanism is provided. To test this assumption, we use logistic regression to model support for infrastructure spending (agree or strongly agree that the federal government should invest in infrastructure across Canada). Our single independent variable is a dichotomous measure of any of the ten infrastructure funding mechanisms (= 1) compared with the control group (= 0). If our assumption is correct, we should find a negative relationship, indicative of less support for infrastructure spending when primed to consider paying for this investment relative to the control group. For ease of interpretation, we present the results graphically (see figure 9.1).[4] The point estimate reports the percentage-point change in infrastructure spending support when primed to consider a funding mechanism to pay for the investment relative to the control group. The tails represent 90% confidence intervals for the estimate.

As expected, support for infrastructure spending drops significantly when individuals are reminded that such investment requires either additional taxpayer funds or a reallocation of existing funds. Overall, the average treatment effect is equal to a 37-percentage-point drop ($p < 0.001$) in the likelihood of an individual supporting infrastructure investments. Put simply, individuals are significantly less likely to support government investment when they are forced to consider how such investment will be paid.[5]

---

4 See chap. 1 for an overview of how to read the results reported in the tables and graphs. See appendix 9.4 for full results.
5 As a robustness check, we ran additional models, which included measures of individual-level of financial awareness, political sophistication, satisfaction with the way democracy works in Canada, and income. In all models, the results were similar to those reported here.

Figure 9.2. Support for infrastructure investment when individuals are given actual versus anticipated costs

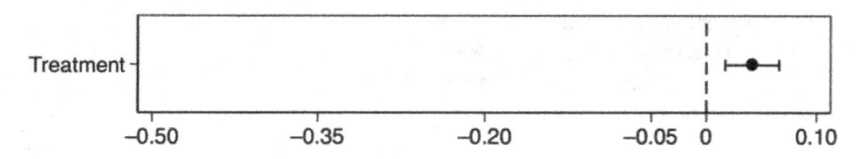

Our second hypothesis assumes that the impact of priming the costs for infrastructure spending will be lower when individuals are given an actual amount of the increase. Recall that this hypothesis assumes that individuals are more likely to overestimate the actual costs when considering personal expenses. To assess this hypothesis, we create a dummy variable that takes the value of "1" if the actual cost is included and "0" otherwise. We use this variable to estimate support for infrastructure spending. If our assumption is correct, the treatment variable should yield a positive coefficient, indicating increased support for infrastructure spending when the costs are known relative to when the costs are unknown. The results from this model are presented in figure 9.2, with the full set of results reported in appendix 9.4.

Congruent with our expectations, individuals are more likely to support infrastructure spending, when primed to consider the costs, when the costs are known relative to when the costs are unknown. The results show a 4-percentage-point increase ($p < 0.01$) in support for infrastructure spending when a specified amount is included. Once again, we tested the independent and conditional effects of financial awareness, political awareness, satisfaction with the way democracy works in Canada, and income on the outcome (see footnote 5). The results (not reported) are virtually the same: independent of levels of awareness and financial well-being, individuals are more apt to support government investment when they know the increased tax, transfer amounts, and/or fees required for the investment relative to when the actual amounts are not specified.

Our final analysis considers the impact of each set of treatments (with and without known costs treatments combined) on support for infrastructure spending relative to the control group. Recall that our general assumption is that citizens will prefer funding mechanisms that minimize personal costs. As noted above, we expect citizens to prefer the redistribution of existing funds over user fees, an increased sales tax, a new special tax, and increased income taxes, in that order. The results

Figure 9.3. Treatment effects on infrastructure investment

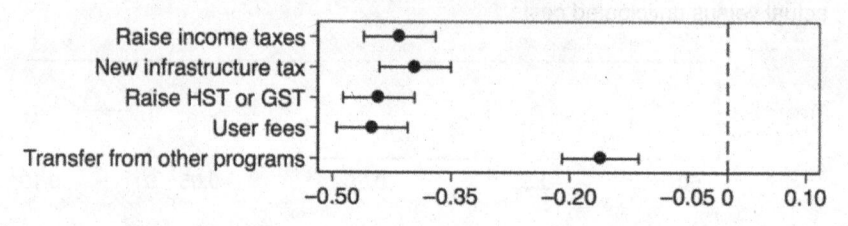

```
Raise income taxes      ├──●──┤
New infrastructure tax       ├──●──┤
Raise HST or GST   ├──●──┤
          User fees ├──●──┤
Transfer from other programs                      ├──●──┤
                    -0.50   -0.35   -0.20   -0.05 0   0.10
```

from this assessment are presented in figure 9.3, with the full set of results included in appendix 9.4.

The results support our assumption that transfers from other programs yield the strongest level of support relative to the other treatments. However, beyond these initial treatments, our hierarchy of preference assumptions appears to be incorrect. For the most part, all the other types of cost offsets have similar effects. The exception is the new infrastructure tax treatment, which yields a somewhat weaker decrease in support relative to the other treatments ($p < 0.05$). Overall, we conclude that, relative to other options, citizens appear most willing to accept transfers from other programs to pay for investments, although the level of investment support is still significantly lower when we cue the costs compared with the control. In regard to the other types of cost offsets, we find limited differences: all treatments significantly reduce support for infrastructure investment.

Discussion and Conclusion

Our results provide empirical evidence of what has often been assumed but rarely tested empirically in Canada: citizens support increased government spending but do not want to pay for it. The assumption is that "hidden taxes" tend to be more popular compared with more visible taxes like a sales tax. Recall the public fallout that the federal Progressive Conservative Party endured after introducing the GST to replace the manufacturers' sales tax, a tax of which citizens had been generally unaware (*Globe and Mail* 2019). The magnitude of the effect in our study was significant: a reduction of 37 percentage points in support for infrastructure investment when citizens were reminded that such investment requires either new funds or a reallocation of existing funds. As expected, individuals were also more apt to support infrastructure investment when the treatment stated the actual cost or increased tax amount relative to the same funding mechanism with the amount withheld.

What are the implications of these findings for winning and keeping power in Canada? Our data suggest that Canadians prefer details to vagueness when it comes to the revenue-collection side of public budgeting. A lack of specifics can make them nervous and more prone to imagining significant increases in personal costs, which can, in turn, trigger loss aversion and a decline in public support for the government. Specific details, on the other hand, provide citizens with more certainty, which can, in turn, discourage them from imagining large increases that impact their personal finances or situation. That said, if maximizing public support is a key concern for political elites, the preferred strategy is to shuffle existing expenditures. However, we did not examine whether the areas from which these funds were transferred mattered for public opinion. It may be that support for transfers from other programs varies according to the programs from which they were taken. Future research might build upon our work to explore this line of enquiry and whether such considerations matter for winning and keeping power in Canada.

REFERENCES

Bartels, Larry. 2005. "Homer Gets a Tax Cut: Inequality and Public Policy in the American Mind." *Perspectives on Politics* 3 (1): 15–31. https://doi.org/10.1017/S1537592705050036.

Beck, Paul Allen, and Thomas R. Dye. 1982. "Sources of Public Opinion on Taxes: The Florida Case." *Journal of Politics* 44 (1): 172–82. https://doi.org/10.2307/2130290.

Beck, Paul Allen, Hal G. Rainey, and Carol Traut. 1990. "Disadvantage, Disaffection, and Race as Divergent Bases for Citizen Fiscal Policy Preferences." *Journal of Politics* 52 (1): 71–93. https://doi.org/10.2307/2131420.

Beeby, Dean. 2017. "Health Canada Report Calls for Big Tax Hike on Cigarettes." *CBC News*, 21 November 2017. http://www.cbc.ca/news/politics/cigarettes-vaping-packaging-tax-tobacco-smoking-target-health-canada-philpott-1.4410518.

Bowler, Shaun, and Todd Donovan. 1995. "Popular Responsiveness to Taxation." *Political Research Quarterly* 48 (1): 79–99. https://doi.org/10.1177/106591299504800105.

CBC News. 2008. "Carbon Tax Plan 'Good for the Wallet,' Dion Pledges." *CBC News*, 19 June 2008. http://www.cbc.ca/news/canada/carbon-tax-plan-good-for-the-wallet-dion-pledges-1.704607.

Edlund, Jonas. 2003. "Attitudes towards Taxation: Ignorant and Incoherent?" *Scandinavian Political Studies* 26 (2): 145–67. https://doi.org/10.1111/1467-9477.00083.

Edlund, Jonas, and Ingemar Johansson Seva. 2013. "Exploring the 'Something for Nothing' Syndrome: Confused Citizens or Free Riders? Evidence from Sweden." *Scandinavian Political Studies* 36 (4): 293–319. https://doi.org/10.1111/j.1467-9477.2012.00300.x.

Geary, Aidan. 2017. "Health-Care Premiums a 'Spoonful of Sugar' to Ease the Pain of Taxes: Expert." *CBC News*, 16 September 2017. http://www.cbc.ca/news/canada/manitoba/manitoba-health-premium-1.4292887.

Globe and Mail. 2016. "The $125-Billion Question." 15 January 2016. https://www.theglobeandmail.com/news/where-will-125-billion-in-infrastructure-spendinggo/article28228477/.

– 2019. "Globe Editorial: Let Us Now Give Thanks for Michael Wilson's GST." 11 February 2019. https://www.theglobeandmail.com/opinion/editorials/article-globe-editorial-let-us-now-give-thanks-for-michael-wilsons-gst/.

Graney, Emma. 2017. "'Patently False': Minister Slams Opposition Claims on Carbon Tax Hike." *Edmonton Journal*, 23 November 2017. http://edmontonjournal.com/news/politics/patently-false-minister-slams-opposition-claims-on-carbon-tax-hike.

Hansen, John Mark. 1998. "Individuals, Institutions, and Public Preferences over Public Finance." *American Political Science Review* 92 (3): 513–31. https://doi.org/10.2307/2585478.

MacManus, Susan A. 1995. "Taxing and Spending Politics: A Generational Perspective." *Journal of Politics* 57 (3): 607–29. https://doi.org/10.2307/2960185.

Steel, Brent S., and Nicholas P. Lovrich. 1998. "Determinants of Public Support for Tax and Expenditure Initiatives: An Oregon and Washington Case Study." *Social Science Journal* 35 (2): 213–29. https://doi.org/10.1016/S0362-3319(98)90041-6.

Tversky, Amos, and Daniel Kahneman. 1992. "Advances in Prospect Theory: Cumulative Representation of Uncertainty." *Journal of Risk and Uncertainty* 5 (4): 297–323. https://www.jstor.org/stable/41755005.

Wingrove, Josh. 2018. "Trudeau Delays Infrastructure Money in Holding Deficits Steady." *Bloomberg Politics*, 27 February. https://www.bloomberg.com/news/articles/2018-02-27/trudeau-delays-infrastructure-money-in-holding-deficits-steady.

Winter, Søren, and Poul Erik Mouritzen. 2001. "Why People Want Something for Nothing: The Role of Asymmetrical Illusions." *European Journal of Political Research* 39: 109–43. https://doi.org/10.1111/1475-6765.00572.

Appendix 9.1. Wording of questions about infrastructure-spending-experiment control and treatments

Control: Please choose the appropriate response for each item.

	Strongly agree 1	2	3	4	Strongly disagree 5
Please indicate the extent to which you agree or disagree that the federal government should invest in infrastructure across Canada (e.g., roads, highways, power lines, etc.).	○	○	○	○	○

Treatment 1: Please choose the appropriate response for each item.

	Strongly agree 1	2	3	4	Strongly disagree 5
Please indicate the extent to which you agree or disagree that the federal government should transfer funding from other programs and services to invest in infrastructure across Canada (e.g., roads, highways, power lines, etc.).	○	○	○	○	○

Treatment 2: Please choose the appropriate response for each item.

	Strongly agree 1	2	3	4	Strongly disagree 5
Please indicate the extent to which you agree or disagree that the federal government should transfer 1% of spending from other programs to invest in infrastructure across Canada (e.g., roads, highways, power lines, etc.).	○	○	○	○	○

Treatment 3: Please choose the appropriate response for each item.

	Strongly agree 1	2	3	4	Strongly disagree 5
Please indicate the extent to which you agree or disagree that the federal government should charge user fees to invest in infrastructure across Canada (e.g., roads, highways, power lines, etc.).	○	○	○	○	○

Treatment 4: Please choose the appropriate response for each item.

	Strongly agree 1	2	3	4	Strongly disagree 5
Please indicate the extent to which you agree or disagree that the federal government should charge user fees (estimated at an average of $500 per year per household) to invest in infrastructure across Canada (e.g., roads, highways, power lines, etc.).	○	○	○	○	○

Treatment 5: Please choose the appropriate response for each item.

	Strongly agree 1	2	3	4	Strongly disagree 5
Please indicate the extent to which you agree or disagree that the federal government should raise the HST/GST to invest in infrastructure across Canada (e.g., roads, highways, power lines, etc.).	○	○	○	○	○

Treatment 6: Please choose the appropriate response for each item.

	Strongly agree 1	2	3	4	Strongly disagree 5
Please indicate the extent to which you agree or disagree that the federal government should raise the HST/GST by 1% to invest in infrastructure across Canada (e.g., roads, highways, power lines, etc.).	○	○	○	○	○

Treatment 7: Please choose the appropriate response for each item.

	Strongly agree 1	2	3	4	Strongly disagree 5
Please indicate the extent to which you agree or disagree that the federal government should introduce a special infrastructure tax to invest in infrastructure across Canada (e.g., roads, highways, power lines, etc.).	○	○	○	○	○

Treatment 8: Please choose the appropriate response for each item.

	Strongly agree 1	2	3	4	Strongly disagree 5
Please indicate the extent to which you agree or disagree that the federal government should introduce a new 1% tax on purchases to invest in infrastructure across Canada (e.g., roads, highways, power lines, etc.).	O	O	O	O	O

Treatment 9: Please choose the appropriate response for each item.

	Strongly agree 1	2	3	4	Strongly disagree 5
Please indicate the extent to which you agree or disagree that the federal government should raise income taxes to invest in infrastructure across Canada (e.g., roads, highways, power lines, etc.).	O	O	O	O	O

Treatment 10: Please choose the appropriate response for each item.

	Strongly agree 1	2	3	4	Strongly disagree 5
Please indicate the extent to which you agree or disagree that the federal government should raise income tax by 1% to invest in infrastructure across Canada (e.g., roads, highways, power lines, etc.).	O	O	O	O	O

Appendix 9.2. Summary statistics

	Control	Treatment 1	Treatment 2	Treatment 3	Treatment 4	Treatment 5
Age	43.91 (16.34)	45.17 (16.19)	47.04 (16.90)	45.84 (16.78)	44.21 (16.15)	44.98 (16.47)
Female	0.49 (0.50)	0.50 (0.50)	0.51 (0.50)	0.53 (0.50)	0.52 (0.50)	0.53 (0.50)
No high school	0.08 (0.26)	0.04 (0.19)	0.06 (0.24)	0.03 (0.18)	0.05 (0.21)	0.06 (0.25)
University graduate	0.34 (0.47)	0.38 (0.49)	0.32 (0.47)	0.34 (0.47)	0.34 (0.48)	0.35 (0.48)
Income	3.77 (1.86)	3.86 (1.78)	3.57 (1.86)	3.69 (1.85)	3.67 (1.80)	3.63 (1.82)
Prairies	0.29 (0.45)	0.24 (0.43)	0.24 (0.43)	0.26 (0.44)	0.26 (0.44)	0.23 (0.42)
Ontario	0.46 (0.50)	0.53 (0.50)	0.50 (0.50)	0.50 (0.50)	0.52 (0.50)	0.49 (0.50)
Atlantic	0.09 (0.28)	0.12 (0.32)	0.11 (0.31)	0.12 (0.33)	0.07 (0.25)	0.12 (0.32)
Satisfaction	0.78 (0.42)	0.79 (0.41)	0.80 (0.40)	0.79 (0.41)	0.76 (0.43)	0.80 (0.40)
Political interest	6.03 (2.57)	6.15 (2.49)	5.95 (2.68)	6.14 (2.64)	5.97 (2.76)	6.08 (2.58)
Political knowledge	0.55 (0.30)	0.56 (0.31)	0.51 (0.31)	0.53 (0.31)	0.54 (0.30)	0.51 (0.31)
Political ideology	5.18 (2.26)	5.03 (2.07)	4.93 (2.07)	4.95 (2.13)	4.89 (2.11)	5.16 (2.23)
CPC PID	0.21 (0.41)	0.21 (0.41)	0.21 (0.41)	0.18 (0.39)	0.20 (0.40)	0.20 (0.40)
GRN PID	0.04 (0.20)	0.04 (0.19)	0.02 (0.15)	0.03 (0.18)	0.04 (0.20)	0.03 (0.18)
LIB PID	0.19 (0.40)	0.24 (0.43)	0.21 (0.41)	0.24 (0.43)	0.20 (0.40)	0.24 (0.43)
NDP PID	0.10 (0.30)	0.08 (0.27)	0.12 (0.32)	0.09 (0.28)	0.09 (0.29)	0.08 (0.28)
Response check	0.91 (0.29)	0.90 (0.30)	0.89 (0.31)	0.89 (0.31)	0.91 (0.29)	0.93 (0.26)
N	411	435	425	437	413	416

Note: The cells report averages, with standard deviations in parentheses. Age is the respondents' age in years. Female, no high school, university graduate, regional variables, PID, and response check are dichotomous measures, coded "1" in correspondence with the variable name. Political interest and political ideology are self-reported positions on an eleven-point scale running from "No interest" to "Great deal of interest" and "Left–Right," respectively. Political knowledge is an index (alpha = 0.61) based on five factual questions: the name of the British prime minister, the level of government that has primary responsibility for education and health care in Canada, the name of the federal finance minister, the name of the governor general, and the number of seats in the House of Commons. The respondents received one point for each correct response. The variable was then rescaled to fit between 0 and 1. N = number of usable cases in each treatment.

Appendix 9.2. Summary statistics (Continued)

	Treatment 6	Treatment 7	Treatment 8	Treatment 9	Treatment 10
Age	45.91 (16.17)	46.74 (17.31)	45.52 (17.01)	46.21 (16.59)	46.04 (17.13)
Female	0.52 (0.50)	0.53 (0.50)	0.50 (0.50)	0.51 (0.50)	0.50 (0.50)
No high school	0.04 (0.19)	0.04 (0.19)	0.04 (0.19)	0.05 (0.22)	0.03 (0.18)
University graduate	0.36 (0.48)	0.33 (0.47)	0.34 (0.47)	0.37 (0.48)	0.33 (0.47)
Income	3.83 (1.80)	3.65 (1.81)	3.65 (1.76)	3.57 (1.82)	3.76 (1.80)
Prairies	0.23 (0.42)	0.26 (0.44)	0.26 (0.44)	0.24 (0.43)	0.26 (0.44)
Ontario	0.54 (0.50)	0.50 (0.50)	0.51 (0.50)	0.50 (0.50)	0.52 (0.50)
Atlantic	0.10 (0.30)	0.11 (0.32)	0.10 (0.31)	0.13 (0.34)	0.10 (0.30)
Satisfaction	0.82 (0.39)	0.82 (0.38)	0.78 (0.41)	0.77 (0.42)	0.78 (0.41)
Political interest	6.25 (2.61)	6.12 (2.60)	6.20 (2.48)	5.94 (2.71)	6.00 (2.52)
Political knowledge	0.53 (0.32)	0.53 (0.30)	0.50 (0.30)	0.51 (0.31)	0.54 (0.31)
Political ideology	5.03 (2.38)	5.05 (2.14)	5.04 (2.20)	5.16 (2.24)	4.89 (2.17)
CPC PID	0.21 (0.41)	0.19 (0.39)	0.22 (0.41)	0.19 (0.39)	0.19 (0.39)
GRN PID	0.03 (0.17)	0.03 (0.16)	0.05 (0.21)	0.04 (0.19)	0.03 (0.16)
LIB PID	0.23 (0.42)	0.21 (0.41)	0.23 (0.42)	0.23 (0.42)	0.27 (0.44)
NDP PID	0.08 (0.27)	0.10 (0.30)	0.08 (0.27)	0.09 (0.28)	0.09 (0.28)
Response check	0.92 (0.27)	0.93 (0.25)	0.89 (0.31)	0.91 (0.29)	0.90 (0.30)
N	400	468	469	423	439

Note: The cells report averages, with standard deviations in parentheses. Age is the respondents' age in years. Female, no high school, university graduate, regional variables, PID, and response check are dichotomous measures, coded "1" in correspondence with the variable name. Political interest and political ideology are self-reported positions on an eleven-point scale running from "No interest" to "Great deal of interest" and "Left–Right," respectively. Political knowledge is an index (alpha = 0.61) based on five factual questions: the name of the British prime minister, the level of government that has primary responsibility for education and health care in Canada, the name of the federal finance minister, the name of the governor general, and the number of seats in the House of Commons. The respondents received one point for each correct response. The variable was then rescaled to fit between 0 and 1. N = number of usable cases in each treatment.

Appendix 9.3. Multinomial logistic regression results for test of random assignment to treatments

	Treatment 1	Treatment 2	Treatment 3	Treatment 4	Treatment 5
Age	0.01 (0.00)	0.01 (0.00)*	0.01 (0.00)	0.00 (0.00)	0.01 (0.00)
Female	0.08 (0.15)	0.10 (0.15)	0.24 (0.16)	0.16 (0.15)	0.24 (0.16)
No high school	−0.74 (0.37)*	−0.27 (0.32)	−0.94 (0.40)*	−0.58 (0.35)[a]	−0.18 (0.32)
University graduate	0.02 (0.17)	−0.03 (0.17)	−0.04 (0.17)	0.03 (0.17)	0.12 (0.17)
Income	−0.01 (0.04)	−0.09 (0.04)*	−0.05 (0.04)	−0.05 (0.04)	−0.06 (0.04)
Prairies	0.19 (0.26)	−0.22 (0.25)	−0.08 (0.25)	0.05 (0.25)	−0.27 (0.25)
Ontario	0.53 (0.24)*	0.17 (0.22)	0.19 (0.23)	0.31 (0.23)	0.12 (0.22)
Atlantic	0.69 (0.32)*	0.17 (0.32)	0.36 (0.31)	−0.11 (0.34)	0.20 (0.31)
Satisfaction	−0.01 (0.19)	0.40 (0.20)[a]	0.03 (0.20)	−0.19 (0.19)	−0.01 (0.19)
Political interest	0.02 (0.03)	0.03 (0.03)	0.06 (0.03)[a]	0.02 (0.03)	0.04 (0.03)
Political knowledge	−0.10 (0.26)	−0.62 (0.26)*	−0.40 (0.26)	−0.25 (0.26)	−0.65 (0.26)*
Political ideology	−0.04 (0.04)	−0.04 (0.04)	−0.05 (0.04)	−0.04 (0.04)	0.00 (0.04)
CPC PID	0.04 (0.22)	0.17 (0.22)	−0.20 (0.23)	−0.05 (0.22)	−0.06 (0.22)
GRN PID	0.17 (0.38)	−0.53 (0.46)	−0.57 (0.45)	0.14 (0.37)	−0.28 (0.42)
LIB PID	0.19 (0.20)	0.11 (0.21)	0.13 (0.21)	−0.06 (0.21)	0.19 (0.21)
NDP PID	−0.20 (0.27)	0.13 (0.26)	−0.37 (0.28)	−0.49 (0.28)[a]	−0.27 (0.28)
Response check	−0.08 (0.25)	−0.06 (0.26)	−0.15 (0.25)	0.08 (0.26)	0.39 (0.28)
Constant	−0.39 (0.51)	−0.18 (0.51)	−0.03 (0.51)	0.32 (0.51)	−0.40 (0.52)

Note: The cells report multinomial logistic regression coefficients, with standard errors in parentheses. Treatment 1 is set as the base outcome. Age is the respondents' age in years. Female, no high school, university graduate, regional variables, PID, and response check are dichotomous measures, coded "1" in correspondence with the variable name. Political interest and political ideology are self-reported positions on an eleven-point scale running from "No interest" to "Great deal of interest" and "Left–Right," respectively. Political knowledge is an index (alpha = 0.61) based on five factual questions: the name of the British prime minister, the level of government that has primary responsibility for education and health care in Canada, the name of the federal finance minister, the name of the governor general, and the number of seats in the House of Commons. The respondents received one point for each correct response. The variable was then rescaled to fit between 0 and 1. N = number of cases with full response set.
*** $p < 0.001$; ** $p < 0.01$; * $p < 0.05$; [a] $p < 0.10$.

Appendix 9.3. Multinomial logistic regression results for test of random assignment to treatments (Continued)

	Treatment 6	Treatment 7	Treatment 8	Treatment 9	Treatment 10
Age	0.01 (0.00)[a]	0.01 (0.00)**	0.01 (0.00)[a]	0.01 (0.00)*	0.01 (0.00)*
Female	0.17 (0.16)	0.18 (0.15)	0.10 (0.15)	0.11 (0.16)	0.07 (0.15)
No high school	-0.50 (0.36)	-0.76 (0.36)*	-0.71 (0.35)*	-0.30 (0.33)	-1.58 (0.47)***
University graduate	0.08 (0.17)	-0.06 (0.17)	0.08 (0.17)	0.23 (0.17)	-0.14 (0.17)
Income	-0.01 (0.04)	-0.05 (0.04)	-0.07 (0.04)	-0.07 (0.04)[a]	-0.02 (0.04)
Prairies	0.06 (0.26)	0.02 (0.24)	0.08 (0.25)	0.09 (0.26)	0.11 (0.25)
Ontario	0.44 (0.24)[a]	0.25 (0.22)	0.38 (0.23)[a]	0.40 (0.24)[a]	0.31 (0.23)
Atlantic	0.42 (0.33)	0.28 (0.31)	0.42 (0.31)	0.54 (0.32)[a]	0.28 (0.32)
Satisfaction	0.13 (0.20)	0.28 (0.20)	-0.14 (0.19)	0.01 (0.19)	-0.11 (0.19)
Political interest	0.04 (0.03)	0.03 (0.03)	0.05 (0.03)	0.01 (0.03)	-0.01 (0.03)
Political knowledge	-0.58 (0.27)*	-0.50 (0.26)[a]	-0.86 (0.26)***	-0.61 (0.26)*	-0.31 (0.26)
Political ideology	-0.03 (0.04)	-0.02 (0.04)	-0.05 (0.04)	0.02 (0.04)	-0.04 (0.04)
CPC PID	0.13 (0.22)	-0.15 (0.22)	0.14 (0.21)	-0.13 (0.22)	-0.04 (0.22)
GRN PID	-0.32 (0.43)	-0.51 (0.43)	0.15 (0.37)	-0.19 (0.41)	-0.64 (0.46)
LIB PID	0.02 (0.21)	0.02 (0.20)	0.06 (0.21)	0.12 (0.21)	0.37 (0.20)[a]
NDP PID	-0.45 (0.29)	-0.25 (0.26)	-0.34 (0.27)	-0.21 (0.27)	-0.53 (0.29)[a]
Response check	0.24 (0.28)	0.36 (0.27)	-0.07 (0.25)	0.05 (0.26)	0.05 (0.26)
Constant	-0.82 (0.53)	-0.82 (0.52)	0.25 (0.50)	-0.48 (0.52)	-0.01 (0.51)

N = 4,011
χ^2 (df = 170) = 179.06
Pseudo R^2 = 0.01

Note: The cells report multinomial logistic regression coefficients, with standard errors in parentheses. Treatment 1 is set as the base outcome. Age is the respondents' age in years. Female, no high school, university graduate, regional variables, PID, and response check are dichotomous measures, coded "1" in correspondence with the variable name. Political interest and political ideology are self-reported positions on an eleven-point scale running from "No interest" to "Great deal of interest" and "Left–Right," respectively. Political knowledge is an index (alpha = 0.61) based on five factual questions: the name of the British prime minister, the level of government that has primary responsibility for education and health care in Canada, the name of the federal finance minister, the name of the governor general, and the number of seats in the House of Commons. The respondents received one point for each correct response. The variable was then rescaled to fit between 0 and 1. N = number of cases with full response set.
*** $p < 0.001$; ** $p < 0.01$; * $p < 0.05$; [a] $p < 0.10$.

Appendix 9.4. Full results for figures 9.1 to 9.3

	Figure 9.1	Figure 9.2	Figure 9.3
Any treatment	−1.60 (0.11)*** [−0.37]		
Actual cost		0.22 (0.08)** [0.04]	
Transfers			−0.66 (0.12)*** [−0.16]
User fees			−2.07 (0.14)*** [−0.45]
Raise HST/GST			−2.00 (0.14)*** [−0.44]
New infrastructure tax			−1.73 (0.13)*** [−0.40]
Raise income tax			−1.84 (0.13)*** [−0.42]
Constant	0.50 (0.10)***	−1.18 (0.06)***	0.50 (0.10)***
Pseudo R^2	0.04	0.00	0.08
N	4,736	3,414	4,736

Note: The cells report logistic regression coefficients, with standard errors in parentheses and marginal effects/discrete changes reported in square brackets.
*** $p < 0.001$; ** $p < 0.01$; * $p < 0.05$; [a] $p < 0.10$.

Chapter Ten

Political Apologies

To the approximately 80,000 living former students and all family members and communities, the Government of Canada now recognizes that it was wrong to forcibly remove children from their homes, and we apologize for having done this. (Prime Minister Stephen Harper apologizing to the former students of residential schools, Harper 2008)

"The goal is to appear more human, foster public empathy and forgiveness and eventually regain public trust and confidence." (Amanda Alvaro, managing director of Narrative PR, quoted in Sylvestre-Williams 2014)

Between 1988 and 2018, Canadian governments issued at least thirty-seven official apologies to various societal groups and individuals: thirteen were issued by the federal government, twenty-one by provincial governments (BC, Alberta, Ontario, Quebec, and Newfoundland and Labrador), and three by municipalities (Toronto, Kingston, and Halifax). The range of issues covered by these apologies has been diverse, including sexual and physical abuse, the relocation of settlements and children, the bombing of a commercial aircraft, forced sterilization, the imposition of taxes specific to ethnic groups, and other discriminatory actions. Similarly, the range of actors affected by these apologies has been diverse and includes immigrants; Indigenous peoples; ethnic minorities such as Japanese and Chinese Canadians, Indians, and Syrians; women; children; and even Canadian soldiers who deserted during the First World War (results compiled by authors).

The apologies that have garnered the most public attention have been those that addressed the treatment of Japanese Canadians during the Second World War, the forced relocation of Indigenous communities and children into residential schools, the imposition of the Chinese head tax, and the Komagata Maru incident off the coast of BC. Given the gravity of and public interest in these issues, political leaders typically issue apologies by making public statements in their respective legislatures, although, at times, they have also apologized in person at historically significant locations. Prime Minister Brian Mulroney, for instance, announced in the House of Commons that "the forced removal and internment of Japanese Canadians during World War II was unjust" and that his government pledged "to ensure, the full extent that its powers allow, that such events will not happen again" (Miki and Kobayashi 1991, 7). Similarly, Newfoundland and Labrador Premier Danny Williams visited Nain, Labrador, in 2005 to apologize for the closure of two northern Inuit communities in 1956 and 1959 (Newfoundland and Labrador Executive Council 2005).

Why do governments apologize? For the optimists, it is because politicians are driven by guilt or genuinely believe that "it is the right thing to do." They hope that an apology will help alleviate a historical injustice in some way and serve as a first step towards reconciliation with the aggrieved group or individuals (Corntassel and Holder 2008; Nobles 2008, 3). For the pessimists, leaders apologize because they are playing politics. Public apologies are political tools that incumbent politicians use to ensure that they do not suffer any lasting harm in the next election for failing to address the grievance (James 2008; Lundy and Rolston 2016, 116–17; Steele and Blatz 2014). Regardless of the psychological motivations that may be driving a particular apology, political leaders are more likely to apologize when faced with significant political pressure from an individual or group that has been victimized or wronged by the government (Blatz, Schumann, and Ross 2009; Nobles 2008). This pressure becomes magnified when members of that group are also prominent members of the current government, when public opposition to government redress on a particular issue is perceived to be low, and when previous apologies for similar historical injustices have failed to generate negative consequences for government actors (Schumann and Ross 2010, 301–5; Bilder 2008, 24–7).

In this chapter, we investigate whether government apologies are an effective tool for managing public opinion in Canada. On the one hand, it seems intuitive that apologizing for a historical injustice, especially if a past government committed it, should increase support for the current incumbent. However, it is also possible that addressing the issue could lead to public backlash by drawing attention to a previously unknown issue. Surprisingly, the empirical literature on the effectiveness of government apologies is virtually non-existent in the Canadian context, and yet apologies are becoming more frequent in Canada. Based on our search of public documents and databases, Canadian governments apologized at least six times during the ten-year period of 1988 to 1999. From 2000 to 2009, they apologized eighteen times, and from 2010 to 2016, they apologized thirteen times. Given this trend, this chapter tries to answer the following questions: Are government apologies effective at managing public opinion? What kinds of apology are most effective? What are the implications of government apologies for the political elites that make them?

Background, Theory, and Expectations

According to Rhoda Howard-Hassmann and Mark Gibney (2008, 2), "There seems to be almost universal recognition that a society will not be able to successfully pass into the future until it somehow deals with its demons from the past." Canadian government officials at all levels seem to recognize this truth, as evidenced by the number and frequency of apologies that they have issued over the last thirty years. At their core, apologies are an attempt to acknowledge, exorcise, and ultimately transform these demons in a way that heals divisions and rifts between governments and societal groups and eliminates any ongoing or lingering harms caused by those demons. In practical terms, "An apology is something we *say* or *utter*, in speech or writing, but it is also something we *offer* and that we offer to *someone* in particular; that is part of what distinguishes apology from confession" (MacLachlan 2013, 187). In essence, words matter. They are spoken to reduce tensions and bring the apologizer and the aggrieved actor into a better relationship that is at least neutral in nature.

Underlying every government-issued apology is a desire to manage public opinion in a way that favours the re-election chances of the incumbent politicians. Apologies are meant not only to satisfy the recipients and reduce their public activism but also to resonate positively with the non-victimized majority population. "Experimental research on negotiations indicates that people evaluate their own side's offers more favourably than equivalent offers by the opposition" (Blatz, Schumann, and Ross 2009, 230). In Australia, for instance, we saw evidence of this trend when public support for an apology towards Indigenous peoples increased substantially after Kevin Rudd and his party formed a majority government in 2007 and offered an apology in 2008. After the apology was issued, survey research found that "69% of the public approved of it"; presumably the apology benefited Rudd and his party among Indigenous and non-Indigenous voters (Tager 2014, 8; see also James 2008, 150). Apologies, therefore, can be effective tools for strengthening public opinion towards the incumbent party, not only among the aggrieved but also among the non-aggrieved members of the population.

Psychologists and political theorists have been at the forefront of investigating the factors that produce effective apologies. These factors can be grouped into three categories: the contexts in which the apologies occur (Bobowik et al. 2017; Bombay, Matheson, and Anisman 2013), the ways in which an apology is delivered (Cels 2015; Philpot et al. 2013), and, most importantly, the contents of the apology itself (Lewicki and Polin 2012). In this chapter, we focus on the latter group of factors, which are the elements within an apology, given their primacy in the empirical and theoretical literatures on government and interpersonal apologies.

Although the normative literature on apologies is quite extensive, the empirical literature, which examines the effectiveness of apologies using experimental designs or observational data, is less developed. Generally speaking, the existing empirical literature on government apologies emphasizes that they should be highly detailed and contain as many elements as possible to maximize their effectiveness. Blatz, Schumann, and Ross (2009, 227), for instance, suggest that governments regularly rely on ten elements when delivering apologies. These elements include using words or phrases to express remorse; accepting responsibility; admitting to the injustice or wrongdoing; acknowledging harm and victim suffering; expressing forbearance; offering to repair the harm; offering praise for the aggrieved group, the majority group, and the present system; and disassociating the injustice from the present system.

Other scholars are more definitive in advocating for elaborate and highly detailed apologies. They argue that effective apologies are ones that, at a minimum, include an acknowledgment of harm, a message of remorse, and a clear statement of recognition that the state committed an act of wrongdoing. The more elaborate the apology, the more likely the public is to perceive it as sincere and remorseful (Steele and Blatz 2014). Wohl, Hornsey, and Philpot (2011) concur with these findings but suggest that elaborate apologies should be constructed in a particular way, using a bottom-up, staircase model to maximize their effectiveness. Each stair, beginning at the bottom of the staircase, should provide a foundation for the next element of the apology. These stairs include accepting collective guilt; setting the historical record straight; discussing reparations; expressing regret, remorse, responsibility, and guilt; and promising to follow up with post-apology actions (see also Hornsey, Wohl, and Philpot 2015).

Table 10.1. Government apology treatments

Treatment	Statement	N
1 – No comment	Provincial government officials have offered no comment on these reports.	699
2 – Apologize only	Today, provincial government officials apologized for the use of the herbicide.	693
3 – Address the issue only	Today, provincial government officials promised to correct the problem by banning the herbicide and providing compensation to the people affected by it.	747
4 – Accept responsibility only	Today, provincial government officials admitted that they did use the herbicide.	702
5 – Apologize and address the issue	Today, provincial government officials apologized for the use of the herbicide and promised to correct the problem by banning the herbicide and providing compensation to the people affected by it.	701
6 – Apologize and accept responsibility	Today, provincial government officials admitted that they did use the herbicide, and they apologized for its use.	623
7 – Accept responsibility and address the issue	Today, provincial government officials admitted that they did use the herbicide and promised to correct the problem by banning the herbicide and providing compensation to the people affected by it.	705
8 – Apologize, accept responsibility, and address the issue	Today, provincial government officials admitted that they did use the herbicide, apologized for its use, and promised to correct the problem by banning the herbicide and providing compensation to the people affected by it.	720
Total		5,590

In this chapter, we assess whether government apologies are effective at managing public opinion and whether the effectiveness of an apology varies according to the components included in it. To do so, we randomly assigned the individuals to one of eight possible treatments (see table 10.1). Each treatment included a preamble that stated, "Multiple reports suggest that the provincial government has been using cancer-causing herbicide to control the growth of mosquitos/weeds across the province. Studies have found that individuals exposed to the spray are more prone to develop cancer and birth defects." This scenario allowed us to treat all members of the sample as potentially aggrieved members and the primary target of the apology, thus improving our ability to assess whether different components of an apology matter for producing positive public opinion towards the government.

The stimulus in our study was to vary the government response to the report, ranging from "No comment" on the issue to offering a public apology, along with full acceptance of responsibility and a promise of action to correct the issue. We asked the respondents to indicate their level of satisfaction with the apology treatment to which they were exposed. We then tested for differences in public support across the various treatments to assess the relationship between government responses and public opinion. We did so by comparing the level of support for the government's response across treatments.

Given the existing literature's emphasis on how the quantity and nature of the components included in an apology matter in how it is received (e.g., Darby and Schlenker 1982; Kirchhoff, Wagner, and Strack 2012; Lewicki, Polin, and Lount, Jr. 2016, 185), our expectations are as follows. We begin by considering whether an apology is likely to have a positive effect on public opinion compared with no apology at all. The empirical literature suggests that it will (Philpot and Hornsey 2008). Steele and Blatz (2014, 276), for instance, found that "compared to no apology, the apology with all five elements, including the promise of forbearance, was perceived by participants as more remorseful" and that "as the apology became more elaborate, it was seen as more sincerely remorseful" (276–7). Thus, we expect that a government-issued public apology will be more effective at fostering public opinion relative to no apology. We also expect that apologies that contain more elements (e.g., acceptance of responsibility and promise of action), regardless of the nature of those elements, will be more effective than apologies with fewer elements (Kirchhoff and Čehajić-Clancy 2014; Wohl, Hornsey, and Philpot 2011). Formally, we expect the following:

H1: Public support will be lowest when governments refuse to comment on accusations of wrongdoing.
H2: Public support will be lowest when governments issue apologies with fewer elements relative to apologies with more elements.

Next, we consider whether the nature of the three components matters: whether the apology offers an expression of regret (e.g., I'm sorry), an acknowledgment of responsibility (e.g., I was wrong), and an offer to repair (e.g., I will fix it). These apology components are frequently found in the apologies offered by the federal, provincial, and municipal governments of Canada and have been identified in the literature as being important. In terms of rank-ordering their importance, we follow the lead of Lewicki, Polin, and Lount, Jr. (2016, 190), who found that the acknowledgment of responsibility was the most important element, followed by the offer of repair and the expression of regret. Given these findings, we expect the following:

H3: Public support will be lowest whenever governments offer no apology, followed by an apology that contains an expression of regret, an apology that contains an offer to repair, and finally an acknowledgment of responsibility.

Methodology

Our research design employs a web-based survey, in which the participants are randomly assigned to one of seven possible treatments or a control group following completion of a pre-survey (see table 10.1 for treatment groups; see chapter 1 for additional sample information and study dates). For all conditions, the participants are provided with a preamble that states the following:

> Multiple reports confirm that the provincial government has been using cancer-causing herbicide to control the growth of mosquitos/weeds across the province. Studies have found that individuals exposed to the spray are more prone to develop cancer and birth defects.

The manipulation was to alter the final line of text, ranging from "Provincial government officials have offered no comment on these reports" (control) to the government offering an apology, accepting responsibility, and promising to address the issue (treatment 8; see table 10.1). Following the preamble, the participants were asked to rate their level of satisfaction with the government's response, ranging from *very dissatisfied* to *very satisfied*. Our interest was not so much in the differences across categories, but whether the individuals were satisfied (or not) with the response. As such, we dichotomized satisfaction to compare those who were satisfied or very satisfied (= 1) against all others. Given that all else was held equal across the treatments, with the exception of the government's response to the reports, we could then directly assess the treatment effects by comparing the respondents' level of satisfaction with the responses across the conditions.[1]

Results

Our sample for this study consists of 5,590 respondents, with an average of 698.75 respondents per group (see table 10.1).[2] Once again,

---

[1] See chap. 1 for further discussion of the strength of experimental designs to isolate causal relationships.
[2] See appendix 10.1 for group summary statistics.

Figure 10.1. Change in public satisfaction with government response compared with "No comment"

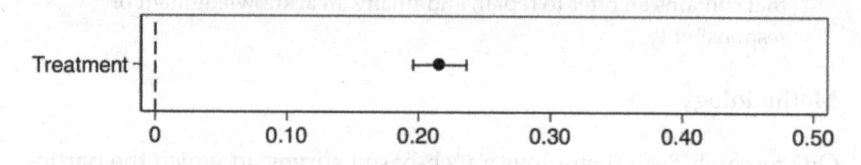

we employ a multinomial logistic regression model to test for random assignment according to socio-demographic characteristics, ideology, partisanship (PID), political sophistication (a combination of political awareness and political knowledge), and the respondents' level of satisfaction with the way democracy works in Canada. The results (see appendix 10.2) show that our randomization process was successful (χ^2 = 104.21; p = 0.83), allowing us to estimate our models net of any controls for differences in group characteristics.

Our first hypothesis is that public support will be lowest when the government offers no comment on the accusation compared with any of the other responses. To assess this hypothesis, we use a logistic regression specification to model the respondents' satisfaction with the government's response (1 = satisfied or very satisfied). We include a dichotomous measure of response type as our predictor variable, with no comment (the control) set to a value of "0" and all treatments coded as "1." A positive coefficient on the dichotomous independent variable will indicate support for our hypothesis; any response is better than none. For ease of interpretation, the results are presented graphically in figure 10.1, and the full results are included in appendix 10.3. The graph reports the change in the probability of the public being satisfied or very satisfied with the government when any response is offered relative to the control group. The results are statistically significant ($p < 0.10$) when both tails fall below or above the "0."[3]

As indicated by these results, our hypothesis is indeed supported: offering any statement increases the likelihood of the public being satisfied or very satisfied with the government's response by 22 percentage points compared with the government offering no comment. As a rule, it would seem that officials are ill advised to refuse to comment on accusations of government wrongdoing.

Is "more" better when it comes to government apologies? As outlined above, earlier work suggests that government responses that include a

---

3 See chap. 1 for further discussion of how to read the results.

Figure 10.2. Change in public satisfaction with government response, compared with "No comment," by number of elements

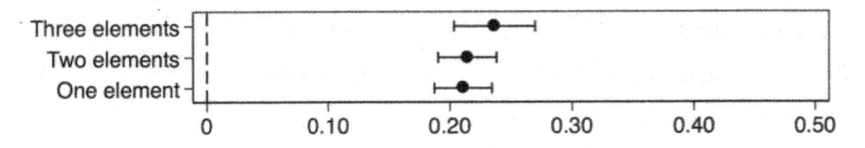

greater number of elements will increase support relative to those that include fewer. To assess this assumption, we once again model satisfaction with the government response as a function of the number of elements included in it (one, two, or three). We set the control (no comment) as our reference category. The results for this model are provided in figure 10.2 and appendix 10.3.

Congruent with expectations, public response does appear to be more positive when governments offer more elements to an apology, although the difference is small and does not achieve conventional levels of statistical significance. As such, we note the pattern but caution against drawing too strong a conclusion based on these results. While any comment regarding wrongdoing is better than no comment, the number of elements included in the response appears to have only a limited (if any) impact on public satisfaction.

Our final hypothesis considers how each of the elements (alone or in combination) influences public support. Following from hypothesis 2, we expect that single elements will have a weaker influence on support relative to treatments that include two elements, which will, in turn, be weaker than the three-element condition. As indicated by our results for hypothesis 1, all government responses are expected to yield positive coefficients relative to the control group of no comment. To test these assumptions, we estimate satisfaction with the government's response as a function of the treatment group. The reference category is the control group (no comment). The results for this final model are presented in figure 10.3 and appendix 10.4.

Our final set of results offers mixed support for our expectations. First, it is noteworthy that all responses are both positive and statistically significant. Clearly, any government response is better than none, regardless of the elements included. However, our results show that the magnitude of the improvement in satisfaction does not follow our anticipated order, in either the number or the type of elements included in the response. Of all treatments, it is the single element of offering to fix the problem that is found to be the strongest, increasing the likelihood

Figure 10.3. Change in public satisfaction with government response, compared with "No comment," by type of element

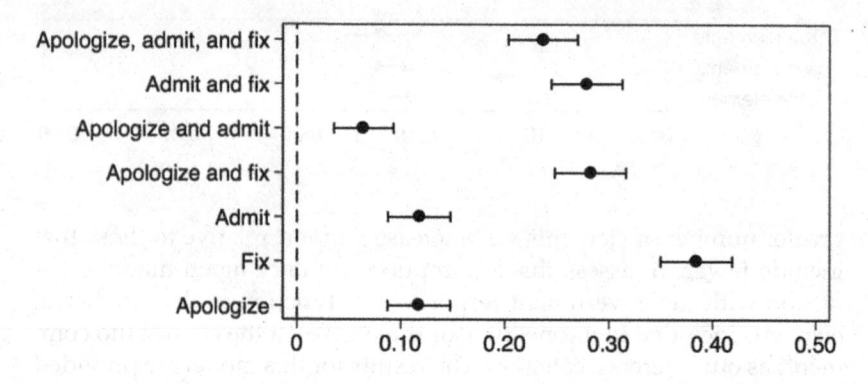

of the public being satisfied or very satisfied by 38 percentage points relative to the control group of no comment. It is also evident that the four treatments that include the promise to address the wrongdoing yield the largest increase in public satisfaction. While admitting and apologizing for government wrongdoings is better than offering no comment, it is the willingness of the government to fix the problem that stands out as most important for improving public satisfaction. While our current study does not allow us to explore how a government apologizing or admitting fault for a previous government – namely, one formed under a different political party – influences public support, we can conclude that governments hoping to retain power in subsequent elections would be well advised to address such issues, even if they are unwilling to admit fault or even apologize for the wrongdoing.

Discussion and Conclusion

In this chapter, we consider how a government's response to accusations of wrongdoing affect public satisfaction. As expected, the public responds more positively to a response over silence. However, the elements, both the number and the type, do not fit with what we expected. In the case of the former, there is virtually no difference in satisfaction between the government including one or two elements and a marginal increase of only 3 percentage points between two and three elements (see figure 10.2). What does seem to matter is what is included in the apology. The bottom line is that the public reacts most favourably to a government willing to fix the problem. This is true regardless of whether the government admits or even apologizes for the wrongdoing.

Of course, this particular study focused on only one type of issue. It may be that different types of issues affect the public differently and that different sets of victims perceive apologies in different ways. We also did not investigate the effect of apologies on non-aggrieved individuals, so it is unclear how members of the Canadian public might react to apologies to groups that are different from them. These are both promising areas of future research, and we hope that others take up these questions in future work.

What are the implications of these findings for winning and keeping power in Canada? When opportunities arise to make an apology for bad or harmful decisions made by contemporary or historical governments, political elites should embrace them. In what will likely please government lawyers interested in limiting the legal liability of their clients but dismay political theorists and civil society actors interested in justice, our results suggest that government officials need not take responsibility for the actions that caused the problem or say the words "I'm sorry" to maximize public support. Instead, they can limit their remarks to a commitment to fix the problem. In practical terms, this might mean providing financial compensation to the victims, giving them opportunities to express their experiences and have them recorded, or creating new programs and services devoted to public education and the provision of public goods to address the needs of those affected by the apology. Based on the evidence marshalled here, it is the promise to fix the problem that matters.

REFERENCES

Bilder, Richard B. 2008. "The Role of Apology in International Law." In *The Age of Apology: Facing Up to the Past*, edited by Mark Gibney, Rhoda E. Howard-Hassmann, Jean-Marc Coicaud, and Niklaus Steiner, 13–30. Philadelphia: University of Pennsylvania Press.

Blatz, Craig W., Karina Schumann, and Michael Ross. 2009. "Government Apologies for Historical Injustices." *Political Psychology* 30 (2): 219–41. https://doi.org/10.1111/j.1467-9221.2008.00689.x.

Bobowik, Magdalena, Darío Páez, Maitane Arnoso, Manuel Cárdenas, Bernard Rimé, Elena Zubieta, and Marcela Murablaistori. 2017. "Institutional Apologies and Socio-emotional Climate in the South American Context." *British Journal of Social Psychology* 1–47. https://doi.org/10.1111/bjso.12200.

Bombay, Amy, Kimberly Matheson, and Hymie Anisman. 2013. "Expectations among Aboriginal Peoples in Canada regarding the Potential Impacts of a Government Apology." *Political Psychology* 34 (3): 443-60. https://doi.org/10.1111/pops.12029.

Cels, Sanderijn. 2015. "Interpreting Political Apologies: The Neglected Role of Performance." *Political Psychology* 36 (3): 351–60. https://doi.org/10.1111/pops.12092.

Corntassel, Jeff, and Cindy Holder. 2008. "Who's Sorry Now? Government Apologies, Truth Commissions, and Indigenous Self-Determination in Australia, Canada, Guatemala, and Peru." *Human Rights Review* 9 (4): 465–89. https://doi.org/10.1007/s12142-008-0065-3.

Darby, Bruce W., and Barry R. Schlenker. 1982. "Children's Reactions to Apologies." *Journal of Personality and Social Psychology* 43 (4): 742–53. https://doi.org/10.1037/0022-3514.43.4.742.

Harper, Stephen. 2008. Canada. Parliament. House of Commons. *House Debates* (Hansard). 39th Parliament, 2nd Session, vol. 142, no. 110, June 11.

Hornsey, Matthew J., Michael J.A. Wohl, and Catherine R. Philpot. 2015. "Collective Apologies and Their Effects on Forgiveness: Pessimistic Evidence but Constructive Implications." *Australian Psychologist* 50 (2): 106-14. https://doi.org/10.1111/ap.12087.

Howard-Hassmann, Rhoda E., and Mark Gibney. 2008. "Introduction: Apologies and the West." In *The Age of Apology: Facing Up to the Past*, edited by Mark Gibney, Rhoda E. Howard-Hassmann, Jean-Marc Coicaud, and Niklaus Steiner, 1–30. Philadelphia: University of Pennsylvania Press.

James, Matt. 2008. "Wrestling with the Past: Apologies, Quasi-apologies, and Non-apologies in Canada." In *The Age of Apology: Facing Up to the Past*, edited by Mark Gibney, Rhoda E. Howard-Hassmann, Jean-Marc Coicaud, and Niklaus Steiner, 137–53. Philadelphia: University of Pennsylvania Press.

Kirchhoff, Johanna, and Sabina Čehajić-Clancy. 2014. "Intergroup Apologies: Does It Matter What They Say? Experimental Analyses." *Peace and Conflict: Journal of Peace Psychology* 20 (4): 430–51. https://doi.org/10.1037/pac0000064.

Kirchhoff, Johanna, Ulrich Wagner, and Micha Strack. 2012. "Apologies: Words of Magic? The Role of Verbal Components, Anger Reduction, and Offence Severity." *Peace and Conflict: Journal of Peace Psychology* 18 (2): 109–30. https://doi.org/10.1037/a0028092.

Lewicki, Roy J., and Beth Polin. 2012. "The Art of the Apology: The Structure and Effectiveness of Apologies in Trust Repair." In *Restoring Trust: Challenges and Prospects*, edited by Roderick M. Kramer and Todd L. Pittinsky, 95–128. New York: Oxford University Press.

Lewicki, Roy J., Beth Polin, and Robert B. Lount, Jr. 2016. "An Exploration of the Structure of Effective Apologies." *Negotiation and Conflict Management Research* 9 (2): 177–96. https://doi.org/10.1111/ncmr.12073.

Lundy, Patricia, and Bill Rolston. 2016. "Redress for Past Harms? Official Apologies in Northern Ireland." *International Journal of Human Rights* 20 (1): 104–22. https://doi.org/10.1080/13642987.2015.1050235.

MacLachlan, Alice. 2013. "Government Apologies to Indigenous Peoples." In *Justice, Responsibility and Reconciliation in the Wake of Conflict*, vol. 1, edited by Alice MacLachlan and Allen Speight, 183–203. Boston Studies in Philosophy, Religion and Public Life. Dordrecht, The Netherlands: Springer. https://doi.org/10.1007/978-94-007-5201-6_11.

Miki, Roy, and Cassandra Kobayashi. 1991. *Justice in Our Time: The Japanese Canadian Redress Settlement*. Vancouver: Talonbooks.

Newfoundland and Labrador. Executive Council. 2005. "Government of Newfoundland and Labrador Apologizes to Relocatees." Press release. 22 January. http://www.releases.gov.nl.ca/releases/2005/exec/0122n03.htm.

Nobles, Melissa. 2008. *The Politics of Official Apologies*. Cambridge: Cambridge University Press.

Philpot, Catherine, Nikola Balvin, David Mellor, and Di Bretherton. 2013. "Making Meaning from Collective Apologies: Australia's Apology to Its Indigenous Peoples." *Peace and Conflict: Journal of Peace Psychology* 19 (1): 34–50. https://doi.org/10.1037/a0031267.

Philpot, Catherine R., and Matthew J. Hornsey. 2008. "What Happens When Groups Say Sorry: The Effect of Intergroup Apologies on Their Recipients." *Personality and Social Psychology Bulletin* 34 (4): 474–87. https://doi.org/10.1177/0146167207311283.

Schumann, Karina, and Michael Ross. 2010. "The Antecedents, Nature, and Effectiveness of Political Apologies for Historical Injustices." In *The Psychology of Justice and Legitimacy: The Ontario Symposium Volume II*, edited by D. Ramona Bobocel, Aaron C. Kay, Mark P. Zanna, and James M. Olson, 299–324. New York: Taylor and Frances.

Steele, Rachel R., and Craig W. Blatz. 2014. "Faith in the Just Behavior of the Government: Intergroup Apologies and Apology Elaboration." *Journal of Social and Political Psychology* 2 (1): 268–88. https://doi.org/10.5964/jspp.v2i1.404.

Sylvestre-Williams, Renée. 2014. "The Art of the Political Apology." *Global News*, 10 January. http://globalnews.ca/news/1072727/the-art-of-the-political-apology/.

Tager, Michael. 2014. "Apologies to Indigenous Peoples in Comparative Perspective." *International Indigenous Policy Journal* 5 (4): 1–18. https://doi.org/10.18584/iipj.2014.5.4.7.

Wohl, Michael J.A., Matthew J. Hornsey, and Catherine R. Philpot. 2011. "A Critical Review of Official Public Apologies: Aims, Pitfalls, and a Staircase Model of Effectiveness." *Social Issues and Policy Review* 5 (1): 70–100. https://doi.org/10.1111/j.1751-2409.2011.01026.x.

Appendix 10.1. Summary statistics

	Treatment 1	Treatment 2	Treatment 3	Treatment 4	Treatment 5	Treatment 6	Treatment 7	Treatment 8
Age	44.89 (16.61)	46.11 (17.05)	46.12 (16.46)	45.60 (16.65)	46.31 (16.43)	46.13 (16.59)	45.31 (17.01)	44.97 (16.67)
Female	0.53 (0.50)	0.47 (0.50)	0.48 (0.50)	0.49 (0.50)	0.50 (0.50)	0.53 (0.50)	0.53 (0.50)	0.55 (0.50)
No high school	0.05 (0.22)	0.06 (0.25)	0.04 (0.19)	0.05 (0.21)	0.05 (0.21)	0.05 (0.22)	0.04 (0.19)	0.04 (0.20)
University graduate	0.33 (0.47)	0.33 (0.47)	0.36 (0.48)	0.31 (0.46)	0.39 (0.49)	0.37 (0.48)	0.33 (0.47)	0.35 (0.48)
Income	3.71 (1.82)	3.62 (1.77)	3.71 (1.85)	3.75 (1.83)	3.71 (1.83)	3.68 (1.83)	3.67 (1.73)	3.70 (1.88)
Prairies	0.25 (0.43)	0.27 (0.44)	0.26 (0.44)	0.25 (0.43)	0.25 (0.43)	0.24 (0.43)	0.26 (0.44)	0.25 (0.44)
Ontario	0.50 (0.50)	0.49 (0.50)	0.51 (0.50)	0.53 (0.50)	0.51 (0.50)	0.52 (0.50)	0.50 (0.50)	0.51 (0.50)
Atlantic	0.11 (0.31)	0.11 (0.31)	0.11 (0.31)	0.10 (0.30)	0.10 (0.30)	0.12 (0.33)	0.10 (0.30)	0.11 (0.31)
Satisfaction	0.79 (0.41)	0.80 (0.40)	0.77 (0.42)	0.79 (0.41)	0.78 (0.42)	0.78 (0.42)	0.81 (0.39)	0.79 (0.41)
Political interest	6.19 (2.59)	6.13 (2.72)	6.22 (2.60)	5.98 (2.65)	6.03 (2.59)	6.00 (2.56)	6.10 (2.49)	6.06 (2.59)
Political knowledge	0.54 (0.31)	0.52 (0.31)	0.54 (0.30)	0.53 (0.31)	0.54 (0.31)	0.54 (0.31)	0.53 (0.31)	0.51 (0.31)
Political ideology	5.02 (2.17)	5.22 (2.25)	4.95 (2.30)	5.04 (2.11)	5.07 (2.20)	5.03 (2.09)	5.09 (2.14)	4.90 (2.21)
CPC PID	0.21 (0.41)	0.23 (0.42)	0.20 (0.40)	0.19 (0.39)	0.21 (0.40)	0.19 (0.39)	0.19 (0.39)	0.18 (0.39)
GRN PID	0.03 (0.18)	0.03 (0.17)	0.04 (0.20)	0.03 (0.16)	0.02 (0.15)	0.04 (0.21)	0.03 (0.17)	0.05 (0.21)
LIB PID	0.23 (0.42)	0.21 (0.41)	0.24 (0.43)	0.22 (0.42)	0.23 (0.42)	0.23 (0.42)	0.24 (0.43)	0.23 (0.42)
NDP PID	0.08 (0.28)	0.07 (0.26)	0.10 (0.30)	0.09 (0.29)	0.08 (0.27)	0.09 (0.28)	0.09 (0.29)	0.10 (0.31)
Response check	0.92 (0.28)	0.89 (0.31)	0.93 (0.26)	0.91 (0.29)	0.91 (0.29)	0.91 (0.29)	0.89 (0.31)	0.89 (0.31)
N	699	693	747	702	701	623	705	720

Note: The cells report averages, with standard deviations in parentheses. Age is the respondents' age in years. Female, no high school, university graduate, regional variables, PID, and response check are dichotomous measures, coded "1" in correspondence with the variable name. Political interest and political ideology are self-reported positions on an eleven-point scale running from "No interest" to "Great deal of interest" and "Left–Right," respectively. Political knowledge is an index (alpha = 0.57) based on five factual questions: the name of the British prime minister, the level of government that has primary responsibility for education and health care in Canada, the name of the federal finance minister, the name of the governor general, and the number of seats in the House of Commons. The respondents received one point for each correct response. The variable was then rescaled to fit between 0 and 1. N = number of usable cases in each treatment.

Appendix 10.2. Multinomial logistic regression results for test of random assignment to treatments

	Treatment 2	Treatment 3	Treatment 4	Treatment 5	Treatment 6	Treatment 7	Treatment 8
Age	0.00 (0.00)	0.01 (0.00)[a]	0.00 (0.00)	0.01 (0.00)[a]	0.01 (0.00)*	0.00 (0.00)	0.00 (0.00)
Female	−0.23 (0.12)[a]	−0.19 (0.12)	−0.13 (0.12)	−0.10 (0.12)	0.04 (0.12)	−0.02 (0.12)	0.09 (0.12)
No high school	0.34 (0.29)	0.02 (0.31)	−0.09 (0.31)	0.08 (0.31)	0.34 (0.30)	−0.09 (0.31)	0.01 (0.31)
University graduate	−0.07 (0.13)	0.10 (0.13)	−0.16 (0.13)	0.18 (0.13)	0.17 (0.13)	−0.05 (0.13)	0.10 (0.13)
Income	−0.02 (0.03)	−0.01 (0.03)	0.02 (0.03)	−0.02 (0.03)	0.00 (0.04)	−0.02 (0.03)	0.01 (0.03)
Prairies	0.16 (0.20)	0.18 (0.20)	0.07 (0.20)	0.03 (0.20)	0.19 (0.21)	0.05 (0.20)	0.11 (0.20)
Ontario	0.15 (0.18)	0.18 (0.18)	0.25 (0.18)	0.04 (0.18)	0.25 (0.19)	0.01 (0.18)	0.17 (0.18)
Atlantic	0.13 (0.25)	0.14 (0.24)	0.10 (0.25)	−0.00 (0.24)	0.31 (0.25)	−0.04 (0.24)	0.18 (0.24)
Satisfaction	0.21 (0.15)	−0.09 (0.15)	0.12 (0.15)	−0.02 (0.15)	0.08 (0.16)	0.17 (0.15)	0.06 (0.15)
Political interest	−0.02 (0.03)	−0.01 (0.03)	−0.04 (0.03)	−0.03 (0.03)	−0.04 (0.03)	−0.02 (0.03)	−0.03 (0.03)
Political knowledge	−0.13 (0.21)	−0.09 (0.20)	−0.04 (0.20)	−0.02 (0.20)	−0.00 (0.21)	−0.11 (0.20)	−0.30 (0.20)
Political ideology	0.03 (0.03)	−0.01 (0.03)	0.01 (0.03)	0.02 (0.03)	0.03 (0.03)	0.02 (0.03)	−0.02 (0.03)
CPC PID	0.04 (0.17)	0.09 (0.17)	−0.08 (0.17)	−0.12 (0.17)	−0.15 (0.18)	−0.08 (0.17)	−0.11 (0.17)
GRN PID	−0.43 (0.36)	0.13 (0.31)	−0.26 (0.34)	−0.51 (0.36)	0.17 (0.32)	−0.42 (0.35)	0.21 (0.30)
LIB PID	−0.06 (0.16)	0.22 (0.16)	−0.00 (0.16)	−0.06 (0.16)	0.05 (0.16)	−0.03 (0.16)	0.04 (0.16)
NDP PID	−0.03 (0.23)	0.26 (0.22)	0.02 (0.22)	−0.08 (0.23)	0.17 (0.23)	0.13 (0.22)	0.21 (0.21)
Response check	−0.18 (0.21)	0.22 (0.22)	−0.14 (0.21)	−0.06 (0.21)	−0.12 (0.22)	−0.27 (0.20)	−0.31 (0.20)
Constant	−0.04 (0.41)	−0.36 (0.41)	0.07 (0.40)	0.03 (0.40)	−0.60 (0.42)	0.18 (0.40)	0.34 (0.40)

$N = 4,709$
χ^2 (df = 119) = 104.21
Pseudo R^2 = 0.01

Note: The cells report multinomial logistic regression coefficients, with standard errors in parentheses. Treatment 1 is set as the base outcome. Age is the respondents' age in years. Female, no high school, university graduate, regional variables, PID, and response check are dichotomous measures, coded "1" in correspondence with the variable name. Political interest and political ideology are self-reported positions on an eleven-point scale running from "No interest" to "Great deal of interest" and "Left–Right," respectively. Political knowledge is an index (alpha = 0.57) based on five factual questions: the name of the British prime minister, the level of government that has primary responsibility for education and health care in Canada, the name of the federal finance minister, the name of the governor general, and the number of seats in the House of Commons. The respondents received one point for each correct response. The variable was then rescaled to fit between 0 and 1. N = number of cases with full response set.
*** $p < 0.001$; ** $p < 0.01$; * $p < 0.05$; [a] $p < 0.10$.

Appendix 10.3. Full results for figures 10.1 and 10.2

	Figure 10.1	Figure 10.2
Any response	1.57 (0.14)*** [0.22]	
One element		1.55 (0.15)*** [0.21]
Two elements		1.57 (0.15)*** [0.21]
Three elements		1.67 (0.16)*** [0.24]
Constant	−2.44 (0.14)***	−2.44 (0.14)***
Pseudo R^2	0.02	0.03
N	5,590	5,590

Note: The cells report logistic regression coefficients, with standard errors in parentheses and marginal effects/discrete changes reported in square brackets.
***$p < 0.001$; **$p < 0.01$; *$p < 0.05$; ª$p < 0.10$.

Appendix 10.4. Full results for figure 10.3

	Figure 10.3
Apologize only	1.04 (0.17)*** [0.12]
Address the issue only	2.30 (0.16)*** [0.38]
Accept responsibility only	1.04 (0.17)*** [0.12]
Apologize and address the issue	1.88 (0.16)*** [0.28]
Apologize and accept responsibility	0.66 (0.18)*** [0.06]
Accept responsibility and address the issue	1.86 (0.16)*** [0.28]
Apologize, accept responsibility, and address the issue	1.67 (0.16)*** [0.24]
Constant	−2.44 (0.14)***
Pseudo R^2	0.07
N	5,590

Note: The cells report logistic regression coefficients, with standard errors in parentheses and marginal effects/discrete changes reported in square brackets.
***$p < 0.001$; **$p < 0.01$; *$p < 0.05$; ª$p < 0.10$.

Chapter Eleven

Reflections, Recommendations, and Future Research

Which electoral strategies are effective for winning power in Canada? What tactics are likely to succeed in fostering public support and maximizing the re-election chances of an incumbent government? In this book, we used experimental methods to collect data that allowed us to investigate a number of widely held beliefs and assumptions about what it takes to win elections and manage public opinion in Canada. Many politicians, party strategists, and journalists have long operated on the assumption that certain strategies are crucial to victory, based on their experiences and observations. Others have made recommendations and given advice based on what they have observed in other countries, such as the United States. To what extent are these assumptions and recommendations justified in the Canadian context? Our studies provided some insight into the validity of these claims and their implications for Canadian politics.

In the first half of the book, we focused on election campaigns and various strategies that party officials and journalists have long believed to be crucial for capturing the vote. In chapter 2, we assessed whether going negative in a campaign was advantageous. While going negative certainly increased public interest in the attacking candidate, generating nearly one full additional information link for the Conservative (CPC) candidate and approximately half a link for the Liberal (LIB) and New Democratic Party (NDP) candidates relative to the attention they received when they spoke of their own strengths, the consequence of that extra attention was weaker support at the ballot box; the probability of the public voting for the CPC, LIB, and NDP candidates dropped by 12, 20, and 20 percentage points, respectively, when they went negative, compared with the vote shares these candidates received when offering a positive message. When we analysed the impact on voter behaviour of the number of candidates engaging in negative and positive campaigns, the results generally held in the case of the information search. However, for vote share, the findings indicated the greatest loss of votes for the lone candidate engaged in a negative campaign. When all three candidates engaged in negative campaigns, the CPC and LIB vote share was no different from when they engaged in a positive campaign, and the reduction in vote share for the NDP was reduced by nearly half compared with the treatment in which the NDP candidate was the only one who engaged in a negative campaign. The moral of the story is that while Canadians seemed intrigued by negative campaign messages, they disapproved of candidates who used them and were willing to punish them accordingly at the ballot box. For candidates opting to go negative, the results suggest that the best course of action is to draw other parties into negative campaigns as a means of minimizing the loss in vote share.

If voters are intrigued but turned off by negative messages, what does this mean for candidates facing accusations of immoral or questionable behaviour? In chapter 3, we investigated this question directly by examining the impact of scandalous news about candidates on Canadian voting behaviour. While attacking one's opponents seemed to generate additional interest in the attacker, exposure to a scandal did not lead to a more detailed information search. In fact, we found the exact opposite. Similarly, scandalous candidates seemed to turn off voters, generating a 3-percentage-point decrease in the probability of voting for the CPC and LIB and a 1-percentage-point drop for the NDP. When we provided voters with different kinds of scandal to consider across treatments, we found that it was financial scandals that had occurred in the personal sphere that had the largest effect, generating a 30-percentage-point drop in voting probability for the LIB and similar results for the other parties. Interestingly, reports of a sex scandal in the private sphere had virtually no impact on the vote probability for the CPC and NDP candidates.

What should we make of these two studies and their results? It is clear that while voters may be intrigued by negativity, this interest does not translate into votes. Canadians are also not supportive of candidates accused of scandalous behaviour, although we note that not all scandals are treated equally and that the impact of the scandalous behaviour varies somewhat by party. Taken together, the results from these two chapters may reflect the public's disappointment with a candidate's failure to live up to its perceptions of how an ideal political representative should behave as a candidate and an elected official. To some extent, we should not be surprised by these findings. The literature on the democratic deficit in Canada suggests that voters have generally been disappointed with their elected politicians, viewing their behaviour cynically during election campaigns and afterwards. In an ideal world, politicians keep their promises, accurately represent their constituents' interests, and work for the greater good. A substantial portion of the general public, however, sees politicians as behaving quite differently: as self-interested and focused only on maximizing their re-election chances (Pammett and LeDuc 2003, 7; Tanguay 2009, 228–9). Our results seem to be consistent with these general trends in Canadian public opinion.

In chapters 4 and 5, we explored these themes further by examining whether and, if so, how voters react to positive rather than negative cues about candidates. In chapter 4, we assessed whether endorsements of candidates by prominent officials had any effect on Canadian voting behaviour and whether that effect varied according to the prominence of the endorser (e.g., local versus national profile). Our findings were somewhat surprising. While exposure to an endorsement reduced the information search that voters engaged in by 0.09 and 0.15 information links for the CPC and LIB, respectively, neither of these results met conventional levels of statistical significance. The results for the NDP indicated no difference between the experimental and the control groups. In other words, an endorsement had no statistically significant effect on whether voters searched out, or did not search out, additional information about the candidate who received it. On the other hand, an endorsement did increase the probability that Canadians would vote for the person who was endorsed. In the case of the NDP, LIB, and CPC, we observed a 13-, 9-, and 7-percentage-point increase, respectively, in the probability of an individual casting a vote for the party when exposed to an endorsement relative to the probability of voting for the same party absent an endorsement. It did not matter, however, whether the endorsement came from a local or national figure. Put simply, endorsements helped candidates win elections.

To what extent does the quality of a candidate matter? Similar to what we found in chapter 4, our results showed a clear increase in each party's relative vote share in the competition in which the party ran a strong candidate compared with its performance when a weaker candidate contested the election. The CPC candidate, for instance, received a 7-percentage-point boost, while the other parties received more than a 10-percentage-point increase in their respective vote shares when fielding a strong candidate. To cue candidate quality, we offered links to information about each candidate from a variety of sources, such as the candidate's biography and a newspaper story about the candidate. Viewing the strong candidate's biography nearly doubled the probability of voters supporting that candidate compared to viewing the newspaper story, although both produced an increase in the vote probability relative to the average candidate treatments: an increase of 31 and 14 percentage points, respectively.

The breadth of the information search that voters undertook, however, mitigated these effects: every additional information link that an individual accessed pertaining to the other candidates or parties *decreased* the probability of the individual voting for the strong candidate by 1 percentage point ($p < 0.05$), net of information pertaining to that candidate. As well, partisanship conditioned some of these effects: relative to their non-partisan counterparts, the probability of leaners supporting the strong candidate was 17 percentage points greater and, for partisans, 14 percentage points greater. For partisans, a strong candidate competing for *their* party boosted the probability of voting for the candidate by 51 points ($p < 0.001$) relative to their non-partisan counterparts. Similarly, leaners were significantly (33 percentage points) more likely to support the strong candidate relative to non-partisans when the candidate was running for the leaner's preferred party. However, when the strong candidate was competing for a party other than the one to which the individual had some ties, we found no difference between leaners and non-partisans and a relatively small and negative impact for partisans. While a strong candidate was likely to generate votes, these votes were most likely to come from individuals predisposed to support the party anyway (e.g., partisans). Still, we did find that non-partisans could be influenced by candidate effects (a 13-percentage-point increase in the probability that they would vote for the strong candidate), although the size of this effect paled in comparison to that observed for leaners supportive of the strong candidate's party.

What should we make of these findings, given the results from chapters 2 and 3? In essence, they are consistent with those studies. Chapters 4 and 5 suggest that Canadians prefer highly qualified candidates who live up to some sort of lofty public service ideal or standard. However, the ability of voters to make those assessments is, at least partly, conditioned by how they access or receive that information. Endorsements are basically information shortcuts or heuristics that allow candidates to quickly (and cost-effectively) convey their qualifications to voters. It would seem that candidates benefit when citizens are exposed to such cues.

Absent endorsements, candidates must somehow convey their qualifications in other ways. The results from chapter 5 indicate that while a third-party source, like a newspaper article, can have a similar effect on the vote share as an endorsement, the most effective way seems to be

Reflections, Recommendations, Future Research 227

to directly communicate one's qualifications; voters exposed to a strong candidate's biography increased the probability of voting for that candidate by more than 31 percentage points. In short, Canadians want to support and elect highly qualified candidates. The key for candidates and parties is to identify the most effective means of conveying information about candidate quality to voters.

What happens when a party wins an election and forms the government? What kinds of strategies are effective at managing public opinion and positioning the incumbent party and its candidates for re-election? The studies reported in the second half of this book examined a variety of strategies that incumbent parties have used and assumed to be effective at accomplishing this task. In chapters 6 and 7, we assessed whether certain pre-election configurations and strategies provided incumbents with a meaningful electoral advantage.

Chapter 6 discussed how, in Canada, our electoral system regularly produces majority governments and, less frequently, minority governments, and political elites assume that these configurations offer different sorts of advantages and disadvantages. Majority governments allow governments to efficiently implement their agenda, while making it relatively simple for Canadians to have a clear idea about who should receive credit and blame for good and bad policy decisions. Minority governments, on the other hand, offer less efficient decision making and agenda implementation, but sometimes offer governments the opportunity to evade responsibility for bad decisions, especially if opposition parties vote against and/or defeat government legislation. Government elites assume that they can sometimes take advantage of these configurations before an election to bolster public opinion and, ultimately, their re-election chances.

Do these parliamentary configurations matter? Can elites manipulate them to provide themselves with an advantage? Surprisingly, when we ignored parliamentary configurations and focused solely on incumbent support when legislation passed versus when it failed to pass, it was the non-governing parties that benefited, with the probability of voting for the governing party decreasing by 7 percentage points. When we compared incumbent vote share when the legislation passed in majority situations (either treatment) against vote shares when the legislation passed in minority and coalition configurations, however, we found incumbent support to be approximately 10 percentage points higher. This result suggests that majority configurations were more rewarding for the governing party for capturing the credit.

Given these findings, what should parties do? They should aim to win majority governments! If this is not possible or seems highly unlikely in the long term, the strategy should be to pursue electoral reform, which should, in turn, produce more minority and coalition configurations. Non-majority outcomes should help these parties have a stronger and more direct influence over the government's agenda, while maximizing their public support. Indeed, the fourth hypothesis in this particular study assumed that a minor coalition partner would reap a greater reward for successful legislation passed under a coalition configuration relative to the other conditions. We found evidence of this phenomenon: the vote share of Party A (identified as a coalition partner only in coalition treatments) increased from 13% under a majority government, when all parties supported the legislation, to 21% under the minority configuration, and to 26% when the party was identified as the minor coalition partner that voted in support of the government legislation. In contrast, when the partner voted against the legislation, its vote share dropped by a significant 12 points ($p < 0.05$), the lowest level of support of all parties in this treatment (see table 6.2). Taken together, these results suggest that the minor partner in a coalition government benefits vis-à-vis successful legislation, but only when it supports the larger, governing party. When the minor partner votes against the legislation, all bets are off.

In chapter 7, we investigated another way in which incumbent parties might manipulate public opinion to maximize their re-election chances: timing elections to coincide with conditions that are favourable to the incumbent, such as when the governing party is experiencing high levels of public support or when the opposition is in disarray. Our study confirmed what other observational studies have found cross-nationally and at the provincial level in Canada, which is that the strategic use of the election-timing power can provide incumbent parties with a boost at the ballot box. In our first model, in which we compared the impact of an immediate election following exposure to a positive incumbent message, the probability of voting for the incumbent increased by 7 percentage points ($p < 0.05$) relative to all other elections. Similarly, when we ran the full model, in which all four treatments were included, we found that the only treatment that yielded a significant change was, once again, the immediate election following exposure to a positive incumbent-message scenario; in this case, we observed a 9-percentage-point increase in incumbent vote probability relative to the control category.

Although the federal government and most provincial jurisdictions have adopted legislation that tries to constrain the election-timing power, our Westminster system continues to provide first ministers with some discretion over its use. It remains to be seen whether a strong norm will emerge to prevent first ministers from using the power opportunistically. Until such a norm emerges, our evidence suggests that the election-timing power provides incumbent parties with a powerful tool for increasing their re-election chances.

The final three empirical chapters in this book moved away from election and pre-election scenarios to examine a number of situations involving incumbent governments managing public opinion while in the midst of their term. In chapter 8, we looked at whether there was any strategic advantage to Parliament passing its political problems or policy issues on to the Supreme Court. Does this strategy provide the government with a mechanism for avoiding negative public fallout that might result from implementing a decision on its own accord rather than having the Supreme Court force its hand? Our results suggest that, generally speaking, the public is more likely to agree (a 4-percentage-point difference) that the Supreme Court should determine Canadian laws relative to Parliament. However, when voters are primed with information about a situation in which the court overrules Parliament, public support for Parliament is higher (6 percentage points; $p < 0.05$).

We then dissect these findings by comparing the change in support when one institution overrules a decision of the other for each institution separately. The results show that Parliament receives a 9-percentage-point boost compared to the control model when it overrules the Supreme Court. Similar conditions for the Supreme Court show the opposite effect. Overall, the results suggest that while the level of support for the court determining Canadian laws may be higher than for Parliament in general, this finding may not hold in cases where the court attempts to assert its authority over Parliament's right to set legislation. Conversely, support for Parliament's right to determine Canadian laws increases when Parliament overrules the court.

These results present an interesting set of considerations for governing elites. On the one hand, they suggest that governments can and perhaps should mitigate public backlash by pushing controversial or difficult issues to the Supreme Court because Canadians seem to support the court more than they support Parliament. If the court agrees with the government and hands down a judicial decision consistent with government legislation and preferences about that legislation, this outcome would be a win for the incumbent party. Should the court disagree with Parliament and strike down the law, however, there may be a strategic advantage to Parliament overruling the court's decision using the various tools available to it, such as the notwithstanding clause or the mechanisms of coordinate interpretation. Indeed, the most advantageous scenario seems to involve Parliament passing a law that the court strikes down and then overruling the court's decision. Our study found that this strategy resulted in a 9-percentage-point increase in public support for Parliament relative to the support it received without the prime. While we did not directly examine how that 9-percentage-point increase might be distributed across the parties, our parliamentary configurations and assigning political responsibility chapter (chapter 6) suggests that the incumbent party in the majority government configuration would likely benefit the most from the bump in support.

While incumbent parties seem to have the option of avoiding difficult or controversial issues by "punting" them to the Supreme Court through the use of the reference power (Puddister 2019) or by providing funding to civil society groups to engage in strategic litigation (Brodie 2001),[1] they cannot do the same to avoid the problems and responsibilities related to revenue collection and expenditure. All governments require adequate revenues to deliver programs and services, build and maintain infrastructure, and develop policies and laws, among other things. Generally speaking, citizens do not like taxes and loathe any sort of tax increase. Hence, the challenge for governments is to somehow implement their agendas, find the funds to do so, and prevent these actions from drastically harming their public popularity and ultimately their re-election chances.

In chapter 9, we investigated Canadian support for various public-spending mechanisms to support government investment in Canadian infrastructure. A sizeable majority (62%) of the control group agreed or strongly agreed that the federal government should invest in infrastructure across Canada. However, when we primed having to pay for the expenditures, the overall level of support dropped by 37 percentage points ($p<0.001$). In all treatments, support fell below that observed in the control. Congruent with our

---

[1] Some might argue that the government is restricted in its strategic use of the Supreme Court in a number of ways. First, reference cases have not happened very often in Canada. Second, most Supreme Court cases are, in fact, initiated by civil society groups rather than the government. Finally, some readers might find the idea of the government strategically playing around with court and Charter rights to be normatively offensive. We agree that these are important restrictions and considerations. However, these constraints and considerations have not stopped the court from strategically using reference cases (see Puddister 2019) and, perhaps more importantly, funding civil society groups to advance a political agenda through the judicial system (see Brodie 2001; Morton and Knopff 2000). Thus, while we agree that it is unlikely that an incumbent party will actively and frequently make strategic use of the courts, this seems more likely to occur in situations where a political or legal issue is extremely divisive, either within the party itself or in the general public writ large.

expectations, we found that the highest level of support for infrastructure spending in our treatments was a transfer of funds from other programs, a method that citizens may think has a minimal impact on their lives. However, it is important to note that this treatment still resulted in a 16-point drop in support for infrastructure spending relative to the control group.

An additional finding from this study reflected how the funding mechanism was presented. In general, we found that citizens were more supportive (4 percentage points) of funding mechanisms when the actual cost was fully disclosed. For political elites, the message is clear. Reallocating existing spending is preferable to increasing existing spending or instituting a new tax or fee. However, if one must pursue the latter option, it is better to provide details about the nature of the increased amount; otherwise, citizens might overestimate the personal costs they must endure to pay for the investment.

Sometimes governments make mistakes or implement decisions that have harmful consequences or generate potentially negative publicity and public reactions. What should governments do? In our final study, we considered the benefits and consequences of public apologies. Generally speaking, our data suggested that any government response was preferable to none, with the former strategy increasing the likelihood of the public being satisfied or very satisfied with the government's response by 22 percentage points compared with the government offering no comment. As a rule, according to our findings, government officials should never respond to a problematic issue or situation with "No comment."

What should governments do when they apologize if their goal is to maximize public support? Surprisingly, rather than offering an apology with multiple elements in it, it is the single element of promising to fix the issue that was found to have the strongest effect on public opinion in our study, increasing the likelihood of being satisfied or very satisfied by 38 percentage points relative to offering no comment. While admitting and apologizing for government wrongdoings is better than "No comment," it is the willingness of a government to address the wrongdoing that stands out as the most important strategy for improving public satisfaction in a situation where a government apology may be expected or warranted.

Collectively, the results from our experiments provide an insightful, window into the dynamics of winning and keeping power in Canadian politics. At the individual level, where we examined the effects of candidate strategies on voting behaviour, we found that Canadians seemed to prefer candidates who met some vague yet conventional quality threshold, not only in terms of their background and qualifications for holding elected office, but also in terms of their actions and behaviour before, during, and after an election campaign. The ability of citizens to make a positive or negative assessment of the candidates, however, depends at least in part on the kinds of information that they receive from individual candidates and how they access that information.

Moving beyond the candidate level, we observed similar effects in chapters 6 to 10, when we focused on the pre-election strategies available to governing parties to influence public opinion and maximize their re-election chances. These chapters demonstrated the importance of winning majority governments and timing elections to coincide with favourable conditions. Once in power, incumbent parties have access to a variety of strategies for maintaining public support, including leveraging the policymaking role of the Supreme Court (chapter 8) and the varying ways that a government might frame tax increases or new spending and apologies for perceived public wrongs undertaken by past or current governments. Canadians seem responsive to positive cues about the performance of the governing party (e.g., chapters 6 and 7, parliamentary configurations and assigning political responsibility and election timing, respectively) and are willing to accept bad news related to that party if the government's response is direct and decisive (chapters 9 and 10, framing public budgeting and political apologies, respectively). Taken together, we believe that the results reported here not only offer insight into current assumptions about winning and keeping power in Canadian politics but also generate a number of possibilities for further research in these areas, a point on which we conclude.

Final Thoughts

As we come to the end of this project, we wish to highlight the work that remains. Each of our studies attempted to empirically test common assumptions about winning and keeping power in Canadian politics. In doing so, we developed our experiments to isolate specific factors. By definition, this means that a number of additional, and potentially important, factors were not considered. For example, in our study of negative campaign tone, we limit our experiment to conditions where it is one candidate directly attacking the others. Would the results change if the attack came from an outside source? Would the findings differ if it were the policies of the other party as opposed to the qualifications of the candidate that were being challenged? What difference, if any, would we find if one or more of the candidates were women? Would the effects vary according to whether a female candidate is criticizing or being criticized by a male candidate? In each chapter, we have suggested ways to expand upon our work and further assess the implications of our findings. We believe that this is only a sampling of the ways in which future research can draw upon experimental research designs to expand our understanding of political behaviour. We hope that our initial set of results encourages such work and the broader use of experimentation to study Canadian politics.

In addition to other considerations that might be added to our experimental designs, we believe that our results can help inform research based on observational data. As we noted in the introductory chapter, the strength of experimental studies is also its weakness: what we gain in internal validity, we lose in external validity. While we attempted to make our studies as realistic as possible, we recognize the limitations of our design. That said, our ability to directly assess factors that influence political behaviour and preferences, as well as the magnitude of the effects, provides a starting point for testing in the real world. As this work draws to a close, we look forward to the work to come and the contribution that it will make to further advancing our understanding of the strategies and tactics for *winning and keeping power in Canadian politics*.

REFERENCES

Brodie, Ian. 2001. "Interest Group Litigation and the Embedded State: Canada's Court Challenges Program." *Canadian Journal of Political Science*. 34 (2): 357–76. https://doi.org/10.1017/S0008423901777931.

Morton, F.L., and Rainer Knopff. 2000. *The Charter Revolution and the Court Party*. Peterborough: Broadview Press.

Pammett, Jon H., and Lawrence LeDuc. 2003. "Explaining the Turnout Decline in Canadian Federal Elections: A New Survey of Non-Voters." Research report prepared for Elections Canada. March. Ottawa: Elections Canada. https://www.elections.ca/content.aspx?section=res&dir=rec/part/tud&document=index&lang=e.

Puddister, Kate. 2019. "The Canadian Reference Power: Delegation to the Courts and the Navigation of Federalism." *Publius: Journal of Federalism* 49 (4): 561–86. https://doi.org/10.1093/publius/pjy034.

Tanguay, Brian. 2009. "Reforming Representative Democracy: Taming the 'Democratic Deficit.'" In *Canadian Politics*, edited by James Bickerton and Alain-G. Gagnon, 221–48. Peterborough: Broadview Press.

Index

Page numbers in **bold** refer to tables; page numbers in *italics* refer to figures.

accountability of political actors, 130–2
Alcantara, Christopher, 152, 153, 155
Alesina, Alberto, 152
Anderson, Christopher J., 131, 132, 140
Arnott, Ted, 73
attack ads, 19, 20

Baker, Dennis, 181
Barnes, Tiffany D., 50
Basi, David, 47
Bennett, Bill, 46
Bernier, Maxime, 73
Blais, André, 49, 105, 117
Blatz, Craig, 210
Bonga, Melissa, 150n2
Bouchard, Lucien, 153
bounded rationality, 190
Bowler, Shaun, 191
Brazeau, Patrick, 45
Brewer, Paul R., 77
Brown, Laura, 48
Brown, Patrick, 73
Brown Rovner, Ivy, 32

Campbell, Kim, 151
Canada Elections Act, 150, 162

Canada's electoral system: call for reform of, 130; majority governments in, 129, 227
Canadian Charter of Rights and Freedoms, 13, 168, 170
Canadian politics: winning and keeping power in, 3, 11, 180, 231, 232–3
carbon tax, 192
Cargill, Thomas F., 152
Carlson, James, 48
Carr, Jim, 104
Chong, Michael, 73
Chowdhury, Abdur R., 152
Chrétien, Jean: calls for election, 151, 153; television advertisement of, 19; use of reference power by, 169, 181; view of politics, 3
Clarity Act, 169
Clark, Glen, 46
Clark, Joe, 151n3
Clement, Tony, 73
coalition governments: assignment of credit and blame to, 131–2, 133, 134, 141–2; definition of, 150n2; lack of tradition of, 13, 129; *vs.* minority governments, 135; minor partners in, 135, 142, 228; passing

of legislation effect on support of, 135, 140–1; responsibility of, 131; vote share and, 135, 141

Conservative Party of Canada (CPC): 2017 leadership race, 73; campaigning strategy, 19–20, 36, 223–4; election cycle legislation, 13; endorsement of candidates of, 74; minority government, 13, 149; recruitment of local candidates, 103

Constitution Act of 1982, 170
Coppock, Alexander, 173
corruption scandals, 46n1, 47, 48
Craig, Stephen C., 23

Darmofal, David, 173
Davey, Keith, 151
Dawood, Yasmin, 129
Deltell, Gérard, 103
De Vries, Catherine E., 132, 134
Dimock, Michael, 48
Dion, Stéphane, 103, 192
Doherty, David, 48, 49
Donovan, Todd, 191
Dowling, Conor M., 48, 49
Duffy, Mike, 45
Duncan, John, 73

Eaton, Nicole, 73
Edwards, Erica E., 132, 134
Eggleton, Art, 46
Ekins, Emily, 173
election campaigning: assessment of tone of, 28–9; average length of, 157; effect on level of attention to a candidate, 25, 26, 30–6, **31, 33**; effect on vote share, 25, 26, 29n6, 31–6, **32, 35**, 223–4; effect on winning and keeping power, 14, 36; in multiparty context, 32–3; partisan behaviour and, 29

election campaigning study: campaign tone treatment, 27, **27**, 29, 43, 44; discussion of, 35–6; Election campaign information screen, 27–8, *40*; hypotheses, 25–6; methodology of, 26–9; newspaper stories examples, 41–2; participants of, 26–7, 28; results of, 29–35, **43–4**

electoral timing study: data collection, 151; discussion of, 161–3; Election campaign information screen, 154, *155*, 156; election-timing treatments, **158**; methodology of, 154–8; newspaper stories used in, 154–5, 156; participants of, 154, 156, 158–9, 158n8; results of, 158–61, **166–7**, 228–9. *See also* timing of election

endorsements: as cognitive heuristic, 75, 76, 77; effectiveness of, 74–5, 77; effect on winning and keeping power, 90; information search and level of, 81, 82, *83, 84, 85*, 87, 90, 99, 100; at local and national level, 76, 78, 82, 84, 87, 90–1; of local candidates, 74; from major newspapers, 73–4, 95–6; from politicians, 73, 94–5; from prominent citizens and groups, 74; scholarly literature on, 75, 76; sophistication of the voter and, *88, 89*, 90, 100, 102; in the US context, 77; vote choice and level of, 81, *86*, 86–91, *87, 88, 89*, 99, 100–2, 225; voter partisanship and, 81; voter sophistication level and, 76, 78, 84–6, *89*

endorsement study: collection of information, 80–1; control groups, **79**, 81–2, 98; Election campaign information screen, 79, *80*; hypotheses, 77–8; methodology of,

78–80; participants of, 80, 81, 97; political sophistication variable, 84n5, 85–6; results of, 81–90
Eso, Michael, 74

Fedoruk, Sylvia, 152
financial scandals: definition of, 47; effect on public opinion, 48; effect on vote choice, 12, 50, 51, 58, *59*, 60; in public and private sphere, 51, 58, *59*; *vs.* sex scandals, 48–9, 50, 51, 55–6; study of, 46
first ministers: election-timing power, 153
fixed-election-date legislation: debates on, 150n2; introduction of, 149–50
Flanagan, Thomas, 19
Ford, Doug, 180
Freeland, Chrystia, 12, 104
Funk, Carolyn, 48

Gabel, Matthew, 173
Ganiel, Gladys, 48
Garthwaite, Craig, 77
Geer, John, 21
Gibney, Mark, 209
Goldfarb, Allan, 151
Goodyear-Grant, Elizabeth, 171
governing party: voter support for, 12, 131, 139, 140, 141–2, 227–8
Gretzky, Wayne, 73, 74
Grossman, Gene M., 75

Harb, Mac, 45
Harper, Stephen: endorsements of politicians by, 74; introduction of fixed-election-date legislation, 149, 150; plan for Senate reform, 168; Senate expenses scandal and, 45; view of politics, 3
Helpman, Elhanan, 75

Herbst, Kenneth C., 77
Hibbing, John R., 48
Hiebert, Janet, 171
Holder, Ed, 73
Hornsey, Matthew J., 210
Howard-Hassmann, Rhoda, 209
Hutchinson, Michael M., 152
Hyde, Mark S., 48

infrastructure spending: cost consideration, 195; in electoral promises, 188–9; public support for, 14, 194–6, *195*, 196, 230–1; questionnaire about, 199–201; reduction of, 196. *See also* public budgeting
Ito, Takatoshi, 152

Jacobson, Gary, 48
Jerit, Jennifer, 173
judicial supremacy, 168, 169, 170

Kahneman, Daniel, 191
Kent, Peter, 73
Kirby, David, 173
Kreviazuk, Chantal, 74

Lau, Richard R., 32, 75, 76, 77
leaners: definition of, 113; effect of quality of candidate on, 114, 115–17, 117n14, 226
Leitch, Kellie, 73
Leslie, Andrew, 104
Lewis-Beck, Michael, 131
Liberal Party of Canada (LIB): 2015 election campaign, 11, 12, 14; campaigning strategies, 19–20, 36, 223–4; candidate endorsements, 74; majority governments, 130; recruitment of local candidates, 103–4; use of election-timing power, 151, 153, 162

local candidates: gap between initial and full support of, 117n14; impact of information search on support of, 106, 110–13, **112**; influence of vote choice, 104, 105, 106, 107, 110, 114–15, 117, 118; newspaper stories about, 108, 123–4; partisanship effects on support of, 106–7, **112**, 113–14, **116**, 116–17; party affiliation of, 108–9, 110; profiles of, 107–8, 121–3; recruitment of, 103–4, 118; support of highly qualified, 110, 227, 231–2. *See also* quality of local candidates

local candidates study: assignment to treatment in, 109–10, **125**; Election campaign information screen, 108, *109*; hypotheses, 105–7; methodology of, 107–9; modelling techniques, 110–11; results of, 109–17, **124–5**; scholarly literature, 104–6

loss aversion cognitive bias, 191

MacCharles, Tonda, 168
MacKinnon, Janice, 152
MacLeod, Alfie, 73
Maier, Jürgen, 48
majority governments: in Canada's electoral system, 129–30; characteristics of, 129, 227; importance of winning, 232; legislation passing effects on support of, 140; vote share and, 132, 140, 142, 228
Manfredi, Christopher, 169
Marsh, Michael, 105
Martin, Lawrence, 3
Martin, Paul, 20, 36, 49
Matthew, J. Scott, 171
McAllister, Ian, 105
McGuinty, David, 74

McLaren, James, 74
Miller, Michael G., 48, 49
Milner, Henry, 150
minority governments: assignment of credit or blame to, 134, 142; characteristics of, 129, 227; *vs.* coalition governments, 135; legislation passing effects on support of, 135, 141, 228; vote share and, 135, 141, 142, 228
Mishra, Abhinav, 77
Mishra, Anubhav A., 77
Moore, Timothy J., 77
Morneau, Bill, 104
Moscardelli, Vincent G., 48
Mouritzen, Poul Erik, 190
Mulcair, Thomas, 74
Mulroney, Brian, 151, 208

Neddenriep, Gregory, 76
negative campaigning: in American context, 22; backlash effect of, 23–4, 34–5; consequences of, 223; directional manner of, 21; evaluative manner of, 21–2; examples of, 42; impact on vote choice, 9, *11*, 22, 23, 25, 31–4, **32**, **35**, 36, 224; level of attention to a candidate and, 25, 30–1, **31**, 32, **33**, 33–4; in multiparty system, 11, 20–1, 24–6; scholarly literature on, 20, 24, 25; in two-party race, 20, 24
negativity: bias effect, 22–3; definition of, 21
New Democratic Party (NDP): campaign strategies, 74; electoral defeat in BC, 19; negative campaigning, 223–4; use of election-timing power, 152–3
Newhook, Kelly, 74
Nicholson, Rob, 149

non-partisans: definition of, 113; effect of quality of candidate on, 106, 114, 115, 117, 117n14, 226
Notley, Rachel, 192
Nownes, Anthony J., 76
Nye, Joseph, 47

Obama, Barack, 77
Ontario provincial election of 1990, 150n3
O'Toole, Erin, 73

Palmer, Harvey D., 152, 155
Park, Jin Hyuk, 152
parliamentary configurations: accountability and, 130–1, 133; effect on clarity of government responsibility, 134, 135–6, 139–40, 142; effect on vote choice, 130, 133–5, 138–9, *139*, 142, **148**, 227; effect on winning and keeping power, 130, 142
parliamentary configurations study: assignment of government configuration treatments, 136–7, **137**; discussion of, 142–3; Election campaign information screen, 136, 137, *145*; hypotheses, 133–6; methodology of, 136–8; participants of, 138; results of, 138–42, **146, 147–8,** 227–8; sample newspaper story, 145; vote share estimates, 139, **140**
Parliament of Canada: authority of, 13–14, 171–2; popularity of, 171; public support for, 13, 170, 172, 175–7, *177, 178,* 180, 229–30
partisans: definition of, 113; effect of quality of candidate on, 106, 114, 115, 117, 117n14, 226
Patterson, Dennis, 73
Pease, Andrew, 77

Pelletier, Jean, 103
Penashue, Peter, 73
Peters, John G., 48
Peterson, David, 150n3
Philpot, Catherine R., 210
political apologies: in Australia, 209; benefits and consequences of, 231; effect on public support of government, 212–13, 214, 215, 216; elements of, 210, 212, 215; implications for winning and keeping power, 60; issues covered by, 207–8; level of satisfaction with, 212, 213, *214, 215,* 215–16, *216*; motivations for, 207, 208; problem of effectiveness of, 14, 208–9, 210, 212; public attention to, 14, 207–8; scholarly literature on, 210, 212; statistics of, 207, 209; as tool for strengthening public opinion, 209, 211
political apologies study: assignment of treatments, 211, **211**; discussion of, 216–17; implications of, 217; methodology of, 213; respondents of, 213; results of, 213–16, **220–2,** 231
political behaviour study: assignment of treatments, 6; design of, 4–5; Election campaign information screen, 6; interpretation of the results of, 8–11; participants of, 7–8; statistical analysis, 5n5, 10; use of experiments in, 4–7; validity of, 5, 5n6, 8n10
political elites: public backlash against, 229; reference to the Supreme Court, 180–1, 229, 230n1
political parties: electoral strategies, 3–4, 223–4, 227–8; financial scandals and, 58, *59,* 60; reaction

to parliamentary configurations, 13; recruitment of local candidates, 103

political scandals: abuse of power and, 49; attention to a candidate involved in, 50, 51, 53–5, *55*, *56*, *57*, 60–1; cost of, 12; effect on public opinion, 46–7, 48–9; effect on vote choice, 48–50, 57–8, *58*, *59*, 60, 61, 224–5; effect on winning and keeping power, 60; endorsement of candidates and, 53; forms of, 45–6; newspaper stories and party statements on, 53, **69**; origin of, 47–8; partisanship and, 49; private and public sphere of, 51, 56–7, *57*; scholarly literature on, 48–50, 50n2; types of, 12, 46n1

political scandals study: discussion of, 60–1; Election campaign information screen, *53*; election instructions screen, 53, **69**; hypotheses, 50–1; limitations of, 60–1; methodology of, 51–4; participants of, 52, 53–4; results of, 54–60, **65–8, 70–2**; treatment groups, **52**, 52–3, *55*, *56*, *57*, *58*, *59*

positive campaigning: advantages of, 35, 36; definition of, 22; directional conception of, 22; examples of, 41; study of, 232–3; vote probability in, 9

positive legislation, 133

Powell, G. Bingham, Jr., 132

Praino, Rodrigo, 48

Prime Minister's Office (PMO), 45

Progressive Conservative Party, 151n3

Provost, VirJiny, 46

public budgeting: assumptions about citizens' view of, 190; detailed treatment of, 193, 197; effect on winning and keeping power, 197; mechanisms of, 14, 189–90, 231; personal costs and, 192, 193, 195, 196; public support of, 188, 189, 194, 196; redistribution of funds in, 191, 195–6; scholarly literature on, 189, 190. *See also* infrastructure spending

public budgeting study: discussion of, 196–7; hypotheses, 191–2, 194; methodology of, 192–3; participants of, 193; results of, 194–6, **202–3**, 230–1; treatment groups, 192–3, **193, 204–5**

public opinion: comparative studies of, 172, 173; fluidity of, 12–13; in relation to judicial system, 170–1

Quebec secession, 169

Rae, Bob, 150n3
Raitt, Lisa, 73
Rankin, Murray, 74
Rayes, Alain, 103
Redlawsk, David P., 75, 76, 77
Reid, Angus, 171, 172
Reid, Scott, 73
responsibility hypothesis, 131
revenue collection, 188–9
Reynolds, John, 73
Richardson, Miles, 74
Rippere, Paulina S., 23
Romanow, Roy, 152
Ross, Michael, 210
Roubini, Nouriel, 152
Rudd, Kevin, 209
Rusin, Peter, 20
Russell, Peter, 169

Sahota, Ruby, 20
Salibi, Elie, 74

Sandals, Liz, 149
Scheer, Andrew, 73
Scheve, Kenneth, 173
Schleiter, Petra, 153
Schumann, Karina, 210
Scotti, Monique, 168
Senate expenses scandal, 45
sex scandals: *vs.* financial scandals, 48, 50, 51, 55–6; impact on vote choice, 12, 49, 50, 58, *59*; in private and public sphere, 51, *59*; study of, 46–7
Sigelman, Lee, 32
Silber Grayson, Marissa, 23–4
Simpson, Jeffrey, 19
single-member plurality (SMP) system, 129–30, 133
Smith, Alastair, 152, 155
sponsorship scandal, 46, 49
star candidates, 12, 103, 118
Stockemer, Daniel, 48
study of public support for Parliament and the Supreme Court: effects of experts opinion, 172–3, 177–9, *178*, 180; hypotheses, 171–3, 180; methodology of, 173–4, 175n5; participants of, 175; political sophistication effect, 179; results of, 175–9, **184–7**; treatment groups, 174, **174**. *See also* Parliament of Canada
Supreme Court of Canada: authority of, 169, 172, 229; governing elites and, 180–1, 229; legislative override, 176, 177, 180; popularity of, 171, 181; public attitudes towards, 13, 170–2, 175–7, *176*, *177*, 180, 229
Survey Sampling International (SSI), 7

Tavits, Margit, 105, 153
taxation, 191–2, 196, 230. *See also* carbon tax

Tell, Christine, 73
Thompson, John, 47
Tillman, Erik R., 132, 134
timing of election: economic conditions and, 151–2; effect on winning and keeping power, 162; electoral advantage due to, 13, 150–1; in Japan, 152; media coverage of government and opposition and, 157, 158, 161; opposition party and, 153; party solidarity and, 152; polling numbers and, 151; prime ministers' control of, 161–2; scholarly literature on, 151–2; vote share and, 157, 159–61, *160*, 162–3. *See also* electoral timing study
Topp, Brian, 19
Trudeau, Justin: on coalition governments, 129; endorsements by, 73, 74; infrastructure spending, 189; limits of power of, 168; recruitment of local candidates, 103–4; view of 2015 election campaign, 11
Trudeau, Pierre, 150n3, 151
Turner, John, 151
Tversky, Amos, 191

Vandenbeld, Anita, 74
Van Loan, Peter, 73
Virk, Robert, 47
voting behaviour: candidate effect on, 114–15; cognitive heuristics in, 75–6; economic conditions and, 132; in European Union, 132; impact of endorsements on, 75; partisan attachment and, 113; political scandals and, 224–5. *See also* leaners; non-partisans; partisans

Wallin, Pamela, 45
Ward, Marianne Meed, 20
Welch, Susan, 48
White, Steve, 152, 153, 155
Whitten, Guy D., 132, 152, 155

Williams, Danny, 208
Wilson-Raybould, Jody, 104
Winter, Søren, 190
Wohl, Michael J.A., 210
Wood, Natalie T., 77